Introducing

Cognitive

Development

WITHDRAWN FROM STOCK

■ Laura M. Taylor

Ψ Psychology Press
Taylor & Francis Group

HOVE AND NEW YORK

First published 2005
by Psychology Press
27 Church Road, Hove, East Sussex
BN3 2FA

Simultaneously published in the
USA and Canada
by Psychology Press Inc
270 Madison Avenue, New York,
NY 10016

*Psychology Press is a part of the Taylor
& Francis Group*

© 2005 Psychology Press

Typeset in Sabon by RefineCatch Ltd,
Bungay, Suffolk
Printed and bound in Great Britain by
MPG Books Ltd, Bodmin, Cornwall
Paperback cover design by Anú Design

*British Library Cataloguing in
Publication Data*
A catalogue record for this book is
available from the British Library

*Library of Congress Cataloging in
Publication Data*

Taylor, Laura M., 1972-
  Introducing cognitive development /
Laura M. Taylor.—1st ed.
    p. cm.
  Includes bibliographical references
and index.
  ISBN 1–84169–352–9 (hard cover)—
  ISBN 1–84169–353–7 (softcover)
  1. Cognition in children. I. Title.
  BF723.C5T39 2005
  155.4′13—dc22
                              2005008361

ISBN 1-84169-352-9 (hbk)

ISBN 1-84169-353-7 (pbk)

For Vera Amy Taylor
1926–2004

Contents

CONTENTS

List of illustrations

Series preface

The Psychology Focus series provides short, up-to-date accounts of key areas in psychology without assuming the reader's prior knowledge in the subject. Psychology is often a favoured subject area for study, since it is relevant to a wide range of disciplines such as Sociology, Education, Nursing, and Business Studies. These relatively inexpensive but focused short texts combine sufficient detail for psychology specialists with sufficient clarity for non-specialists. The series authors are academics experienced in undergraduate teaching as well as research. Each takes a topic within his or her area of psychological expertise and presents a short review, highlighting important themes, and including both theory and research findings. Each aspect of the topic is clearly explained with supporting glossaries to elucidate technical terms. The series has been conceived within the context of the increasing modularisation that has been developed in higher education over the last decade and fulfils the consequent need for clear, focused, topic-based course material. Instead of following one course of study, students on a modularisation programme are often able to choose modules from a wide range of disciplines to complement the modules they are required to study for a specific degree. It can no longer be assumed that students studying a particular module will necessarily have the same background knowledge (or lack of it!) in that subject. But they will need to familiarise themselves with a particular topic rapidly as a single module in a single topic may be only 15 weeks long, with assessments arising during that period. They may have to combine eight or more modules in a single year to obtain a degree at the end of their programme of study. One possible problem with studying a range of separate modules is that the relevance of a particular topic or the relationship between topics might not always be apparent. In the Psychology Focus series, authors have drawn where possible on practical and applied examples to support the points being made so that readers can see the wider relevance of the topic under study. Also, the study of psychology is usually broken up into separate areas, such as social psychology, developmental psychology, and cognitive psychology, to take three examples. While the books in the Psychology Focus series will provide excellent coverage of certain key topics within these "traditional" areas, the authors have not been constrained in their examples and explanations and may draw on material across the whole field of psychology to help explain the topic under study more fully. Each text in the series provides the reader with a range of important material on a specific topic. They are suitably comprehensive and give a clear account of the important issues involved. The authors analyse and interpret the material as well as present an up-to-date and detailed review of key work. Recent references are provided along with suggested further reading to allow readers to investigate the topic in more depth. It is hoped, therefore, that after following the informative review of a key topic in a Psychology Focus text, readers not only will have a clear understanding of the issues in question but will be intrigued and challenged to investigate the topic further.

Acknowledgements

Much love and thanks to all of those who were denied the attention that they deserved while I wrote this book. They know who they are and I am eternally grateful for the fact that I have such a fab bunch of people around me.

My brother Nathan deserves a special mention here (and a big hug!) for the time that he spent reading drafts and preparing the figures that illuminate this text.

Chapter 1

Introduction

What is cognition?

THE WORD "COGNITION" is defined by the *Oxford English Dictionary* as "the mental action or process of acquiring knowledge through thought, experience and the senses". So, cognition is an umbrella term that refers to all of the mental activities that we engage in; our thoughts and our thinking.

Thinking itself is not a simple process, or even a single process. Thinking (or cognition; the two terms are interchangeable) is a complex procedure that is made up of many other processes. Identifying the different processes that are involved in thinking about both different things and in different situations is one of the main aims of those studying cognition. This is not an easy task, as we can't actually observe thoughts. We can only observe the behaviours and actions that result from them and the brain function that accompanies them.

Before we can engage in any actual thinking we need to have something to think about. Thinking involves the processing of information and therefore we need information before any processing can occur. Some theorists suggest that we are born with some *innate* knowledge, but much of our knowledge comes about as a result of learning. To learn things we need to interact with our environment and commit our experiences to memory. Things that we have experienced in the past are stored in our long-term memory. Some theorists argue that all our experiences are committed to memory; other theorists disagree and suggest that only a proportion of our experiences are stored in memory. This is a contentious issue that we do not need to consider here. Either way, we often call on the information that we *have* stored in our memory; our knowledge. Sometimes we reminisce about specific events or experiences just because we want to or because we want to tell other people about them. At other times we use our past experiences to help us interpret the situation that we now face. This is all thinking and it is this that will be the focus of this book.

When we have no previous experiences or knowledge relevant to the task at hand, we have to work with the information that is currently available. In such situations the only information that we can process is the information that our senses are receiving at the time. Although there is a lot of controversy about whether we have different types of memory and what these might be, it is generally accepted that information that is being received and attended to is held in our working memory and that this is distinct from long-term memory. Information that is recalled from long-term memory when needed to deal with a cognitive task is also stored in our working memory during the time that it is being processed. When thinking we often integrate environmental information and information that we have previously stored in our long-term memory in this way.

All of the knowledge that we have and use when thinking is represented in our brains in some form. The pieces of information that we manipulate when thinking are therefore known as *representations*. We can represent information at different levels. Whereas most of what we think of as knowledge we can access voluntarily and on a conscious level, some knowledge is stored at a level that precludes its availability to consciousness. Reflex behaviours are an example of lower-level representations of this sort. Sometimes we do things in response to environmental stimuli seemingly without thinking or, to use the proper term, *automatically*, because we are not consciously aware of any knowledge being involved. For instance, the other day someone asked me which of my kitchen taps was cold and which was hot. I use these taps on a daily basis and consistently turn on the one that will provide me with the temperature water I require. Despite this, it took me a long time to answer the question, as I hadn't really thought about knowing this before, although I obviously do. This is because I had stored the information at a behavioural level, something that was further evidenced by the fact that I had to visualise getting a glass of cold water and act out my actions to answer the question. Automatic responses are very similar to reflex behaviours in a way because in both cases we act upon knowledge as to how to behave in response to a particular environmental cue. The difference between the two is that reflex behaviours are innately preprogrammed whereas automatic behaviours have been learned, albeit subconsciously.

Before we can form representations of our experiences we obviously need to experience things. Experience depends upon us both perceiving and attending to the information that we receive when we interact with our environment (Figure 1.1). Our senses pick up a lot of information and we often need to interpret this. The interpretation of raw sensory input involves imposing some sort of order upon what might otherwise be a confusing bombardment of information. The actual sensory input that we receive is fairly chaotic. As we move around our world we experience a constantly changing array of sights, sounds, smells, feelings and tastes. To make any sense of this we need to organise things. For example, we need to identify objects *as* objects and therefore we need to work out which features "go together" and form whole objects as distinct from other objects. We also need to understand that the same objects can give rise to several different types

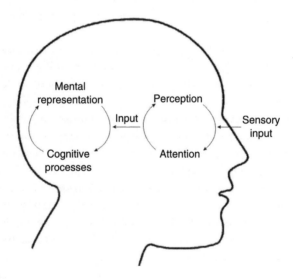

Figure 1.1 The relationship between sensory input and information processing

of sensory input, and we need to know how these relate to each other. For example, we can see, hear, smell, taste, and feel a bowl of Rice Krispies™ and we integrate this knowledge into an experience. We do not experience the different bits separately. Given that these abilities seem fundamental to the formation of complete and accurate representations it seems likely that we would be able to interpret sensory input at an early age. We might even be preprogrammed to be able to do such things from birth (we will return to this issue in Chapter 2).

Having imposed order upon sensory input we then need to attend to it. Even though we may recognise many objects in our surrounding environment *as* objects, we don't always pay attention to all of them! Although our attention can be focused intentionally, that is we can consciously control it, we also attend to a lot of things that we are not consciously aware of paying attention to. Our understanding of this aspect of cognition underlies things such as television reconstructions of crimes. Often we attend to information without knowing it and triggers are needed to bring that information to a consciously accessible level. After all, we can't deliberately recall things that we don't *know* we know.

Attending to information on some level, whether that is consciously or subconsciously, is necessary for information to be committed to memory. As previously mentioned, our working memory is where much of our cognition occurs. When we are actively thinking about something, whether that be recalling a memory or solving a problem, it is our working memory that is being used. If a cognitive *process*, such as using a strategy to solve a problem or to remember something, is applied to information in working memory this often triggers its transference to our long-term memory store. Whether this is always the case is debated but evidence suggests that it does help.

The simple retrieval of a previously stored memory can be said to constitute thinking at a low level (for example, recalling the events of a Friday night out involves *thinking* about what happened) but we often go beyond the information given and fill in gaps and interpret events. Such interpretation often involves us making use of information that we have previously acquired and stored in our long-term memories. For example, the way in which we interpret the behaviour of another person will depend on our knowledge of that person. Similarly, our knowledge about an individual will be based on similarities in that person's behaviour over time and in different circumstances. This is a much more complex process than the retrieval of memories because it involves both this and the integration of this knowledge with new knowledge, and thus it involves more information processing. As such, it is considered to be a higher-order process. The passage of information from our working to long-term memory is therefore two way. We often use knowledge we already have to interpret new information. Similarly, new information can help us to make sense of and organise memories that we have previously acquired. Given that we hold a lot of information in our long-term memories and that we often need to access this information at a moment's notice (and that we can do this quite easily) it is probable that we organise our long-term memories; that we have some sort of mental filing system.

Thinking is not just a matter of remembering and recalling information, as we have seen. We often have to go beyond what is given and engage in some sort of reasoning process. Such reasoning allows us to *make use* of information and generate new ideas based on information we have acquired elsewhere. All the cognitive activities that we engage in are geared towards obtaining information, understanding and interpreting this information and modifying our existing knowledge on the basis of new information so that it provides an accurate description of objects and explanation for events that happen in the outside world. That is, we appear to be preprogrammed to learn and develop our knowledge. Only this flexibility of thought appears to distinguish us from other species and allow for the complexity and ever-changing nature of human society. Human cognition involves a constant interaction between incoming information and information that we have already stored away in our long-term memory. The process of using old information to interpret incoming information often results in changes being made to the knowledge stored in our long-term memory. This allows for cognitive development, something that appears to be a more complex and lengthy process in humans than in other species.

Individual differences in cognitive development

If cognition is thinking, then the term *cognitive development* refers to the way in which our thinking changes with age. Given that we appear to be internally motivated to learn, and that human cognition is flexible and develops in response to environmental experiences, it would seem obvious that every individual, because of their different experiences, will follow a different developmental pattern.

All children are different from the outset. Any parent of more than one child will tell you that they have different temperaments and that these are apparent very soon or even before birth. Such temperamental differences are a reflection of genetic tendencies and are therefore inherited.[1] The temperamental differences of children affect cognitive development in that they specify how the child interacts with his or her environment. They also affect the way in which the environment responds to the child. For example, an active baby might receive more stimulation from his or her caregivers than a baby who cries a lot, who might elicit more negative responses. Given that environmental input and experience is where much of our knowledge comes from, any differences in experience will effect the cognitive development of the child. Other factors that affect experience, such as cross- and within-cultural differences in childrearing and expectations of development, all have an impact upon the precise path of development. We will discuss this issue in more depth later in this book.

Despite individual differences in development, development does seem to follow a predetermined path, with children reaching specific developmental milestones at remarkably similar ages, both across and between cultures. Because of this, the focus of this book will be on the process of normal development and general trends and changes in cognitive abilities. However, factors that contribute to individual differences in development will not be glossed over completely because they can often help us to identify factors that contribute to development.

---

[1] Temperament differs from personality in that whereas temperament is genetically determined, our personality develops as a result of the interaction between our innately specified temperamental predispositions and environmental feedback and experience.

Cognitive development

It is obvious that newborn infants are not capable of complex thought patterns but also that they are born with the capacity to *develop* the ability for complex thought. This ability appears to be a uniquely human capacity.[2] Newborn babies appear to be equipped with all that they need to be able to learn. They enter the world ready and able to extract information from their environment and thus they can immediately begin to form representations of this information (these abilities will be discussed in more detail in the next chapter). But development involves more than just collecting pieces of information. Whereas learning itself can be a passive process, the learner merely taking "photo-shots" of reality and committing them to memory, for humans at least cognitive development goes way beyond this. Human cognition is an active process that involves interpretation and organisation so as to provide an explanation for, and interpretation of, what is seen to be reality. As such, cognitive development involves the constant reorganisation of knowledge so that new incoming information is consistent with what the learner already knows. This has the knock-on effect of enabling the learner to develop new and more effective ways of dealing with and explaining the world.

It is not only the amount of information that we have learned (and have stored in our memory) that increases with age. The degree to which it *can be* and *is* consciously accessed and controlled also changes with development. Thinking does not just get better, faster and more efficient with age, the processes involved actually change in nature. Moreover, the *way* in which information is represented changes as we develop.

Why study cognitive development?

Understanding the nature of cognitive development, the factors that contribute to it and the way in which internal and external factors

---

[2] Some of the great apes have shown *some* higher-order cognitive abilities such as problem solving (Premack & Woodruff, 1978).

interact and result in changes to the way that children think, allows us to develop ways of teaching children so that their development is maximised. Similarly, knowing what constitutes *typical* cognitive development allows us to identify those children who are not developing as expected. We can then use our knowledge of development to help the child development as best we can. For example, if a child's reading age is below normal we can look at the environmental and biological factors that we *know* contribute to reading development (assuming that it is only the child's reading that is affected). We know that certain brain regions are implicated in reading and so these might be damaged. If this is the case then we might be able to develop strategies that do not rely on these parts of the brain but would enable the child to develop reading abilities. We also know that motivation to learn and the encouragement of caregivers and access to reading materials are important factors in the development of reading abilities. If these appear to be contributing to the problems being experienced by the child then we could take the appropriate steps and try and remedy the situation (we will discuss reading development in much more detail in Chapter 6).

If the factors that contribute to development in a particular area are biologically or genetically determined, the extent to which we can intervene in development is obviously going to be limited. This is often the case with children who have genetic syndromes such as Down syndrome, which put an upper limit on cognitive development. Despite these limitations, we can aim to maximise development and make sure that children fulfil their biologically limited potential. The study of genetic syndromes can be helpful in informing our understanding of cognitive development. If a specific biological impairment can be associated with specific cognitive impairments then we have evidence to suggest that biological mechanisms have a large part to play in cognitive functioning in the impaired area. We will discuss how studies of brain function can help our understanding of cognitive development later in this chapter.

Developmental psychologists study cognitive development to understand it. The theoretical models and research findings that have contributed to and arise from such an understanding also have a lot of practical value for educators and clinical child psychologists.

Likewise, studies that look at the effects of intervention programmes that have been developed from theories of development can provide useful feedback and inform subsequent theories and models. The relationship between theory and practice is therefore two way and continuous.

Traditional approaches to the study of cognitive development

Traditionally, the *behaviourist* school of thought argued that children came into the world with no knowledge or capabilities, except the ability to learn. "Blank slate" theories such as this see development as little more than the gradual acquisition of knowledge; the child simply receives input from the external environment and internalises it. The *nativist* view, by contrast, argued that we are born with *innate* abilities that are preprogrammed into the brain at birth and so determine development. For proponents of this approach, the environment of the child has little effect on the child's cognitive development as it is therefore thought to be dictated by a biological timetable within which there is little room for manoeuvre; a view known as *genetic determinism*.

Both the nativist and behaviourist accounts of development described children as passive participants in the process of development; they are either entirely at the mercy of their biology (the nativist view) or dependent on what they are taught (the behaviourist view). Neither of these is correct. We now know that environmental and biological factors interact and the child has an active role to play in his or her own development. This is a constructivist position and it is the constructivist perspective that Jean Piaget pioneered.

Many consider Piaget to be the founder of developmental psychology because he was the first to suggest that children of different ages think in different ways. This sounds obvious today, but for many years it was assumed that children think in the same way as adults—they are just not as good at it. Piaget's theory acknowledged that both innate predispositions and environmental factors have a role to play in cognitive development. Piaget believed that children's thinking is constrained by brain development and tendencies rooted in the child's biological make-up and that these put an upper limit on the child's cognitive capabilities. However, he also suggested that the information that the child is presented with, as well as the *way* in which it is presented, affects the child's thinking and how this thinking develops. Thus he acknowledged the role of the environment. Piaget's theory represents a compromise between the radical nativist and behaviourist theories and suggests that cognitive development is *transactional*, that is, that it results from an interaction between environmental input and knowledge and structures that are inside the child. Piaget claimed that children are preprogrammed not only to learn, but also to organise their mental representations and to adapt their existing knowledge base on the basis of new information; that children *actively construct* knowledge.

Piaget saw the process of development as a continuous one with new cognitive developments emerging from earlier ones. Piaget claimed that children are born with only a very limited amount of knowledge. This knowledge is said to be *behavioural* in nature and therefore it is not available to consciousness. What he meant by this is that newborn infants possess only knowledge of how to *do* certain things such as demonstrate simple reflex behaviours in response to specific features in the environment. They are not aware that they have such knowledge though; it is used *automatically* when necessary. Several reflex behaviours are demonstrated by newborns, they grasp objects, suck, blink, etc. Piaget claimed that these reflex behaviours form the foundations for all subsequent knowledge acquisition. As the child interacts with the environment (by *doing* things to it) the child is said to modify and add to his or her existing knowledge base (such as is the nature of cognitive development).

Piaget coined the term "schema" to refer to units of knowledge (or representations) and he saw development as a gradual increase in both the amount of schema (things that are known and therefore represented) and in the complexity of these schemas. According to Piaget, these mental structures are the representations through which the child "knows" the world. For example, whereas newborns might be able to grasp objects (grasping being one of the few reflex behaviours that Piaget saw as being preprogrammed into the brain at birth) they only grasp in one way, which means that the range of objects that can be held is limited. As infants interact with new objects they need to modify their "grasping" schema. As adults, our grasping schema would be rather complex, we have stored information (based on our experiences with objects) to enable us to pick up objects ranging from a pin to a sofa. So, with development, reflexes become more flexible, easier to generalise to new situations and also more under conscious control (they are no longer automatic).

Schemas are revised and added to as a result of a process that Piaget called *adaptation*. If the schema (knowledge) that the child has is sufficient for him or her to cope with or explain a situation then the child is said to be in state of *equilibrium*. If, however, children are confronted with a situation that they cannot cope with or explain then they are thrown into a state of *disequilibrium*. This state is a negative one and, as with many other negative mental states, it motivates children to return to a positive state (equilibrium). To return to equilibrium they must learn something new or modify existing knowledge: They have to *adapt* their schema. Through this *active* process the structures of thought change.

Piaget not only proposed that the complexity and number of schemas increases with age, he also proposed that the *way* in which knowledge is represented changes as we grow older. According to Piaget's theory, information is represented at a very basic behavioural or perceptual level during the first 18 months or so of an infant's life. So, although infants might *behave* in a way that suggests that they *know* something, they only know things at a level that links a perceptual experience with behaviour. Infants of this age don't actually *know* that they know anything. Any cognitive activity that occurs does so without the infant being aware of it. For example, young babies smile at their parents, giving the impression that they recognise them and that they have a memory of them. But such a memory can be accessed only in the presence of the parents, their presence automatically triggering a behavioural response (the smile); the infants don't actually know that they recognise the parents (although most parents would want to believe that they do!). Whereas newborn infants are limited to behavioural representations, behavioural representations are not limited to infancy. Even in adulthood behaviours can be triggered automatically by perceptual stimuli. Do you remember the tap example mentioned earlier?

According to Piaget, it is during the second year that the capacity for symbolic thought develops and it is this that he claimed allows for the representation of knowledge in a format that is accessible in the absence of related perceptual or behavioural cues. Any conscious recall of information, such as thinking about something that happened last week, requires the ability to store information at a mental level.

The final representational format described by Piaget was *operational*. Operational representations are more complex still because they are organised into a coherent system. It is only when this system is in place that we develop the capacity for logical thinking. Piaget claimed that these changes in representational ability come about as a result of the structural development of the brain.

The basic claims made by Piaget—that the child plays an active role in cognitive development, that it is not just the amount of knowledge that a child has that improves with age, and that development comes about as a result of an interaction between environment and biology—are generally supported by evidence, both research and observation. Cognitive development seems to be *epigenetic*, that is it results from developing brain systems that respond to and develop in response to environmental input. Whereas the structure of the brain at any point in development affects the way in which environmental input is interpreted, environmental influences also affect the development of the brain. Although we cannot assume that brain development and cognitive development are directly related it is highly likely that they are related in some way. The nature of this relationship is much debated; some theorists (like Piaget) believe that cognition reflects changes that occur in the brain at a structural level, others believe that the mind and brain are not as directly related because this and that structural changes are not necessarily reflected in thinking. The relationship between the mind and brain is an issue that is not easily resolved, as we cannot conclusively relate abstract thoughts to physical brain structures. This is a problem for those studying cognitive development but one that needs to be investigated. One of the primary aims of cognitive psychologists is working out how brain structure and cognition are related and how each of these relates to behaviour. Given that only behaviour and brain structure can be directly observed, we can do no more that make informed guesses as to how cognition fits in to the overall picture.

Although many of the points made by Piaget have been incorporated into current thinking, many recent theorists have contested some of his claims. Piaget organised his description of children's development into distinct stages, each characterised by a different way of thinking of things. This stage-like description of development, the importance that Piaget accorded to genetically preprogrammed brain development and the relationship between cognitive activity and brain structure have all been argued against. We will address these issues in the remainder of this book.

Constructivist theories

Constructivist theories, such as that of Piaget, assume that cognitive development comes about as a result of complex interactions between biological factors (that operate from the inside-out) and experiential factors (that operate from the outside-in). Our biology affects the way in which the world is perceived, interpreted and explained. Likewise, our experiences can affect our biology.

The "dynamic systems approach" (Thelen & Smith, 1994) is a constructivist theory *par excellence*. It proposes that development results from a complex interaction between many different aspects of both the environment and the child (at both biological and psychological levels). The dynamic, ever-changing nature of development is emphasised and it is suggested that you can't meaningfully separate out cognitive processes from the context in which they are embedded. As a result, dynamic-systems theories attempt to identify all the interacting influences on development and organise these into a coherent explanation for development. Although such an aim is admirable, it is an incredibly ambitious one given the apparent complexity of human cognition.

It is now generally acknowledged that innate tendencies and abilities might well be preprogrammed into the brain at a genetic or biological level but that they are not "useable" at birth. It is therefore thought more useful to look at the influence of nature (genetic factors) in terms of how they *constrain*, as opposed to dictate, cognitive development. This suggests a rejection of the genetic determinism preferred by traditional nativist theorists. Elman et al. (1996) propose three types of innate constraints on development. First, there are *representational* constraints. These are innate constraints on the child's ability to represent information or the way in which they represent information. These are the type of constraints referred to by Piaget when he proposed that brain development constrains the type of representations that can be supported. Second, there are *architectural* constraints. These are constraints on thinking that are determined by brain structure. For example, the number of neurons in various areas of the brain will determine the way and speed with which information is processed. It might well be that different areas of the brain have developed to different extents at birth so that the child is more likely to process some types of information over others. This leads us on to the third type of innate constraint: *chronotopic* constraints. These are innate constraints on the ordering of specific cognitive developments. It might be that children are preprogrammed to learn specific things at specific times. Genetic programmes that specify the order in which specific cognitive developments occur are said to be innate constraints that exist at a genetic level and become apparent as a result of either biological maturation or as a result of environmental factors that trigger development.

Nowadays, competing theories disagree about the *relative* influence of nature and nurture, the specific aspects of nature and nurture that affect development and *how* these result in and constrain cognitive development. Indeed, most now attempt to define the precise *way* in which various factors interact and how patterns of interaction give rise to cognitive development.

Domain generality/specificity

During our lifetime we acquire knowledge about many different things. Much of this knowledge is subject specific (e.g. maths, science, language) and thinking about different types of knowledge can involve different processes. A *domain* is an area of knowledge that is said to be separate from other areas of knowledge. It comprises of a set of representations of acquired facts. We might also have representations of processes that we use *only* to process knowledge within a specific domain (because they are not relevant to the processing of other sorts of information). Alternatively, it might be that the same cognitive processes are applied to information in different domains.

Domain-general theories of cognitive development propose that *general* psychological changes affect development in all domains simultaneously. Piaget's theory is one such theory. Piaget proposed that biologically based "functional invariants", such as the development of the capacity for logical thinking, were the result of the operation of a single, integrated cognitive system that controls all thinking. As these functional invariants become operational, all domains are affected. So, for example, if a child's development has reached a point whereby they are capable of logical reasoning then a domain-general theory (such as Piaget's) would argue that this capacity for reasoning would become apparent across different domains soon after the development of this domain-general ability. So if a child can reason logically about scientific phenomena that child should also be able to interpret social situations in a logical way. However, theories such as Piaget's acknowledge that domain-general abilities tend to be innately specified to some extent and therefore that they usually put an upper limit on performance within a given domain. The importance of domain-specific knowledge and experience is acknowledged but the importance of these is seen as minimal when compared to domain-general constraints.

Domain-specific theories suggest that development in different domains is completely independent. As a result, development in some domains might proceed at a much faster rate than development in another. Similarly, whereas development in one domain might be dependent on innate factors, development in another could depend more on learning (an environmental influence). This doesn't mean that development in one area cannot affect development in other areas, though. For example, learning to talk or understand the language spoken by those around you opens up new opportunities for learning and development in other areas.

Most current theories of development adhere to neither of these two strict positions; rather they acknowledge the coexistence of both domain-general and domain-specific *mechanisms*. It also doesn't necessarily follow that the effect of domain-general and domain-specific mechanisms on the operation of the cognitive system are the same at different developmental points. This is something that needs to be borne in mind when studying cognitive development. It also makes things a lot more complicated!

Evolution and development

Theories suggesting that children are born with domain-specific innate mechanisms that trigger or help development in specific areas often use evolutionary theory to back up their arguments. It is suggested that, over the course of evolutionary history, our brains have developed in a manner that will maximise our chances of survival, and therefore that any abilities present at birth, or that become available shortly after, are likely to be those that are the most useful. Obviously, the amount of innately specified abilities and knowledge is limited by the size of the human brain at birth and this is limited by the size of the mother's birth canal. If our heads were any bigger than they are at birth, birth itself would be impossible for the mother. Maximum head size therefore limits brain size, which in turn limits our cognitive capabilities. Evolution seems to have done a very good job in this respect because it has prioritised the development of cognitive abilities in terms of their likelihood of ensuring our survival. High-level cognitive functions, such as being able to reason in a scientific way, aren't essential for survival and so they are relatively late achievements (if at all; this is a hotly debated area that we can't go into now but will return to later). Attending to specific aspects of the environment, however, is very helpful and tunes us in to those things that we should learn about very quickly. Focusing on other people, for example, allows us to form attachments with those who care for us during the early years and allows us to develop the ability to communicate with our caregivers so that our basic needs are met. Given that other people can contribute considerably to our cognitive development, the ability to form relationships with them is an important one to have and evolution has acknowledged this.

Domain-specific abilities therefore are those that allow for specific developments in specific areas. The more essential the area of development in terms of our survival, the more likely we are to have innate predispositions that trigger development in that area. Similarly, those abilities we have at birth are those that are likely to trigger later developments.

It is unfeasible for us to think that all cognitive development could be attributable to domain-specific, innately specified abilities. Perhaps *because* of our advanced cognitive capabilities, we have developed new ways of thinking, such as those required when programming a computer or playing a computer game. The demands made on our cognitive system by the technology surrounding us changes at an alarming rate and to function effectively in today's society we have to keep up with these developments and adapt our ways of thinking. Obviously, evolution could not restructure our brains at a rate that would enable us to keep up with the current "mode" of thought. Unfortunately for those of us who can't get their head around what appears to be the bizarre thinking demanded by most computer games (last time I played one, someone suggested that I pick up a chicken and throw it at a wall; something I would have never considered myself!), we have to *learn* to think in an appropriate way. Here there is no help from any domain-specific innate tendencies, unfortunately.

More recent approaches to the study of cognitive development

Early theories of cognitive development were based on studies of children's abilities. Typically, these involved presenting children with a specific task and asking them to give a response. Many of the tasks that were used to substantiate the claims made by theorists such as Piaget required children either to do or to say something in response to a specific test question or situation. By relying on responses such as these it was inevitable, to some extent, that children's cognitive capabilities would be underestimated (as recent studies have now shown to be the case). This is because children might well *know* something but not be in a position to *show* this knowledge to the researcher. There are many possible reasons for this. First, the children might not have the language skills necessary either to understand the questions put to them or to explain themselves. Second, the children might not have the motor co-ordination to act on their thoughts. Finally, children might well have considerable skills in the area under study but not know that these are the ones that they need to use because the nature of the task being presented or the situation in which they find themselves is rather alien; they might know the answer but just not understand the question.

Failure to acknowledge that there are limitations on children's ability to *demonstrate* their cognitive abilities in a way that they can be recognised by researchers led many early theorists to underestimate children's capabilities. We cannot be too harsh when judging these early efforts, though, because the methodologies available to researchers were limited. Recent technological advances have allowed us to devise new ways of looking at the cognitive abilities of children. Not only have these revealed competencies in children at ages much younger than was previously supposed, they have also added significantly to our understanding of the area, the processes involved in cognitive development and the factors that contribute to it.

One procedure that is often used to study the cognitive abilities of very young children is the *habituation* technique. This technique cashes in on the fact that we get bored with things that we have seen or heard many times before and that we pay more attention to novel experiences; just think about how easily your attention is drawn to objects and events that deviate from the norm. The existence of such a tendency makes perfect sense if we consider that human cognition enables us to deal with the outside world in an effective way. To do this we need to accumulate as much knowledge as possible about our environment. Concentrating on things that we have not experienced before allows us to learn *new* things and therefore expand our knowledge base.

From a very early age infants demonstrate the tendency to get bored by things that they have experienced before, preferring instead to attend to the new. Numerous studies have shown that with the repeated presentation of the same stimuli infants' responses steadily decrease. Given that the ways in which very young infants can respond to stimuli are limited, researchers have to take this into consideration and look at behaviours that we *know* even neonates are capable of. As babies aren't capable of much, most studies looking at early representational abilities rely on children's ability to either suck on a dummy or move their eyes in the direction of a particular stimulus. Both of these abilities are instinctive reflex behaviours that require no conscious effort. It is assumed that babies will suck harder to see, hear or feel something that they prefer and that they would similarly spend more time looking at something that they find interesting.

Habituation involves presenting infants with a stimulus until they no longer find it interesting, as indicated by a decrease in the proportion of time they spend looking at it or the amount of sucking that they do so as to be able to look at it. Once habituated to a stimulus, the infants are shown another stimulus. If their looking time increases or they suck at a faster rate it is assumed that they have recognised the difference between this stimuli and that to which they had previously been habituated.

Cognitive science

The cognitive science approach to the study of human intelligence (cognition) was recognised as a separate discipline in the 1970s. It resulted from technological advances that allowed us to observe cognitive processes in a more direct manner. We can now observe the workings of the brain directly using non-invasive techniques such as neural imaging (which allows for the recording of brain activity during various cognitive activities). Invasive techniques such as *positron emission tomography (PET)* (in which radioactive materials are injected into the brain so that those areas of the brain in which activity is occurring can be identified) have also informed our understanding of cognition, although techniques such as this are not really suitable for the study of "normal" children because their invasive nature would be very frightening. Despite this, the use of such techniques has informed our understanding of cognitive development because studies with children who are showing signs of dysfunction, and are therefore subjected to brain function analysis for diagnostic reasons, have allowed us to identify the brain areas and patterns of activity associated with specific cognitive functions.

We also have the computer technology to "model" brain processes. By developing electronic devices that perform functions previously only associated with the human brain (such as remembering) we can learn about how our brains *might* perform the same functions as their artificial equivalents.

Whereas before we could only guess what was going on inside people's heads from what they said or did, and thus we could only study human cognition at a theoretical level, we can now actually access and model these processes. We are no longer limited to the study of the way in which human cognition is used and expressed; we can now go deeper and look at the brain mechanisms that are involved in thinking. This has allowed us to develop a more thorough understanding of the nature of thought. The study of cognition at one level can inform our understanding of thinking at another. For example, understanding brain function has allowed us to develop new theories to explain the nature of thought. Similarly, understanding how we reason through problems has informed our theories as to how information is represented and organised in the brain (at an architectural as opposed to a representational level). So discoveries made at each individual level inform theories and research about the other levels.

Because human cognition is so complex, not only do we have to study it at different levels to get a full explanation, we also have to break it down into individual processes and study these separately. Thus, the cognitive science approach to the study of thinking separates out different aspects and levels of cognition, studies them in isolation and then reconstructs them so as to generate a consistent explanation of the mechanisms and processes that underlie thought. The integration of the mind and the brain is both recognised and emphasised by cognitive scientists.

Developmental cognitive science

Developmental cognitive science looks at the development of cognitive processes from the scientific perspective outlined above. Whereas early theories of cognitive development were based only on the observable aspects of children's cognition (which are obviously limited!), cognitive developmental science allows for a more holistic explanation. Modern-day theories of development go beyond the simple *description* of cognitive processes and the way in which these are utilised and now include references to the neurological processes that underlie these.

In addition, we have developed techniques for the study of cognition that do not rely on other developments (for example, language and motor development). Such advances have been particularly useful for studying the thoughts of infants (infants being children who have not yet developed language). By monitoring behaviours that we know infants are capable of, such as sucking and looking in a particular direction, we now know that infant cognition is far more sophisticated than was previously thought.

Taken together, the fact that we can now study cognition at a physical level and we can also measure the abilities of children without having to rely on them *showing* us what they are capable of, has resulted in significant leaps forward in terms of our understanding of cognitive development.

Cognitive neuropsychology

Methods such those described in the previous sections have enabled researchers to directly investigate how changes in the structure of the brain relate to cognitive development. Brain development is not just a matter of increasing size. Different parts of the brain develop at different rates and this is, at least in part, related to their function.

There are two main areas of the brain. The cortex is on the outside and the subcortex sits within the cortex at the top of the spinal column. Generally speaking, the subcortex comprises structures that control biological functions and instinctive behaviours, whereas the cortex is where the structures that support cognition reside. Given that the cognitive abilities of humans are considerably more advanced than those of other species, our cortex takes up a greater proportion of our brain. Whereas our subcortex develops before birth according to a genetic blueprint that is only minimally affected by environmental factors, much of the development of the cortex occurs after birth. This is reflected in the developing child's increasing cognitive abilities.

The cerebral cortex is divided into different areas (Figure 1.2), each one being responsible for different aspects of cognition. Of these areas the prefrontal cortex is the least developed at birth. This is the part of our brain that is responsible for the regulation and planning of behaviour and thinking or what has become known as *executive function*. Executive function is not a single cognitive skill, it is a complex set of processes that monitor and control other lower-level thought processes (Shallice & Burgess, 1991). We will discuss the nature of executive function in more detail later in this book. For now, what is important is the fact that executive function is a complex cognitive activity that develops postnatally and in response to environmental feedback. Generally speaking, more complex cognitive skills are dependent on more postnatal development and more environmental factors feature in the development of the brain areas that support them. It is for this reason that human brains undergo more postnatal development than the brains of other species.

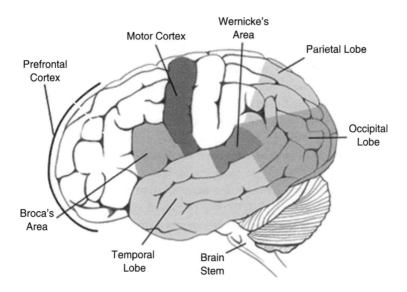

Figure 1.2 **The human brain**

Within each of the key brain areas there are more specific structures that are associated with specific functions. Engaging in different mental activities gives rise to distinct patterns of activity across different brain areas. These *functional specialisations* suggest that the brain is made up of a number of distinct *cognitive modules;* each one controlling a different cognitive function. What is unclear, though, is whether these cognitive modules are innately specified at a genetic level or whether the brain becomes progressively modularised with development and as a result of interaction with the environment. *The modularity issue*, as it has become known, is a strongly debated issue and will therefore be discussed further at various points in this book.

Much of our brain is made up of neurons. These are specialised nerve cells that communicate with each other by *electrochemical transmission*. Electrical signals travel through the neuron and trigger the release of a chemical that passes between points of communication between neurons (known as synapses). This triggers an electrical reaction in the next neuron. Before birth, neurons are born through a process of cell division, they then migrate to different parts of the brain. Having settled in their final resting place they begin to *differentiate*. Differentiation is the process through which neurons specialise so as to perform the functions associated with the particular brain area that they have settled in.

Well before they are born, children are equipped with a full complement of neurons; about a million million (Rakic, 1995) but these are not all connected to each other. With development, neurons reach out and form connections with other neurons (a process known as *synaptogenesis*). At different points in development, different parts of the brain are active in this way. After an initial burst of connection-forming activity, neuronal connections then undergo *pruning*. Synapses between those neurons that have not communicated with others tend to die off (Figure 1.3). This means that at earlier points in development there are often more synapses than there are at later developmental points. So why do some neurons communicate with each other and others not?

As we have already seen, different parts of the brain perform different cognitive functions; it is modularised. How this happens and how neurons specialise to perform the functions associated with the

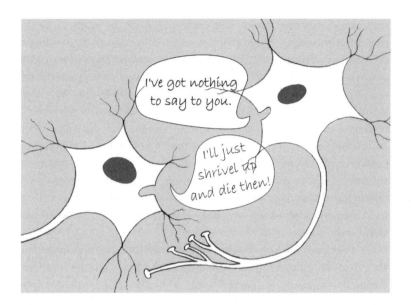

Figure 1.3 **Shrivelling dendrite: The effects of pruning**

different brain areas occurs is not, however, clear. *Selectionist theories* (e.g. Changeux, 1985) suggest that each individual neuron is preprogrammed to react to (be activated by) a specific feature of the environment. Each perceptual experience that a child has therefore gives rise to a specific and distinct pattern of neuronal activity. These patterns of activity are known as *neural circuits*. Those synapses that are not utilised in the neural circuits weaken and are eventually lost through the process of pruning. With development, neural circuits become progressively more isolated from other circuits. This results in the specialisation of brain regions for different functions.

It was suggested earlier that the study of people with known genetic syndromes could be useful in helping us to understand cognition and its development. The study of the brain activity of people with such syndromes has informed our understanding of both the syndromes themselves and patterns of typical development.[3] Studies of

---

[3] We will consider specific syndromes in more detail later in this book.

such syndromes have shown how certain areas of the brain are better suited to processing certain types of information and that any genetic defects that affect specific brain areas affect specific types of cognitive activity. This is evidenced by the consistency in the patterns of impairments of those with genetic syndromes. However, we have also learned that areas of the brain not typically associated with the processing of different types of information can take over the role usually associated with the impaired areas if this is necessary. Although processing might not be as effective in such cases, the fact that brain areas are not limited to only one function shows us that the path of development is not as fixed as the nativist theorists would have us believe and that brain modules are not innately specified, at least not completely.

The study of people who have experienced brain damage has also contributed to our understanding of the brain and its plasticity during development. If damage occurs while the brain is still developing, other brain areas can take-up the role usually adopted by the damaged areas. If damage occurs later in life this is not the case. The progressive specialisation of brain areas means that as development occurs it becomes more difficult for atypical brain regions to adopt roles that they are not normally associated with. This suggests that modularisation is progressive.

Modelling cognitive development

Many of the more recent theories of cognitive development have made use of the advances in computer technology that have occurred over the past few decades. Of particular note are information-processing accounts of development. Information-processing accounts are based on the assumption that cognition and information processing is one and the same thing; that thinking *is* information processing and vice versa. Information processing is said to be dependent on domain general, biological brain structures, the most important being working and long-term memory. These brain structures are said to be relatively stable components of the information-processing system and, as such, their overall structure is not thought to change with age. That is not to say that there are *no* structural changes to these components; at a neuronal level, more information is represented. The changes are quantitative rather than qualitative though. So, if the principal brain structures that are involved in cognition don't change with age, what does? After all we already know that cognition *does* develop and that it is far more than the acquisition of knowledge.

According to information-processing theorists, the extent to which the brain structures that support cognition can be *used* is thought to change with development. The ways in which structures are used when thinking are known as *processes* and it is the way in which these change with development that is of interest to information-processing theorists. The strategies that children employ when trying to interpret, explain and deal with incoming information, given that their attempts to do so are limited by the development of the afore-mentioned cognitive structures, are often the focus of research and computer simulations.

To simulate a specific cognitive development on a computer, you have to be able to both model the internal workings of the human mind and input into this system inputs of the kind that children receive over the course of development. If system works then it suggests that the model is based on sound theoretical claims about the interaction between the internal workings of the mind and information from the environment.

We must, however, be cautious when interpreting successful models of cognitive processes. Whereas the successful operation of a computer simulation might suggest that a cognitive development *could* occur as a result of an interaction between clearly defined internal mechanisms and environmental input, it does not necessarily follow that it does. We must always bear in mind that computer models look at one aspect of development in isolation, and this is not how the human mind works. During development a child does not just concentrate his or her efforts on developing in a particular area, many different types of input and situation have to be learned about at the same time.

Siegler's (1996) "overlapping waves" theory has resulted in accurate computer simulations of cognitive processes. These are based on Siegler's suggestion that the process of cognitive development is similar to the process by which species adapt as a result of evolution. He proposes that at any one time children have available to them a number of different ways of thinking or approaching a problem; that is, they have different *strategies* that can be applied to the same situation. These compete against each other and eventually the more adaptive ones become those that are more frequently used. This is where the evolutionary analogy comes in. Characteristics that are useful survive whereas those that are not gradually die out. Having implemented a particular strategy, information as to its speed and accuracy is fed back into the cognitive system. This results in the modification of existing knowledge, which in turn alters the likelihood of it being used in the future. If a strategy has proven successful in the past then the child might well choose this strategy as opposed to other available strategies. However, it could be that this strategy is only of use in certain situations. As a result, the child might well go through a period whereby he or she attempts to use a strategy in inappropriate situations. The feedback generated from these poor attempts is then used to up-date knowledge.

The connectionist approach to modelling cognitive development attempts to simulate the neurological activities that give rise to cognition at a structural level. According to Plunkett (1996), connectionist models are made up of a number of information-processing units or *nodes*. These are organised in layers: There is an output layer, an input layer and a layer in the middle (known as the *hidden* layer). The nodes are connected so that each one can communicate with all of the others. The researcher controls the information that is input into the computer system and this results in the activation of a specific pattern of nodes. This strengthens the connections between those nodes that are activated at the same time.

Connectionist models learn by comparing the output generated by the system (the answer to a problem) with the correct answer. This results in the modification of existing knowledge. Knowledge, according to connectionist accounts, is distributed across the network (so several nodes and the connections between them, are involved in the representation of any piece of knowledge). Any modifications made to connections between nodes are therefore indicative of a change in the knowledge represented within the system.

Connectionist models have successfully replicated a number of different cognitive processes. This, teamed with the obvious resemblance of the information-processing nodes to neurons, has increased the popularity of these models in recent years. These models also demonstrate how development can appear stage like but not actually reflect any underlying structural change to cognition. After all, in these simulations the structure of the information-processing system does not change. Such a position is very similar to that of Siegler in that neither adheres to the idea of stages of development.

Neo-Piagetian theories, like information-processing accounts, take a computational approach to the explanation of cognitive development and emphasise the interaction between structures and processes. However, they also bear some resemblance to Piaget's theory in that they suggest that development is stage like. Fischer's (1980) and Case's (1985) theories fall into this category.

Both Fischer's and Case's theory suggest that architectural constraints on information processing put an upper limit on a child's cognitive capabilities at any given developmental point. Both also suggest that environmental input influences development.

Fischer (1980) concentrates on children's *skill* development. Skills are said to be patterns of thought and action that enable us to respond to specific situations in an organised way. If a specific skill proves effective, the child will demonstrate this skill at its *optimal level*; this level being dictated by biological constraints on information processing. Given that the environment supports the development of some skills more than others, children's cognitive development will appear domain-specific despite the fact that domain-general changes to information-processing and representational abilities always limit cognitive development. So, although a child might be capable of logical reasoning, this would only be apparent (i.e. the child would only use this skill) in some domains. The domains in which children would perform at their optimum level would be those in which the environment had provided the child with sufficient experience. Fischer's approach then appears to incorporate an aspect of behaviourist theory in that it proposes that learning is important for cognitive development.

Case (1985), like Fischer, believes development to be constrained by domain-general changes to information-processing capacity. Also like Fischer, he sees environmental input as a key factor in determining a child's cognitive abilities within a particular domain. The acquisition of domain-specific knowledge allows domain-specific mental processes (strategies) to become automatic within a given domain. Automatic processing requires no cognitive effort and thus makes no demand on working memory. As more working memory space is cleared, the child has more mental resources available allowing him or her to engage in more complex cognitive activities and keep more information "in mind" at any given time. As a result, a child will only perform at an optimum level in domains with which he or she is familiar.

Theory theories (and this isn't a typing error, they are a type of theory) of cognitive development (Gopnik & Meltzoff, 1997) propose that cognitive development occurs because children are born with an innate tendency to explain their world. To do this, they construct theories. For theory theorists, children are little scientists, who actively come up with theories, test these out through experimentation and then modify them so that they provide a good explanation for the evidence. According to theory theories, the basic processes of development (theory generation, testing and change) do not change over the course of development; it is the nature and complexity of children's representations that change. Such theories are similar to Piaget's in that they suggest that children actively modify knowledge when confronted with evidence that contradicts it (similar to Piaget's concept of adaptation). Unlike Piaget, theory theorists emphasise the existence of both domain-specific knowledge and domain-specific constraints upon the extent to which information can be processed.

Summary and conclusions

Traditional approaches to the study of cognitive development, such as nativism and behaviourism, could not accommodate research evidence that suggested that although children's cognitive development occurs in a remarkably consistent way, no two children develop in exactly the same way. As a result, current theories acknowledge an interaction between innate, genetically preprogrammed constraints on development and environmental influences. Recent technological advances that have allowed us to study brain function have shown us that brain development constrains cognitive development and that it is somewhat dependent on experience. There thus seems to be a complex interaction between internal and external influences on the development of cognition. Given that human thought is limited in terms of the structures and procedures that are available for use when thinking, and is flexible in that different cognitive resources can be called upon in different situations, cognitive developmental psychologists have a difficult task ahead of them. Not only do they need to explain how brain activity, cognition and behaviour are related but also how each of these is affected by environmental influences and experience, as well as genetically based predispositions, abilities and limitations.

The rest of this book

Many basic domain-general abilities, such as the speed with which information can be processed, increase with age and as such they do not change in function over the course of development. This book will focus on the more complex abilities that *change* rather than just improve with age. How changes to domain-general abilities affect abilities in specific areas will be given due consideration, however, because they often constrain development, as we shall see.

Given that representations underlie thought, the early chapters (2 and 3) will focus on how infants represent their world, how they perceive and interpret both objects and events, and how these abilities develop over the early years.

As a child's ability to represent information develops and his or her store of mental representations increases, some sort of organisation system becomes necessary. This allows for much easier access to representations that might be of use when interpreting new information. How this occurs will be considered and we will see that with age the tendency to extract only the necessary information from experiences becomes more efficient and this results in the formation of *conceptual prototypes*, which are prototypical representations that refer to categories of objects or events. As children's cognitive capacities increase, children also become more *aware* of their own thinking. While evidence suggests that infants don't consciously think in the same way as adults or older children, because they can't access mental representations on demand, the degree to which we can exercise control over our mental processes increases with age and experience. Such control allows for the implementation of strategies that can increase our ability to learn about, interpret and reason about the world around us. As this occurs, the capacity for logical thought develops (this will be discussed in Chapter 4). Recent evidence relating to the afore-mentioned cognitive developments will be presented in an attempt to describe the nature of cognitive development and identify the specific developments that occur. Attention will be paid to the structures (biological) of thought and the way in which thinking operates (its function). Theoretical explanations for development will also be presented.

In the latter part of the book (Chapters 5, 6 and 7), we will consider specific areas of development, these being language development, reading development and the development of an understanding of the nature of mind.

When looking at each area of development, theoretical explanations and models of development will be considered and research findings from experimental studies will be used to evaluate the claims made by competing theories. Attention will also be paid to disorders and problems associated with development in some of the areas studied, as studies of the specific deficits and neurological bases for these disorders can shed light on the processes and structures involved in "normal" thinking.

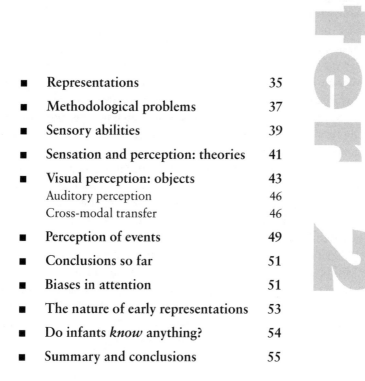

Chapter 2

The starting position

THE TERM "STARTING position" is often used by developmental psychologists to describe the knowledge and abilities of newborn babies. It is this knowledge and these abilities that allows for subsequent cognitive development. The term "starting position" is a strange term and it could be seen to imply that development is a race. It certainly isn't. On the contrary, humans take their time to develop. As discussed in Chapter 1, the cognitive abilities of humans are not only considerable they are also flexible. Human cognition develops in response to an ever-changing environment and for this reason innate constraints upon development are limited to those that "kick-start" development. Environmental information then feeds back into the developing system, resulting in cognitive development.

In Chapter 1 we looked at the basic stages involved in the processing of information; we looked at what cognition *is*. Representations are the pieces of information that we hold in our minds and thus these underlie our thoughts (or cognition). Our representations are the basic structures through which we *know* the world. As soon as we can say that a child has access to representations, then we are saying that they have some knowledge of the world with which to work. Whether any cognitive activity occurs as a result of this (i.e. whether these representations are subject to any manipulation or processing) is another issue and one that will be addressed later. For now, we will concentrate on whether neonates *can* represent knowledge.

We experience the world through our senses and, as we shall see, these are fairly well developed at birth. Although some environmental input is needed to "finetune" a neonate's sensory abilities, this appears to be minimal, suggesting that sensory abilities are to a large extent genetically preprogrammed. This makes sense if we consider the evolutionary argument that suggests that those abilities that we are born with or develop early are those that are the most useful for our subsequent development. Receiving sensory input is fundamental for learning and if our senses were poorly developed at birth any sensory input that we then went on to represent would be a poor representation of reality and therefore would not be of much use. To learn about the world in which we live we have to have accurate information.

As adults, we can attend to only a relatively small amount of the information that we are confronted with every day because our information-processing capacities are constrained (as they are throughout development). Some of the time we actively engage in the process of attending to that information that is the most relevant to us whereas at other times we to do this instinctively. Given that newborns have had very few experiences upon which to base any judgements about what to attend to and what not to, any biases in attention that exist are likely to be attributable to innate constraints on development.

In Chapter 1 we considered the possibility that babies enter the world equipped with predispositions to attend to some environmental stimuli over and above others. These, it was argued, would have developed as a result of evolutionary forces that determine which abilities develop first. This would be those that are the most important in terms of ensuring survival. In terms of Elman et al.'s (1996) description of innate constraints on development we need now to consider the starting point of the neonate with regards to the representational, architectural and chronotopic constraints on development.

Representations

It must be assumed that the ability to form representations is innately specified, so that no learning is necessary for the ability to become apparent. The ability to learn *has* to be innate because it can't be learned. How could you possibly learn to learn? If this is the case then the question is when does this ability "kick-in"? Are neonates capable of forming representations and, if so, are there limitations on how long they can be held for and on the nature of the representation formed?

Any limitations on the receipt and processing of information at birth must be a result of our biology. As we saw in Chapter 1, the human brain is far from developed at birth. Because of this it is obvious that the cognitive abilities of a newborn are going to be very constrained. The question is *how* constrained? Do infants enter the world ready to learn or must they wait for their brain to develop to an extent that allows them to form representations?

Research evidence suggests that newborn babies can form representations, and that this ability is in place even before birth. DeCaspar and Fifer (1980), for example, found that 12-hour-old babies learned to suck at a specific rate to hear a tape of their mother's voice rather than that of a stranger demonstrating that they could both recognise the mother's voice and that they preferred it to other sounds. Although it is possible that the babies in this study learned to do this in the 12 hours between being born and being tested, a further study by DeCaspar and Spence (1986) suggests otherwise. In this study, mothers-to-be read a story to their baby (or their tummy, depending on how you want to look at it), each day for the last 6 weeks of their pregnancy. Once born, the neonates demonstrated a preference for these stories over others, as indicated by their learning to suck at a specific rate so as to be allowed to hear the familiar stories. The possibility that the infants were responding to the mother's voice rather than the story itself was ruled out because DeCasper and Spence found that the preference persisted even when an unfamiliar voice was reading the story. The infants in this study had clearly formed a representation of the story read to them while still in the mother's womb. In a later study, DeCasper, Lecanuet, Busnel, Granier-Deferre and Maugeais (1994) found that even when still in the womb, a preference for familiar over unfamiliar stories was apparent. Fetal heart rate was found to decrease when a familiar rather than a novel piece of prose was read to the unborn baby.

It is obvious that any learning pre-birth is going to be limited by the amount of environmental input the child is exposed to. Once born, the neonate is suddenly exposed to a much richer environment. When in the mother's womb babies can hear sounds from the outside world but they can't see it. Because of this it would be reasonable for us to assume that a neonate is likely to have formed more auditory than visual representations. It is very difficult to test for the formation of visual experiences while in the womb, but we do know that neonates begin to form representations of visual experiences very soon after birth. Slater (1997) reviewed the evidence and came to the conclusion that newborn babies can form representations of objects and that they can distinguish between objects of different sizes, shapes and colours. This suggests that not only were infants representing objects as whole objects but also that they had perceived and represented the properties of these objects. The ability to recognise size irrespective of the distance from which it was viewed has also been demonstrated in newborns (Slater & Morrison, 1985). In a habituation study, newborn infants demonstrated renewed interest in objects of different sizes even when these were presented at a distance that would result in a retinal image that was the same size as that projected onto the retina by the object which the infant was initially habituated. This suggests that *size constancy* is innately specified; that newborns are born with the ability to use perceptual cues to perceive depth and to work out sizes of objects on the basis of this. In a similar study, Slater, Matlock, and Brown (1990) found that *shape constancy* is also an innate ability.

It seems, then, that the brain structures required for the representation of different aspects of the environment, and thus for the formation of simple memories, are in place before birth. Neurological evidence supports this, as the basic neural architecture of the brain does not change with development (as discussed in Chapter 1). What does appear to change is the amount of information represented and this is a result of learning and experience. For the human brain to be equipped in such a way makes perfect sense if we consider that the capacity for representation must be in place before further cognitive development can occur. If representations were not available to children then there would be nothing for them to manipulate and therefore apply cognitive processes to. As a result, evolution has deemed this to be a developmental necessity.

Methodological problems

Although the brains of newborns preprogrammed to allow for the formation of representations from the moment of birth, some areas of the brain are far from fully developed, for example those responsible for motor control (the basal ganglia and motor cortex). Whereas the prioritisation of specific developments testifies to the existence of innate constraints in that those abilities that develop earlier are the most useful, limited abilities in specific areas can be problematic for those studying the cognitive abilities of infants. The limited motor control of neonates is just one problem that researchers face when attempting to study early capabilities. Babies can't actually *do* much and thus getting babies to demonstrate what they know is rather problematic.

We have to rely on behaviours that we *know* children are capable of when conducting studies. As we shall see, *not* doing so has led to misconceptions as to the extent of infants' abilities in the past. As babies aren't capable of much, most studies looking at early representational abilities (such as those of Slater et al., 1985, 1990, described earlier) rely on the babies' ability to visually attend to stimuli or suck on a dummy. Both of these are instinctive reflex behaviours that require no conscious effort. However, although we know that babies are capable of these behaviours, we cannot claim to know what they *mean*. We can't be *sure* that infants look at novel stimuli more than they do familiar stimuli, or that they will suck harder on a dummy to see or hear things that they want to see or hear; they might suck harder or look for longer for reasons that we haven't considered.

Whereas many studies conducted with infant participants rely on reflex behaviours, many don't. Researchers therefore need to be very careful when designing studies that rely on other abilities, and make sure that infants are actually capable of these. Given that we can never be sure of the meaning of an infant's behaviour, any conclusions we draw from research studies must be drawn tentatively. We can only ever infer infants' behavioural responses and there may well be a difference between what infants know and what they can show us that they know.

Reaching conclusions as to whether specific abilities are present at birth is complicated by the fact that it is unethical to study infants the minute they enter the world (although rumour has it that Piaget inflicted such things on his children and on his poor wife, whose newborn was subjected to a few basic tests very soon after birth!). As a result, many studies look at the abilities of neonates several days or weeks after birth. This, of course, begs the question, when considering such research findings, of whether the specific ability under study was present at birth or whether it was learned rather quickly, that is between birth and the time of the study. Having said that, this issue is not as important as it first might seem. While this question was considered to be fundamental in the days when the nature/nurture issue was a hotly debated topic, we now know that genes and the environment interact in complex ways and that it is these interactions that give rise to cognitive development. If we consider the arguments presented in Chapter 1 relating to what is meant by innateness and how innate abilities have been prioritised by evolution, early development of a specific ability suggests that it is an important ability to have in terms of survival and maximising subsequent development. Given this, it is not possible for us to draw a definite distinction between abilities that are present at birth and those that develop shortly after because it is impossible for definite conclusions to be drawn in terms of the precise ages at which specific skills become apparent. More importantly though, we know that this isn't that important in the greater scheme of things. What *is* more important is determining the nature of development and the order in which specific developments occur. It is this that will enable us to determine the relative roles of environment and biology and look at the domain-specificity or generality of specific abilities and processes.

New technology has allowed us new insight into the representational abilities of neonates. For a long time this was considered to be an almost impossible area of study, given that it is impossible to access thoughts because thoughts are abstract and have no concrete basis. The thoughts of children are even more difficult to access because children often cannot make their thoughts known to us, as they have no language and a rather limited behavioural repertoire. New technology has enabled us to observe mental processes more directly. Although studies of neural activity in infants are limited for reasons already discussed, we have *begun* to accumulate knowledge about the biological and neural structures involved in infant cognition.

Sensory abilities

To form a representation you first need to have some information to represent. The fact that neonates are capable of forming representations suggests that their senses are in working order. After all, you need to be able to see, hear, feel, and so on, to receive any sensory input that you then go on and store. The sensory abilities of young babies appear to be linked directly to the ability to form representations. The auditory system is developed well before birth. Joseph (2000) found that 6 to 7 weeks into pregnancy, embryos respond to sounds from the mother's environment suggesting that they can hear. By 30 weeks into pregnancy, babies responded selectively to environmental sounds, reacting more to those that are unfamiliar as measured by fetal heart rate. Not only does this suggest that the auditory system is well developed but also that the brain areas that support the formation of auditory representations are similarly well developed. The unborn babies in this study had obviously formed representations of familiar sounds, allowing them to discriminate and react differently to different noises.

The visual system is less developed and still not fully functional at birth. Newborn infants have rather blurry vision and can only focus on things that are very close to them. This might serve an important function in that it focuses attention on certain aspects of the environment. If newborns could see as well as adults they would be bombarded with visual information and this might be too much for their little brains to cope with. Limiting the amount of information that can be attended to could be helpful, as could the gradual loosening of this biological constraint.

This prioritisation of developments makes perfect sense. It wouldn't be worth developing abilities before they can be put to good use. Hearing develops before birth, allowing for the formation of auditory representations that could help orient the child once born. Similarly, the development of visual abilities is limited to the extent to which they allow for the formation of those visual representations that are likely to prove the most essential for later development.

That young infants can form representations of specific objects and events in their environment also suggests that, contrary to James' (1890) description of the infant's world as a "buzzing, blooming confusion" in which there is no perceived sense, neonates appear to be equipped with some innate knowledge that enables them to impose some order on what would otherwise appear to be a chaotic array of sensory information. To form a representation of a sight or sound you need to be able to isolate that sight or sound from a bigger sensory experience. Thus, some perceptual abilities appear to be hard-wired into the brain and available for use at birth.

The way in which we (as adults) interpret sensory input depends to some extent on what we already know. We therefore have to acknow-

ledge that learning and therefore the environment are important influences on the development of perceptual abilities. For example, we
adults can easily recognise familiar objects even if the features that
distinguish them are for some reason obscured. To do this we look at
contextual cues and often make informed guesses about the identity or
nature of objects. The flow of information within the cognitive system
therefore seems to be bi-directional: Information that is received by the
senses forms the basis for representations while previously acquired
knowledge contributes to interpretation of sensory input.

Sensation and perception: theories

Newborn infants have a very limited store of knowledge (about specific things) to refer to when interpreting the raw sensory data that they
receive. They have, after all, had very little experience of any sort.
However, this does not necessarily mean that they cannot *perceive*
their surrounding environment. It might well be that they are born
equipped with innate tendencies and principles that allow them to
decipher sensory information to some extent. The question that needs
to be addressed here is the *extent* to which neonates interpret the world
around them and, as such, what their representations consist of.

The fact that newborn babies have been shown to form representations of objects and selectively attend to some over others so soon
after birth suggests that infants have some knowledge as to what an
object actually *is*. If neonates didn't know what an object was they
would not be able to pick an object out from an array and form a
representation of that object as distinct from the context in which it
was presented. This implies that the world that an infant perceives is
not nearly as chaotic as the early blank slate theories of development
would have had us believe. These theories, such as those of James
(1890) and Skinner (1957), suggested that children are born with no
knowledge at all, including no knowledge of how to interpret the
environmental information that they are confronted with. According
to these theories, a newborn's first task was to learn how to interpret
this information. Even Piaget (1954) subscribed to this idea: He too
thought that neonates could not impose any order on sensory input

and that the ability to *perceive* develops as a result of cognitive activity and learning. More recent research evidence suggests that this is not the case and that children are born with innate knowledge and abilities that enable them to make sense of their environment. From an evolutionary perspective this makes perfect sense. Surely if evolutionary development were to equip us with one ability that could pave the way for subsequent development it would be the ability to interpret sensory data. After all, to form a useful representation you have to attend to meaningful information. You can only have meaningful information if you can impose some meaning on the sensory data that is being received.

The fact that neonates *are* able to interpret sensory input and perceive their environment fits Gibson's (1979) description of the perceptual abilities of newborns. Gibson argued that perception is a direct, innately specified response to stimulation and that no cognitive interpretation of sensory input is required. Gibson proposed that the human brain is pre-wired to interpret sensory data using perceptual cues. These cues are implicitly understood and used to interpret the two-dimensional image projected onto the retina so that a three-dimensional world is perceived. According to Gibson, experience just finetunes an innately specified system; a view that contrasts with Piaget's assertion that experience is necessary for the development of perceptual abilities. Evidence shows that neonates have shape and size constancy and that they form representation of objects separate from the context in which they were presented. This suggests that infants do have substantial perceptual abilities and that these are specified at a biological level. However, Gibson claims that we do not cognitively process the sensory data that we perceive and therefore he suggests that we always perceive the world as it is. Given that he does not allow for cognitive interpretation, his interpretation suggests that we could never misinterpret visual reality. This obviously is not the case as we often succumb to visual illusions.

So what is the extent of infants' interpretative abilities? What order can infants impose on their environment and how does this pave the way for subsequent development? There are two main things in the world that infants need to represent before they can begin to accumulate knowledge: objects and events. We will now consider the research evidence and try and ascertain the extent to which they can represent these.

Visual perception: objects

Spelke (1988, 1998) suggests that neonates possess innately specified "guiding principles" that enable them to impose some order on their visual environment. These allow the babies to work out which visual features in their environment belong with one another and therefore to the same object. This perceptual isolation of individual objects is the first step in the formation of representations of objects: To form a representation of an object we need to identify it as *an object*. Spelke proposed that infants assume that parts belong to one object if the outline of the object is clearly defined. This seems reasonable enough, but this assumption alone would not get us very far in the real world because we very rarely see clear outlines of objects as other objects often get in the way. This hiding of parts of objects by other objects is known as *occlusion*. How do infants cope with this?

To investigate, Kellman and Spelke (1983) presented young infants with a moving rod that was partially occluded by another object so that the two ends of the rod were poking out from behind the occluding object, and the rod was moving behind this object. What they were interested in was whether the infants would recognise the rod as a single object, that is as one rod rather than two rods. To test this, the babies were habituated to the original (occluded rod) stimulus. They were then shown two simultaneous visual displays. One of these was a single rod of the same size and shape as that used in the first phase of the experiment. The other stimulus was two shorter rods, positioned so as to be *visually* identical to the ends of the rod as *seen* in the first part of the procedure. By 4 months, infants showed a preference for the second of these stimuli as measured by looking time. This suggests that they perceived this to be the more novel of the two stimuli. Thus, they appeared to have formed a representation of the rod ends, in the first part of the procedure, as being part of *one* object.

Although 4-month-old infants perceived the partially occluded rod as one object they could not do this when the rod was held still (rather than moving) until 7 months of age. This suggests that movement plays an important role in early object perception and that in the absence of movement, infants have problems identifying occluded objects. Further evidence for the importance of movement in the early perception of objects comes from a second study.

Kellman and Spelke (1983) found that when the aforementioned experiment was repeated with irregular shapes that were presented so that the non-occluded parts of the object were different shapes and colours, young infants still perceived the non-occluded parts as part of the same object. This is not what adults would do. As adults, other principles are often accorded more importance than movement. For example, we assume that objects are usually consistently shaped and coloured. If both colour consistency and movement were available as cues we would usually place more importance of the first of the two available cues. The fact that movement is so important for object perception during the early stages of development suggests that there might be innate constraints on attention and that infants are predisposed to attend to moving objects over and above stationary ones. We will return to this possibility later.

It is evident that innately specified abilities have a vital role to play in the early perceptual abilities of infants. Whereas environmental input and learning also have a role to play in the development of these abilities, the basic principles outlined above enable the young infant to put the sensory information that they receive into some sort of order. This is obviously something that is necessary before they begin to learn about specific objects and events in the environment. Although the neonate's ability to identify objects is guided by only a few simple rules, the acquisition of knowledge allows for these rules to be modified. As our knowledge of objects increases we make use of this knowledge. If we recognise an object as a specific type of object we no longer have to call upon these principles to interpret sensory input (see Figure 2.1 for examples). Here we have another example of how the flow of information from one part of the information-processing system to another is bi-directional. The sensory input that we receive determines that what we can represent whereas the representations we have acquired determines the interpretation placed upon sensory input and thus their content and complexity.

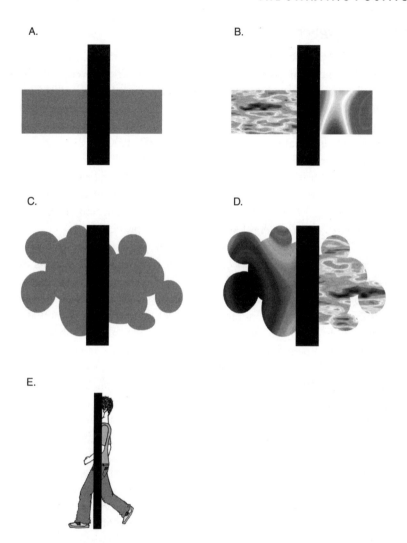

Figure 2.1 **Various occluded objects**
According to Kellman and Spelke (1983) 4-month-olds can perceive all objects as one if movement is also a cue, whereas adults would perceive A, B, C and E as one object, even if stationary. D would not be recognised as one object because shading is seen as important and the object is unrecognisable.

Auditory perception

Can infants differentiate between sounds (auditory events) in the same way that they can distinguish between objects (visual events) in the visual field? What we all actually *hear*, infants and adults alike, is a constant stream of noise from which we have to extract individual sounds before we can represent them: Just think of how we can "tune in" to an individual's voice when several people are talking or pick out a single beat to dance to, from a song that consists of many overlapping beats. Earlier we looked at evidence that showed that auditory representations are formed and stored while the child is still in the womb, suggesting that the ability to form representations is present before birth and as such is hard-wired into the brain.

Forming a representation of the mother's voice while still in the womb might well be an easier task than forming representations of other sounds after birth. The womb is not a particularly noisy environment and as such there would be less background noise from which the sound of the mother's voice would have to be perceptually distinguished (only the mother's internal gurgles and womb sounds would be competing for attention!). However, by the age of 1 month babies can discriminate between very similar speech sounds (Trehub & Rabinovitch, 1972). Individual sounds (known as phonemes) are spotted in a variety of voices by 2 to 3 months of age (Marean, Werner, & Kuhl, 1992) and by 6 months infants can discriminate between multisyllable sounds and respond to target sounds even when they are in the middle of words (Fernald & Kuhl, 1987). The early emergence of the ability to identify individual sounds from a continual stream of noise is a useful one and one that is necessary for language development. Given that being able to understand language opens up new possibilities for learning, it is not surprising that we see evidence of the early emergence of abilities related to language development (these issues will be explored further in Chapter 5).

Cross-modal transfer

So far we have considered visual and auditory perception separately and looked only at whether infants are capable of imposing order on the sensory data that they receive. In real life we don't often consider information from each of our senses separately. We combine information from several sources into one coherent *experience*. For example, when we are having a conversation with someone we usually both see and hear them, sometimes we smell and touch them as well (we don't often taste them though!). As adults, we combine the information received via the various routes effortlessly and therefore we know that the same object (the person, in this example) is being both seen and heard. Perception involves integrating information from different modalities (each modality being tied to a specific sense) to enable us to see the world as a coherent whole. The ability to integrate information received by the various senses is known as *cross-modal transfer*. The question is whether neonates integrate information in this way.

The evidence discussed so far suggests that the format in which representations are stored matches the sensory modality through which they are experienced; auditory events are represented in an auditory code and visual ones in a visual code. As adults, we often convert from one to the other. When asked to recall someone's telephone number, we might think of the sounds made by pressing the buttons on the keypad or we might actually type out the number with our fingers and convert this information into numerical information based on our knowledge of where specific numbers lie on the keypad. As adults we are consciously aware of what we are doing when we convert information from one modality into another. Although it is highly unlikely that young infants can exercise such control (for reasons that will become apparent in due course), it might be possible for them to make links between such things instinctively (without the need for conscious active cognition).

Spelke (1976) found evidence of cross-modal transfer in 4-month-old infants. They were presented with a soundtrack and two visual images, one of which "went with" the soundtrack and one of which didn't. The infants seemed to prefer (as measured by the amount of time they spent looking at) the visual image that went *with* the soundtrack because they spent considerably longer looking at the right visual image. This suggests that they understood that the sights and sounds were related and therefore that they had a basic understanding of what visual images go with what sounds. Even neonates appear to have some understanding of this relationship and turn their head in the direction of a sound even when they are in the dark (Turkewitz, Birch, & Cooper, 1966). Although at birth this understanding appears to be only an instinctive behavioural response to a stimulus, with learning and experience this ability develops rapidly.

These abilities are not limited to the combination of auditory with visual information. Meltzoff and Borton (1979) gave 4-week-old babies one of two types of dummy to suck: One that had a standard smooth teat or one that had knobbly protrusions. The babies sucked these dummies for only a minute and a half and the researchers made sure that the infants did not see the dummy that they were sucking on. When pictures of the two types of dummy were simultaneously shown to the infants, the infants demonstrated a preference for the dummy that they had previously been sucking. Again it seems that information from one modality had been converted so that it was available to another. The fact that the infants didn't see the dummy meant that they must have actually created a representation of the visual characteristics based upon a purely "touch-based" (or *proprioceptive* to use the "proper" term) experience.

Further evidence that suggests that very young infants can transfer information across modalities comes from studies looking at early imitative abilities. Meltzoff and Moore (1983) found that neonates of between only 1 and 3 hours of age are capable of imitation, although this is limited to the imitation of facial gestures that they can already perform, such as poking out their tongue or opening their mouth. They also can only reproduce these actions in immediate response to seeing someone else perform them. The fact that young infants can mimic these actions suggests that they can match their own bodily actions with those of other people without any effort. The limitations on this ability suggest that no conscious control of actions is involved and that infants have no conscious access to representations of actions. If they did they would be able to call upon these representations in the absence of the perceptual trigger, here the actions of the model.

Perception of events

It seems logical to assume that the perception of objects in the environment is an easier cognitive task than the perception of relationships between such objects and thus it seems likely that such ability would develop later. Whereas cross-modal transfer depends upon the ability to perceive relationships between different sensory inputs that occur simultaneously, the perception of *events* requires the ability to perceive relationships across time.

Rovee-Collier, Sullivan, Enright, Lucas, and Fagen (1980) found that 3-month-old children could not only learn how to activate a mobile by kicking their feet, they could remember the relationship between their action and the actions of the mobile for between 2 and 8 days. One foot was connected to the mobile by a piece of string in the first phase of the procedure. As babies have a habit of kicking their feet this inevitably resulted in the activation of the mobile; accidentally at first. With time, the infants seemed to work out and remember the relationship between their kicking and the actions of mobile. It seems that the infants had not only perceived the *relationship* between their action and the effect of it but also that they had represented this event and that this representation guided their actions. Although these representations seemed to fade with time, with some children apparently forgetting how to activate the mobile 2 weeks after the event, contextual cues such as the same cot bumper being present both when the child initially learned the action required to activate the mobile and when they were required to activate the mobile again, extended the length of time that a child could remember the initial event. So, whereas even young infants can represent events and represent them for while, these representations are very fragile and fade quickly.

Clifton et al. (1991) conducted a study that suggests that by the age of 6 months infants are capable of forming representations of events that can be retained over much longer periods of time than those shown in Rovee-Collier et al.'s (1980) study. They compared performance of two-and-half-year-old children on an object location task in which they had to find a rattle in the dark using only the rattle's sound as a clue. Half of the children tested had performed the task when they were six-and-a-half months of age. Those children who were familiar with the task performed significantly better than those who were not. This suggests that these children had access to a previously stored representation of the event and that this was triggered by recognition of the task required of them.

Although infants' memories for casual events is fairly sophisticated, the ability to represent non-causal events is not quite as developed (Mandler & McDonough, 1995). This again suggests that innate constraints on event perception exist and that infants are predisposed to learn about causal events before they learn about other types of event. This makes sense if we consider that children need to develop an awareness of "self". An understanding of self includes information about who you are, where you begin and other environmental features, and also about what you are capable of as an individual. Learning about the effects of your actions on other objects in the environment is likely to contribute to such an understanding and is therefore an important ability to develop. An understanding of causal relationships does not just help explain social events and behaviour though. It also underlies the child's developing understanding of the objects that make up the physical world; after all it's not just animate objects that can affect other objects, inanimate objects also can, although some intervention is usually necessary because inanimate objects can't move themselves!

Mandler (1990) points out that although infants' representational abilities are considerable, the representations formed by young infants are not available to consciousness and therefore the children don't know that they have learned anything. In all of the studies outlined above, the existence of a representation is measured by the children's behavioural reaction. These reactions are not within the children's control and as such they are similar in kind to the conditioned responses demonstrated by animals. They are instinctive reactions to environmental stimuli and cannot be controlled by the children; they are involuntary.

Conclusions so far

The fairly sophisticated perceptual abilities of neonates, and the rapid development of these abilities, is an indication of their importance for subsequent development. Evolution seems to have resulted in innate constraints on development that places the ability to identify specific features of the environment at the top of the priority list. This makes sense given that the ability to form representations of objects and events in the environment is necessary before cognition can occur. However, the perceptual abilities of infants are far from *fully* developed. The guiding principles described by Spelke appear to be applied to sensory information of all types (auditory, visual, etc.) although the age at which they become apparent differs from one modality to the next. This suggests that whereas some cognitive processes are innately specified and domain-general, the acquisition of domain-specific knowledge determines whether, and the extent to which, these processes are available to the child.

So are newborns fully equipped to deal with the variety and complexity of perceptual information that they are exposed to? It seems not. Although they are obviously preprogrammed to be able to impose some order on perceptual input, the extent to which they can do this is constrained by their lack of knowledge and experience and also by their neurological make-up.

Biases in attention

Having established that infants are capable of perceiving their environment and that perceptions form the basis of representations, the next thing to consider is how *much* and more importantly *what* information a young baby actually attends to. After all, we attend to only a relatively small amount of that which we perceive. Given that we have already seen that young infants have no conscious access to their representations and that they cannot consciously control their behaviour, any biases in attention that do exist must be innately prespecified.

If newborns do have innate tendencies to attend to some things over others then it is likely that those that are attended to are those that need to be learned about fairly quickly. As a result, infants would accumulate domain-specific knowledge about some things more quickly than they would about others. We have already seen that, during the first few months of life, babies pay particular attention to things that move, but why? Well, not only is movement a useful cue to object boundaries but also things that move are those things that are more likely to cause you some sort of physical danger (a rock being hurled at your head would be one such example). Objects that can move themselves, or *animate* objects, as they are better known, are an especially important category of objects for infants to learn about. We have already discussed how it is particularly useful for babies to recognise other humans (and even more specifically, their caregivers) at a very early age. Not only would this ensure physical care (just think of how a baby showing that they recognise one of their parents can effect the parent–child relationship) but it would also "tune the child in" to people. Given that other people will be able to contribute to the child's cognitive development in that they can actually teach them things, this has got to be a good thing!

From birth, babies seem to respond differently to people and objects (Poulin-Dubois, 1999). Neonates prefer speech to other sounds and they seem to learn about (and therefore form representations of) voices and speech quicker than they learn about other sounds (Mehler, Lambertz, Jusczyk, & Amiel-Tison, 1986, cited in Thornton, 2002). Fantz (1961) and many others have shown that neonates prefer to look at faces rather than other equally complex patterns. At birth, this seems to be a preference for the overall shape of a human face but within days neonates turn their attention to facial features (Bushnell, 1982) allowing them to form representations of and therefore distinguish between different people very quickly (Bushnell, Sai, & Mullin, 1989).

Overall, then, the evidence seems to suggest that although environmental input and learning are important in the development of attentional preferences, innate biases also exist. These appear to be limited to a preference for movement and for faces (and more specifically, human ones). Such preferences are instinctive and, as such, infants can't consciously choose to pay more attention to specific objects. It seems that infants are born predisposed to collect information about specific things and that these things have been carefully selected by evolutionary forces to be those that are most likely to prove adaptive.

The nature of early representations

Early representations are based purely on perceptual experiences; representations of sights, sounds, feelings, smells, or tastes. In response to these experiences, infants often demonstrate specific behavioural reactions. This suggests that young infants have learned a response to a stimulus and that the presence of this stimulus is sufficient to trigger an automatic response. Thus they recognise stimuli. We have also seen that infants' ability to recognise stimuli is fairly sophisticated in that they can transfer information from one modality to another; they engage in cross-modal transfer. Despite these early accomplishments, the representations of young infants are limited in one very important respect. Whereas as adults we have conscious access to a lot of the knowledge that we have represented in our minds (and we can call this information to mind at will), early infant memories are *implicit* in nature. Implicit memories are not as useful as explicit memories because they are not available to consciousness. As a result, they can be accessed only when something in the immediate perceptual environment triggers them. So, infants recognise an object or event only when that object or event is being perceptually experienced; newborn babies don't remember that they have seen or heard something until they see or hear it again. Even then, they don't actually *know* that they know something, although the behaviours that they demonstrate suggest that they do. Information is stored at a behavioural level; specific behaviours being triggered automatically by exposure to familiar things.

The behavioural (or procedural) nature of early infant cognition is demonstrated by the fact that infants know how to *do* things but little more. The evidence that suggests that infants are only capable of representing information at this low level has led some to suggest that biological constraints upon development preclude the acquisition of what is known as *declarative* knowledge. Declarative knowledge is knowledge that we know we know about and (therefore we can declare that we have). Such an interpretation of the research findings is similar in some ways to Piaget's description of early cognition. He claimed that infants are confined to working with representations that are purely procedural up until the age of about 18 months. More recent evidence suggests that this is not the case and that the ability to represent information at a mental rather than a behavioural level is present much earlier. This will be considered in more detail in the next chapter.

Despite the limitations of early cognition, it is clear that from birth infants are learning and accumulating knowledge. The extent to which they do this differs between domains and depends on both opportunity (exposure to specific information) and biological predispositions to attend to some information preferentially. These biases in attention tune the child to information that is more likely to prove useful. The rapid development of the cortex during the early years of life reflects the rapidity with which infants accumulate knowledge. Similarly, the differential development of different cortical areas effects reflects the fact that children concentrate on learning about different things at different points in time.

If every experience that a child has were encoded separately the brain wouldn't be able to cope. As the amount of information represented in the mind grows, some sort of organisation becomes necessary. As this is a fairly essential ability, because not being able to categorise would limit the amount of information represented somewhat, we would expect evolution to have equipped us with the ability to categorise experiences at a time when this would be necessary and/or adaptive. This will be considered in the next chapter.

Do infants *know* anything?

Given that the representations of neonates and young infants are perceptual in nature, that their perceptual experiences are fleeting, and that there is no evidence to suggest that young infants are capable of representing information in a format accessible to consciousness, we cannot argue that infants actually "know" anything in the sense that we, as adults, tend to use the word. If we can't call something to mind we do not claim to have stored it on another level. Instead, we (usually) admit to not knowing. Young infants do, however, have representations (and therefore, memories) of sorts but these are implicit and procedural. Whereas these might trigger behaviours as a result of learned associations, there is no conscious control over these actions and no explicit awareness of any link between perception and action. Despite this, young infants do appear to know some things. They know how to respond behaviourally to a variety of stimuli and they know to respond to and attend to different things in different ways. Although neonates know nothing of many things, to claim that they know nothing at all because their knowledge is stored at an implicit level seems too harsh a judgement. The answer to the question of whether infants know anything seems to depend on whether you acknowledge that implicit knowledge *is* knowledge. Many theorists in the past have denied that it is, claiming instead that true cognition begins with the development of the capacity for explicit representation. The development of explicit mental representations will be the focus of the next chapter.

Summary and conclusions

Infants possess the ability to encode perceptual information at birth (and before) and thus they are equipped with the basic apparatus for learning. Initially, this ability is limited to the implicit coding of perceptual information. At this early age infants' representations are still both implicit and procedural.

We have considered research evidence that suggested that newborn babies attend to specific aspects of the environment over and above others, that is, they are born prepared to learn those things that are going to benefit them the most. In addition, we acknowledged that there seems to be a predetermined order to early cognitive development. The age at which specific things are learned seems to have been predetermined and prioritised. This could, we concluded, be the result of evolutionary forces that have resulted in us being born with a set of highly specialised psychological mechanisms, for specific purposes.

Cognitive development over the first year or so seems to come about as a result of complex interactions between environmental input and innate constraints on information-processing abilities. The structure of the human brain at birth allows for perception and learning. As the child accumulates knowledge within specific domains, this knowledge is used to interpret incoming information. This has the knock-on effect of making the processing of incoming information somewhat easier, in terms of the demands made upon the cognitive system. This allows for the acquisition of more information at a greater rate.

Chapter 3

Mental representation

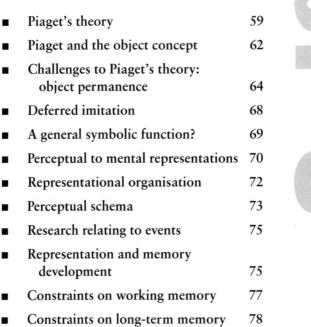

OVER THE COURSE of the last two chapters, we have seen that the capacity for learning (and thus the ability to form representations) develops before birth and that newborn babies make good use of these abilities. Indeed, infants acquire knowledge about their world at an amazing rate. We have also come to the conclusion that the representations of young infants can only be accessed by recognition, which means that direct perceptual input is needed to trigger an automatic behavioural response. The mental representations of young infants are therefore implicit and unavailable to consciousness and, as such, we cannot claim that they think in the way that we, as adults, do most of the time (although that's not to say that we don't store representations at a procedural level). Young infants do not represent information *mentally*; no mental images of objects or events are created and stored in their minds. When we can say that an infant is capable of storing representations so that they are accessible in the absence of direct perceptual input we would have evidence that a mental representation has been formed. We would need to see evidence of the ability to remember and recall information when required to be able to reach such a conclusion.

The development of the ability to recreate objects and events in their minds is obviously going to have an enormous impact upon children's understanding of their world. Being able to recall previous experiences at will and compare them with new ones would allow for the perception of similarities and differences between new and past experiences. This is a very useful skill to have, as it would enable children to organise the knowledge that they have acquired. It could also mean that old knowledge could be used to interpret incoming sensory data and therefore generate appropriate behavioural reactions in novel situations.

It doesn't necessarily follow that the development of the ability to call on knowledge that you have previously stored would result in the type of cognitive activity described above. Just because children can bring a previous experience or event to mind it doesn't mean that they will mentally represent similarities and relationships between perceptual experiences. To do this they would also have to understand the *meaning* of their experiences. Understanding the meaning of objects and events will allow for the development of descriptions of, explanations for, and therefore a more integrated understanding of the world around them.

We need to look not only at the format in which information is stored (implicit or explicit) but also at what children know, how this knowledge is stored and how it is organised. In the last chapter we considered how even young infants organise their experiences into perceptual categories. As soon as infants begin to incorporate meaning into their representations, such categorisation would no longer be based on perceptual categories but on conceptual ones (a concept being a meaningful category into which experiences can be sorted, for example, perceiving the similarities between the behaviour of someone on different occasions would enable us to form a concept of that person).

With development and learning, infants begin to incorporate meaning into their representations and so representations become more than just perceptual snap-shots of reality. Not only does the format of them change from procedural to mental, so does their content. Piaget believed that these changes occur simultaneously, procedural representations being meaningless but mental ones incorporating meaning. More recent evidence suggests that things are not as clear-cut as this and that the extent to which representations contain meaning is not as inextricably tied to their format as Piaget thought.

Piaget's theory

Piaget claimed that the capacity for mental representation, or as he called it the *symbolic function*, does not develop until the second year of a child's life. Piaget proposed that innate domain-general structural constraints preclude the formation of mental representations before the age of about 18 months. He did acknowledge that there would be some variation in the age at which such abilities appear because environmental factors and experience also have a role to play, but he thought that this was limited. He cited the high degree of consistency in the age at which symbolic abilities are demonstrated in young children to support his claim. Piaget only studied children in Western cultures, with shared similar environments, and therefore his conclusions would have been somewhat presumptive. More variation in experience could result in less consistency in the age at which this ability develops.

According to Piaget, symbolic thought is evidenced by the ability to retain a mental representation in the absence of perceptual input. If infants could be shown to have formed a representation of an object or event some time after that object or event has been perceived then Piaget claimed that we would have evidence of the child's ability to mentally represent. Most psychologists would agree with this.

Early mental representations are accessed automatically; a behavioural response being triggered by exposure to a specific perceptual feature or event in the environment. Such automatic reactions to perceptual input do not demonstrate that a mental image of an object or event has been stored in a format that allows for voluntary recall. Consciously recalling an object or event in such a way requires that information is stored at an explicit rather than an implicit level.

Piaget saw the development of the symbolic function as resulting from the internalisation of external perceptions and behavioural responses. This internalisation results in the formation of a mental image that is available *when required* rather than when automatically triggered by a perceptual experience. Piaget labelled mental images in which previous experiences are recreated mentally *reproductive mental images*, which he contrasted with the later-developing *anticipatory* mental images that allow for the consideration of hypothetical events and objects. The symbolic function also allows for the development of other abilities that require the ability to use symbols, for example, language, drawing and pretend play. The fact that all of these abilities appear during the second year of life, at around the same time, seems to support Piaget's propositions that the symbolic function both develops at this time and that it is a domain-general process. However, these abilities do not emerge at *exactly* the same time. This could suggest that the acquisition of domain-specific knowledge might have a role to play in determining the emergence of symbolic abilities within different domains (we will return to this issue later).

Piaget focused much of this work on the development of symbolic thought on the emergence of two specific abilities; object permanence and deferred imitation. *Object permanence* is the understanding that an object continues to exist even when it can no longer be experienced. As adults, we know that when someone walks past us in the street and turns the corner they continue to exist but do infants realise that this is the case? Evidence we looked at earlier suggests that infants don't understand such things and that representations can be accessed only involuntarily (automatically) and when they are triggered by recognition.

Deferred imitation involves the reproduction of a behaviour that the child has seen modelled by someone else at an earlier point in time. To do this they must have represented the imitated behaviour in a format that allows for it to be consciously accessed at a time when a trigger stimulus is not present. An example would be a child pretending to shave after having watched his or her father shave earlier in the day. In both cases (deferred imitation and object permanence) the important thing is that the child is invoking a mental representation *actively*; the child is making a conscious decision to behave in a specific way. The fact that the child is making such a decision and that it has become clear in recent years that children can do this from a very young age is one of the things that contributed to the rejection of nativist and behaviourist theories, both of which propose that the child is a passive participant in the developmental process.

In the last chapter we saw that very young infants appear to understand something of the nature of the physical objects that make up their (and our) world. An understanding of the permanence of objects was *not* demonstrated, though, and an early understanding of objects was found to be apparent only when the object itself was being re-experienced; that is, children only had recognition memories. However, the early abilities of infants do appear rather sophisticated and their development proceeds quickly. In the light of this we must question Piaget's claim that the symbolic function does not develop until 18 months of age. We also need to question whether there is a *general symbolic function* and also whether the abilities that Piaget talked about are indeed evidence of the ability to symbolise. Before we do this, we need to look at how Piaget reached the conclusions that he did.

Piaget and the object concept

Piaget coined the term "object concept" to describe our understanding of the physical environment (which is made up of objects). He claimed that this develops during the first 18 months or so of life. This stage of development Piaget called the sensorimotor period, as he suggested that it is characterised by the formation of representations that are not stored at a mental level but rather at a procedural one; such representations only specifying relationships between sensory experiences and behavioural reactions.

Piaget claimed that infants learn about objects through interaction with the environment and did not acknowledge the existence of any innate knowledge about objects. Although he claimed that a child's understanding of objects develops gradually, he proposed that the development of the symbolic function was necessary for the child to understand that objects are *permanent*, that is that they continue to exist even when they are no longer being experienced.

Piaget supported his account of the development of *object permanence* with research findings that showed that infants do not attempt to retrieve a toy that is covered with a cloth (right in front of the baby) until about 8 months of age (Piaget & Inhelder, 1969). At first sight, it is easy to reach the conclusion that if a child doesn't attempt to retrieve a hidden toy then he or she can't be holding in mind a representation of that toy and its continued existence. Therefore we could conclude that although 8 month-olds can't hold a mental representation of the hidden toy, those older than that can. Piaget did not accept this obvious interpretation and presented further evidence that he claimed showed that even the 8-month-olds had not based their retrieval of the hidden toy on a mental representation.

When infants were shown a toy being placed under a cloth (cloth A) several times and *then* placed under a second cloth (cloth B) (the two cloths were only centimetres apart and directly in front of the infant) the infants tended to attempt to retrieve the toy from under cloth A rather than from under the cloth that they had just *seen* it placed under (B). Piaget's explanation for this was that rather than the infants having stored a mental representation of the object to be retrieved, the infant (at 8 months) had stored only a procedural representation of what to do when their toy disappeared. As a result, they weren't invoking a mental representation of the missing object; they were reproducing an implicitly learned behaviour—something along the lines of "toy disappears, reach to cloth A"; after all, this action had apparently made the toy reappear in the past. The child is therefore assuming (implicitly of course) that simply enacting a specific behaviour (reaching to cloth A) is sufficient to recreate the object. By 12 months, though, Piaget showed that infants no longer make what has become known as the *"A not B" error*.

Piaget claimed that although *not* making the A not B error seems to suggest that a mental image of the object as a permanent entity has been formed, at this stage the child's mental representations are still extremely fragile. For example, if the object was moved from one place to another, out of the sight of the child (a procedure called an *invisible displacement*) the child will not search for the object if it is not found in the place that they had seen it hidden. Not until 18 months of age will children systematically search for an object until they find it, and only this, according to Piaget, suggests a fully developed understanding of the permanence of objects; that they can't just disappear and "must be around here somewhere". It could, however, be that young infants' ability to concentrate on the search task is limited and that their attention is easily distracted. Alternatively, it could just be that they are lazy and can't be bothered to search for the toy! Although these interpretations seem unlikely, we must always bear in mind that there *are* always alternative interpretations and that when we are dealing with infants we can't rule out unlikely interpretations purely because they seem unlikely from an adult perspective.

Nobody contests Piaget's findings and they have been replicated hundreds, if not thousands, of times. The amount of importance accorded to the development of object permanence and what it can tell us about the ability to represent information mentally is similarly accepted. The assumption that the search behaviour of the infants in the experiments described above accurately reflects the infants' representational abilities *has*, however, been challenged by more recent findings. It is to these that we will now turn. We will then look at whether Piaget was right to suggest domain-general constraints on the ability to represent information mentally and at alternative interpretations.

Challenges to Piaget's theory: object permanence

To retrieve the hidden toys in the aforementioned series of experiments, infants not only had to have access to a mental representation of the object but they also had to know *how* to act upon this knowledge and be physically capable of carrying out the required action to reach their aim of retrieving the toy. It could be, therefore, that infants *knew* that the object existed even when they couldn't see it, but that they couldn't *show* us that they know this because either their motor responses were insufficiently co-ordinated (Willatts, 1989) or because they couldn't co-ordinate the search for the object even though they knew that it still existed (Baillargeon, Spelke, & Wasserman, 1985).

Bower, Broughton, and Moore (1971) devised a test of object permanence that did not require a motor response from the child. Infants were shown a toy train passing along a track in front of them. Halfway along the track there was a screen. The infants' eye-gaze was monitored as they watched the train disappear behind the screen, whereupon the experimenter stopped it. Infants as young as 2 months of age expected the train to reappear from behind the screen, as indicated by their direction of gaze. This suggests that they understood that while that train was out of sight it still existed.

Although Bower et al.'s (1971) study appears convincing, a later variation of the procedure (Bower & Patterson, 1973) found that if the train was stopped *before* it disappeared behind the screen, infants still moved their gaze along the track in the direction in which the train was travelling. Such a finding suggests that infants, having started to follow the train with their eyes, can't (or just don't) stop this action when the train stops. Maybe, as Diamond (1985) suggests, infants have difficulty stopping doing something that they have already started doing because of brain limitations. Stopping an action you have already started is known as *inhibiting a pre-potent response* (we will return to this issue later).

Baillargeon et al. (1985) devised a rather ingenious experiment to investigate object permanence. In their study, 5-month-old infants were shown a cardboard screen that was rotated through 180 degrees (so that it started flat on the table in front of the child and was raised away from the child until it was again flat on the table). Once the infants had been habituated to this display, a wooden block was placed on the table in a position that would not allow for the full 180-degree rotation of the screen. In one condition the infants were shown the screen rotate until the block stopped it, as we would expect it to do. In the other condition the block was surreptitiously removed so that the screen rotated fully. This is an *apparently* impossible event, given that the block was removed without the child's knowledge. The infants demonstrated surprise (as measured by an increase in the amount of time that they looked at the display) when the screen rotated all the way, suggesting that they understood that the block remained in the position it had been placed in. They seemed to understand that it was permanent.

To rule out the possibility that infants looked at the full 180-degree rotation for longer than the partial rotation simply because it took longer, a second version of the procedure was devised in which the block was placed in a position that would *not* impede the screen and the screen was rotated. The infants in this version of the test spent an equal amount of time looking at 120- and 180-degree rotations of the screen, suggesting that it was the presence of the block in a position that *would* impede the screen's rotation that had caused the extended looking times in the first study. Not only do these experiments provide fairly convincing evidence of object permanence in 5-month-olds, they also suggest considerable understanding of the *nature* of objects, because the infants understood that one object would impede the movement of another object. The foundations of such an understanding were discussed in the last chapter, where we saw how very young infants appear to be equipped with some innately specified guiding principles that allow for the identification of individual objects in their environment (see p. 43).

Baillargeon (1986) conducted a similar study to that of Bower in which a car (rather than a train) was seen to travel along a track and behind a screen. When a block was positioned behind the screen but *on* the track, infants showed surprise if the car reappeared from the other side of the screen (the block was moved out of the way by the experimenter; psychologists can be very sneaky at times it seems!). If, however, the block was positioned *near to* rather than *on* the track, infants showed no such surprise when it reappeared, confirming Baillargeon et al.'s (1985) findings that not only is an understanding of object permanence present but also that 5-month-olds possess considerable spatial awareness and an understanding of object properties.

Some people have suggested that because the experiments described above are so complex, the findings of them are difficult to interpret. Simpler procedures have resulted in findings consistent with those described above and as such have put pay to such a claim. For example, Hood and Willatts (1986) showed infants a toy and then placed it on the floor to one side of the child. The lights were then turned off and, via infrared cameras, the actions of the children were monitored. It was found that infants reached for the toy even though they could no longer see it; again providing evidence of object permanence in 5-month-olds. Shinskey and Munakata (2003) recently presented evidence to suggest that infants find it easier to search for an object in the dark than they do to search for an object hidden under a cloth in daylight. The reasons for this are unclear. It could be that, when searching for a hidden object under a cloth, the fragile representation of the hidden object is displaced from working memory and replaced with a representation of the cloth under which the object is hidden. This would make sense given that we have already seen that infants' representational abilities are limited and that perceptual features easily distract children. Another suggestion could be that the understanding of the continued existence of objects when it is dark develops before an understanding of the permanence of hidden objects for evolutionary reasons. Given that we have to contend with darkness on a daily basis, whereas we don't generally have to deal with people hiding our possessions every day, it would make sense for us to be preprogrammed to develop an understanding of darkness and its lack of effect on our possessions at a very early age. This interpretation was supported by the findings of Scher, Amer, and Tirosh (2000), who found that 9-month-olds with a good understanding of object permanence slept better than those with a less developed understanding.

Whatever interpretation we place upon Hood and Willat's evidence, it is clear that physically reaching for an object is not a problem for 5-month-old infants. So, if the reaching involved in Piaget's procedures wasn't masking infants' true abilities, what was?

There are several possible answers to this question. Harris (1973) suggested that poor performance on the A not B task could be the result of a memory problem. He found that infants who were allowed to search for the hidden toy straight away had no problem with this task, whereas those who were prevented from doing so for 5 seconds often reached to cloth A (the classic A not B error). Given that infants had seen the toy being placed under cloth A several times before it was placed under cloth B, he suggested that their memory for this hiding place would be stronger and therefore would over-ride the weaker memory for the second hiding place. Diamond (1985) expanded on Harris's work. She suggested that the mental representation of the second hiding place was being held in the infants' working memory, whereas the memory of the first hiding place had most probably been transferred to the infants' long-term memory. As the representation in working memory fades rapidly, the infants have to act on the basis of the only mental representation of the objects location that they hold; of it being under cloth A. As working memory abilities are dependent on the development of the prefrontal cortex, Diamond argued that it was the limited development of this area that impeded infants' performance on the A not B task (rather than a lack of object permanence). Further evidence for this interpretation comes from Milner (1963), who found that people who had suffered lesions to their prefrontal cortex made similar errors. As discussed in Chapter 1, the prefrontal cortex is associated with executive function and this is a late developing cognitive structure that governs high-level cognitive functions. It seems feasible then that deficiencies in executive function limit performance on object permanence tasks.

Butterworth (1977) refuted such an interpretation, showing that infants make the A not B error even when the covers used were transparent. In this variation of the procedure, no memory skills are necessary to successfully complete the task; they can actually *see* the object that they are to retrieve. Instead of memory limitations, Butterworth suggested that infants' problem with the A not B task stems from an inability to update information about spatial locations. He claimed that infants can represent the position of objects in one of two ways: Either in relation to where they (the infants) are or in relation to another object. If infants represent the location of the cloth in one way and the location of the toy in another they could easily be confused and search in the wrong place. Only when infants code objects in their environment in a consistent way (using one or other of the two possibilities) could they pass this task.

Whatever the reason for children's problems with the search tasks devised by Piaget, it seems clear that infants understand the permanence of objects earlier than he proposed (by 5 months). Although the findings of his studies still hold true, the tasks obviously require more than just the ability to hold a representation of the object in mind and access this in the absence of perceptual input. Other cognitive and motor abilities are called on and limitations in these areas mask the child's understanding of object permanence.

Deferred imitation

Piaget (1951) claimed that infants' imitative abilities develop alongside their understanding of object permanence; something that he said substantiated his claim that the development of a domain-general function resulted in the capacity for mental representation. On the basis of his observations, Piaget reported that although imitative abilities begin to develop during the early months, it is not until the age of about 18 months that children show evidence of *deferred imitation*; the reproduction of a previously seen behaviour some time after they have witnessed it.

For Piaget, the delay between witnessing behaviour and reproducing it is of key importance. Whereas direct imitation only requires the child to represent information at a perceptual level (and automatic behaviour being triggered by a perceptual event in the environment), deferred imitation requires the *recall* of a specific event and thus access to a mental representation (see Chapter 2). Piaget's (1951) theory was entirely based on studies of his own children, something that caused many to be sceptical of his account of the development of imitation (not that there was any real reason to suppose that his children were not representative of children in general). This scepticism appeared unfounded, though, as any studies with larger more representative samples initially confirmed his account (Uzgiris & Hunt, 1975).

Meltzoff (1985) and others have since found evidence of deferred imitation in infants at a younger age than Piaget claimed. Although the results from such studies are rather mixed, taken together they seem to suggest that deferred imitation occurs from around the age of 9 or 10 months and increases over the second year, both in terms of the complexity of the imitated behaviour and the amount of time that a mental representation of the modelled behaviour can be held in mind before the behaviour is reproduced. The ability to learn by imitation is an important development and evidence shows that infants learn a lot by watching others.

A general symbolic function?

Piaget's focus was on deferred imitation and the development of object permanence. From his studies of these abilities, he came to the conclusion that children develop the capacity for mental representation at around the age of 18 months. Piaget claimed that these developments occurred as a result of structural changes that allow for the representation of knowledge at a mental rather than behavioural level. He also claimed that it was the development of this ability that enables the development of language, pretend play and drawing, as all of these abilities are dependent on the ability to *symbolise* that is, form a mental representation (in his view). Piaget claimed that, like deferred imitation and object permanence, these abilities develop at around the age of 18 months and that this suggests that they are all the result of a domain-general change in cognitive abilities. Therefore Piaget claimed that domain-general processes constrain development in all of the aforementioned areas of development

We have reviewed plenty of evidence that suggests that Piaget's theory is not an accurate description of development. Not only do imitative abilities and an understanding of object permanence develop at earlier ages than he supposed, they do not seem to occur simultaneously or coincide with the development of the other abilities he listed as demonstrative of the development of a general symbolic function. This does not necessarily mean that the symbolic function is *not* a domain-general process. It is possible that it is but that domain-specific constraints on development result in it being applied inconsistently across domains. It could be that domain-general constraints on the ability to mentally represent knowledge exist but that they are lifted during the child's first few months. Once lifted, infants' performance on tests that require mental representation could then be constrained by a lack of domain-specific knowledge. This would explain why abilities that all require the capacity for mental representation appear in different domains at different times.

Nobody contests that Piaget was correct in highlighting the importance of deferred imitation and object permanence, because they do show that infants are capable of forming explicit mental representations within certain domains. As a result, a lot of research has focused upon these abilities. What is not accepted is Piaget's suggestion that these abilities demonstrate an underlying structural development that generalises across domains. It seems that his explanation was far too simplistic and that he overlooked the importance of knowledge and concentrated too heavily on the processes that are applied to knowledge.

Perceptual to mental representations

So far in this chapter our discussion has centred on the *format* of representations, whether they are perceptual or mental in nature, whether they are implicit or explicit. But *what* exactly do infants represent? What do they know and understand?

Young infants' understanding of objects and events is considerable. Innate constraints on development both equip infants with some guiding principles that enable them to impose order on their environment (see Chapter 2) and to some extent determine which things are going to be learned about and in what order. Infants' early abilities are, however, limited to the perception of specific *features* in the environment. What we need to consider now then is the age at which infants begin to represent things in a *meaningful* way. To represent meaning, the infant must be able to perceive not only individual features but also how these features relate to one another.

Baillargeon et al. and Bower et al.'s findings suggest that infants do represent meaning by 5 months of age. They obviously have some awareness of spatial relationships, as evidenced by their ability to mentally represent the position of an object in relation to another object and to understand that the position of one object might impede the movement of another. However, the infants' ability to form mental representations was the main focus of these investigations and, as such, it was their *mental* representations that were meaningful. Although Piaget believed that only mental representations contained meaning, we now have substantial evidence to suggest that the perceptual representations available to infants prior to the development of such abilities also contain meaning.

Quinn (1994), for example, found that 3-month-old infants could represent spatial relationships between objects. When habituated to a bar with a dot above it, they preferred a bar with a dot below it, thus demonstrating that they recognised this stimuli as novel and therefore had represented not just the perceptual features of the visual display but also the relationships between features. In the last chapter we considered evidence that suggests that very young infants are also capable of representing relationships between events and that they can categorise simple perceptual forms, both of which involve the perception of relationships (between features or events).

Mandler (1988, 1992) suggests that there is an intermediary stage between simple perceptual representation and mental representation, a stage in which perceptual representations incorporate meaning; these he calls *image schema*. Mandler suggests that these representations are not explicit in nature. The evidence described above suggests that he is right.

Representational organisation

The ability to represent meaning and therefore the ability to recognise relationships between events underlies conceptual development. To construct prototypical representations of what is *usually* true of a particular category of objects or events, we need to be able to perceive similarities and differences. For example, to construct a prototypical mental representation of a cat we have to be able to distinguish between those characteristics that are typical of cats and those that distinguish one cat from another. My cat Norman is black and white and very naughty, and all that information gets stored as a concept of Norman. My concept for cats, however, specifies that cats have whiskers, meow, etc., both of which Norman does but, given that this information is true of all cats, I don't replicate this information in my head and store these details alongside my schema for Norman, or any of the other cats that I know and therefore have a separate concept for. Prototypical mental representations are known as *schemas*.

Prototypical mental representations of events are known as *scripts*. Each script specifies what is typical of an event. For example, our script for "going out for a meal" would include details of things that usually happen when you do: You go in, get seated, are given a menu, you order, you are given your meal and you eat it, etc. If someone asked you how your evening went because they knew you had been out for a meal the night before you would omit all these "typical" details and only tell them about those things that distinguished *your* going out for a meal from any other trip to a restaurant (for example, you might mention that the waiter poured wine all over you or that your partner forgot his or her credit card and you ended up paying).

The ability to form prototypes, both scripts and schemas, is an important development because it allows for the effective organisation of information. We extract those details that deviate from the schema or scripts when forming mental representations of objects or events, thus cutting down on the amount of information that we hold in our memories.

Perceptual schema

Most of the objects that make up our world are structurally very complex. As a result, the ability to form representations of objects depends on both the ability to perceive relationships between features and the representation of these relations. Perceiving similarities between objects that you are currently confronted with and those that you have come across before has obvious advantages. Avoiding situations or objects that are similar to those that have harmed you in the past, for example, is probably a good move and this is dependent on the perception of meaning. Although Piaget argued that perceptual representation lacks meaning, this does not appear to be the case.

Cohen and Caputo (1978) showed 7-month-olds a variety of stuffed animals. Initially, the infants showed a renewed interest in each toy that they were shown (as measured by an increase in looking time). After a while, the infants were no longer interested in stuffed toys (although toys of the non-stuffed variety *were* still considered interesting). This suggests that they had formed a prototypical mental representation of what a stuffed toy *is*. However, it could be that they were habituating to only *one feature* of the toys (e.g. their eyes) rather than the inter-relations between features. Either way, the results of this study might explain why many babies aren't remotely interested in playing with soft toys. Stuffed animals seem to be a rather common (and unimaginative) gift for a newborn. By the time they have developed enough motor control to be able to actually play with them they are probably sick of the sight of them!

In a further study, Younger and Cohen (1983) showed 10-month-olds cartoon animals that differed in terms of five attributes (they had different tails, bodies, legs, heads, and ears). During a habituation phase the infants were shown animals in which three of these five critical features varied. Two features varied together (e.g. had either short legs and long body or long legs and short body) and one independently (e.g. ear size) (Figure 3.1). In the test phase of the procedure, the infants showed a renewed interest only in those animals whose features violated the learned relationship between features (those that had a short body and short legs). It seems, then, that the prototypical constructions of infants at this age are fairly sophisticated.

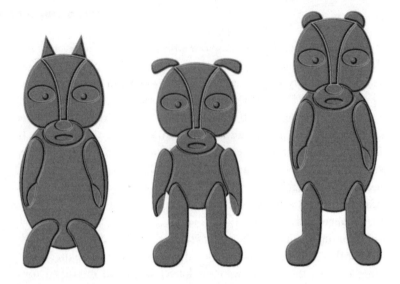

Figure 3.1 **Animals that have covarying and non-covarying features**
In Younger and Cohen's study, infants were presented with several stimuli
that covaried on two features but varied on one. Pictures A and B covary on
body size and leg length but have different ears. Picture C violates the rule
specifying a relationship between leg length and body size and would be
identified as novel in Younger and Cohen's procedure. (*Note*: These are not
the actual stimuli used in Younger and Cohen's study.)

Younger (1985) took things a stage further and showed that
infants with different perceptual experiences formed different prototypes. Those who had a broader experience of stimuli, because there
was no obvious covariance of features in the stimuli that they were
shown, formed one prototype based on an average, whereas those
given a narrower experience because there was an obvious covariance
of two features (as in the previously described study) formed two more
specific prototypes. It seems, then, that taken together these studies
suggest that infants construct prototypical representations of object
properties and features at a very young age. These prototypes, while
perceptual in nature, also incorporate meanings, thus supporting
Mandler's (1980) suggestion that there exists an intermediate form
of representation; one that isn't purely perceptual but that isn't yet

mental in nature. These representations, according to Mandler, are perceptual and yet contain meaning.

Research relating to events

The ability of infants to categorise relationships between events has often been studied by looking at their ability to transfer knowledge of how to do something from one situation to another, that is, their ability to learn by analogy. Chen, Sanchez, and Campbell (1997), for example, taught 10- and 13-month-old children a sequence of actions to obtain a toy. To do this they had to remove a barrier, lift a cloth and then pull a string. When they were presented with problems that required the same series of actions, the infants appeared to see the similarity between the problem they had been taught to solve in the first scenario and the problem that they currently faced. That is, they transferred their knowledge. The 10-month-olds, however, needed more perceptual cues for action to be transferred and so the "new" problem had to look very similar to the initial one if they were to solve it successfully. These findings suggest that infants possess the ability to mentally represent relations as well as properties, and therefore that meaning is incorporated into the still perceptual organisation of representations. However, given that such knowledge is represented only implicitly, it provides further evidence to contest the assumption made by Piaget; that only mental representations are meaningful.

Representation and memory development

What does the emergence of the ability to mentally represent information tell us about the increasing memory abilities of infants? These two are inextricably linked of course. Whereas implicit memories are not mental in nature, explicit memories are, as evidenced by McDonough, Mandler, McKee, and Squire's (1995) finding that adult amnesiacs who fail explicit memory tasks but perform well on tests of implicit memory also have problems with deferred imitation, an ability that requires the capacity for mental representation. These results suggest that not only are the capacity for mental representation and explicit memory one and the same, but also that different brain areas control explicit and implicit memory.

Early evidence from the field of cognitive neuropsychology (e.g. Schacter & Moscovich, 1984) suggested that memory is a modular system and therefore that different parts of the brain control different aspects of memory. It was argued that whereas the brain structures that underlie implicit memory develop during the early months, those that underlie explicit memory do not develop until later. The development of the limbic system (which consists of several inter-related brain structures) was seen as essential for the formation of explicit representations and evidence suggests that this isn't fully developed until around the age of 2 years (Greenspan, 1997).

More recent evidence, although supporting Schacter and Moscovitch's (1984) suggestion that implicit memory and explicit memory call upon different areas of the brain, suggests that memory is not modular in nature. Nelson (1995) reviewed the literature and came to the conclusion that two types of memory system start to develop in infancy, one that supports implicit procedural representations and one that supports explicit representations. These two are not distinct, however, and the representations supported by the implicit system often become explicit as the hippocampus and related regions of the cortex become integrated into the memory system as a whole. This development is gradual; the hippocampus is incorporated into the system before the related cortical areas.

Implicit memory seems to be a fairly basic, low-level cognitive function that even pigeons possess (Vaughan & Greene, 1984). From the evidence we have discussed in this chapter (and the last), it appears that this type of memory is in full working order before birth. Implicit memory abilities also don't seem to develop with age whereas explicit memory does (e.g. Brown & Scott, 1971; Carroll, Byrne, & Kirsner, 1985; Russo, Nichelli, Gibertoni, & Cornia, 1995). As a result, implicit memory abilities will not be discussed any further.

The development of explicit memory allows not only for the encoding of information in a format that will be accessible later but also for the formation of many more different "types" of memory. Neurological evidence suggests that different types of memory are represented in different areas of the cortex, for example we store memories for events in our episodic memory and information about the meaning of things (e.g. words) in our semantic memory. However, this does not imply that memory is modular, rather that different cortical areas have different neurological structures and that this makes some areas of the brain more receptive to the formation of different types of memory (Johnson, 1997a).

Different types of memory are often studied in isolation and, as such, they are *disembedded*; that is the formation of different types of memory are studied outside of the context in which our memory normally works. Whereas a single experience might well result in the formation of an episodic memory, it is also likely that information from the episode represented is incorporated into other types of memory, such as semantic memory. It could be argued, therefore, that any results obtained from such studies are unrealistic, as in the everyday world our cognitive processes don't work one at a time.

Constraints on working memory

Given that our working memory is where active cognition occurs, any changes to its capacity or functioning are going to have an enormous impact on the child's overall cognitive abilities. Our working memory is where we interpret sensory information. Any increase in knowledge stored in our long-term memory is bound to have an effect on what exactly goes on in our working memory because it affects the way in which sensory information is interpreted and processed.

Working memory capacity increases as a function of age (Case, 1985; Dempster, 1981). However, whether this is a real or an apparent increase is not clear. The capacity of working memory can be extended by the grouping of units of information into meaningful chunks. For example, we can retain as many words as we can letters (Miller, 1956). In real terms, what this means is that our working memory capacity is extended as a result of knowledge that we have acquired and strategies that we employ to organise information. Domain-specific knowledge increases the extent to which working memory capabilities are utilised.

The amount of time that information can be held in working

memory can also be increased through the use of strategies. Although information that is not subject to any cognitive processing tends to decay after between 15 and 30 seconds, that which is being processed is kept in working memory for as long as active processing is occurring (Baddeley, 1990). One way in which we can increase the capacity of our working memory is through rehearsal. By repeating information we can keep it in mind; just think of those times when you have to remember a telephone number for as long as it takes for you to get to a phone to dial it or to a piece of paper to write it down.

The capacity of working memory also seems to be affected by strategy use. Whereas the average number of units that can be retained by an adult is about seven "plus or minus two" (Miller, 1956), young children appear to be able to retain fewer items (Dempster, 1981). The suggestion that strategy use affects working memory capacity implicates executive function in the apparent increase in working memory abilities with age. This is because, as we have seen, executive function allows for the planning and regulation of cognition and behaviour. The extent to which strategies can be implemented is therefore dependent, to some extent, on the development of executive function. By contrast, Baddeley and Hitch (1974) suggest that it is the extent to which children can make use of what they refer to as the *phonological loop* that constrains working memory capacity. Baddeley and Hitch suggest that when rehearsing information we repeat it to ourselves using an "inner voice". This repetition circulates the information to be remembered around the phonological loop, which has a limited capacity. The faster you can repeat this information, the more information you can fit onto the loop and therefore keep in mind (in your working memory). Speech rate does appear to be related to working memory capacity (Baddeley & Hitch, 1974).

Constraints on long-term memory

Long-term memory, as we have seen in Chapter 1, is where we store our knowledge. It is generally acknowledged that this is structurally distinct from working memory (refer back to the neurological evidence presented in Chapter 2). It is also assumed that our long-term memory is organised in some way. As information that is related to other knowledge seems to be connected neurologically, which results in modularisation, it seems likely that our long-term memories are organised so that similar memories are stored alongside each other.

Whether we should draw distinctions between different types of knowledge and therefore different types of memory is contentious. It is obvious that we do store memories of different *types*, though; for example we have memories of word meanings, personally relevant events, people that we know or have known and . . .; the list goes on. Whether similar memories are stored in different parts of the brain (suggesting modularity), or whether they are organised into domains that are not necessarily independent of each other, is still debated. No clear conclusions have been reached because to do so would require concrete evidence that links brain structures with specific knowledge.

With development and experience we are bound to accumulate more knowledge. Recalling relevant information when we need it is therefore going to get more difficult the more information that we have stored in our memory; we have more information to sift through to find that which is relevant. To be able to effectively locate relevant information when we need it, some sort of organisation is necessary.

Obviously the organisation of memory is going to depend on the formation of *concepts* of events and objects. The formation of concepts, as we have seen (see Chapter 2) is dependent on the perception of similarities between different instances of the things that we experience. We have to be able to recognise that one event or object is another example of something that we have experienced before.

Early episodic memories (memories of events) seem to be organised in terms of scripts. Scripts are prototypical descriptions of specific types of event. We have already seen that infants are capable of perceiving relationships between individual events that are separated in time (that is, they are temporally separated) and that a sensitivity to events that are causally related precedes the development of an ability to relate non-causally related events to one another (see Chapter 2). Obviously, the ability to remember events is going to build on this understanding and we would expect that causally related events would be easier to remember and therefore would be remembered from a younger age. If this were the case, we would expect domain-specific knowledge to play an important role in the development of episodic memories. This makes intuitive sense: To organise information effectively we need to understand the meaning of it. It is highly likely, therefore, that the ability to organise our long-term memories is more dependent on knowledge than processes.

Bauer and Shore (1987) engaged young infants in a play scenario and "gave teddy a bath". Seventeen-month-olds could both immediately model the sequence and reproduce it 6 weeks later. This suggests that infants are capable of forming scripts for events but also that memories for events are temporally organised, because they were able to remember the order in which the different actions involved in giving teddy a bath occurred. Bauer and Shore might have overestimated the competencies of 17-month-olds in that they suggested that only minimal modelling of the "bath sessions" resulted in the formation of a temporally organised event memory. Given that children of this age are probably already familiar with the sequence of events associated with having a bath, they could well have constructed a script for "bath time" before they participated in the study. Although this would undermine the suggestion Bauer and Shore made about the ease with which coherent event memories are formed, it does not call into question the infants' apparent ability to both organise their memories and retain them over time. In a similar study, Bauer and Mandler (1989) found that causally related events are easier for 16- to 20-month-olds to remember, suggesting that causality and time are used as principles around which to organise information.

Nelson (1988) argues that infants have an innately specified tendency to remember events that occur frequently over and above "one-off" events, that is, that scripts are formed before exceptions to scripts. She argues that this tendency enables the infant to predict the likelihood of future events and eventually engage in planning. It is therefore an adaptive strategy. She also suggests that the basic ways in which we structure, represent, and interpret reality are consistent over the course of development (Nelson, 1993). This is because these abilities are dependent on structurally based abilities that are available from birth and do not change. Any development in the ability to remember events is said to result from the acquisition of domain-specific knowledge rather than any domain-general changes to the processes applied to knowledge.

Fivush and Hammond (1990) take this argument further and suggest that the development of scripts *enables* the development of memories for novel events. They suggested that infants could form memories of individual events only once scripts for events that occur frequently have been formed. All early memories are grouped together and similarities and differences between them are extracted so that concepts and scripts can be formed (for the reasons given by Nelson). Once scripts are formed, events that deviate from them are represented individually. If this were the case we would expect that individual events that deviate rather than conform to scripts would be more likely to be remembered. Evidence to support this suggestion comes from studies that compare children's abilities to remember proto-typical and novel events. Fivush and Hammond (1990) found that the ability to remember events that conformed to scripts was better than the ability to remember one-off episodes, suggesting that the children were merging their representations of events into scripts. By contrast, Farrar and Goodman (1990) found that novel events were recalled more frequently than prototypical events. In Fivush and Hammond's study, the one-off events considered were those that would have been par-ticularly relevant to the child—emotionally charged events such as births and deaths of family members. In Farrar and Goodman's research the events considered were events that would not have been as emotive. Usher and Neisser (1993) found that the perceived import-ance of events predicted memory formation. In their sample, the earli-est memory for the birth of a sibling was age two, whereas for the death of a family member or a house move it was 3 years of age. Indeed, few people can remember more than a few isolated events that they experienced before the age of about 3 years (Perlmutter, 1986). These limitations on early autobiographical memory formation are not attributable to an inability to form long-term memories in general, as we have seen that young children *can* form long-term memories, they just don't very often. This apparent lack of memory of our early years has been labelled *infantile amnesia* (Howe & Courage, 1993). So why are our early memories so few and far between? It seems that Nelson might be right to suggest that infants have an innate tendency to form script-based memories rather than memories of isolated events.

The tendency to merge similar memories into scripts might in part explain why young children are so susceptible to memory failures and inaccuracies in recall when they are subjected to repeated questioning about events (Ceci & Bruck, 1993). Memories of individual events might be blurry and suggestions made by those posing the questions could be incorporated into still developing scripts and schemas. The latter interpretation appears to have confirmed by Clubb, Nida, Merritt, and Ornstein (1993), who found that children are less susceptible to suggestion when questioned about events for which they have already developed scripts.

In sum, young children can and do form memories of isolated events, but these are very few in number. Those that are formed are those that are particularly significant to the child. Most event memories formed during early childhood appear to be subsumed in script memories. Two different innate tendencies determine which early events are remembered and which are not. Scripts for events that occur frequently are created and reinforced by experience. Events that are accompanied by emotional reactions also seem to be remembered.

Language also seems to be related to the development of autobiographical memory. The development of language is obviously dependent on long-term memory, because it requires the storage and retrieval of information about word meanings (as well as knowledge of grammatical structure, linguistic conventions, etc. We will discuss this further in Chapter 5). The development of language in turn enables us to share our experiences with other people (Nelson, 1996). Given that we appear to be social beings who are innately preprogrammed to form attachments with others, communicate, and learn from and about others through interaction, the development of language gives memory more purpose. We can trade memories with others and use the trading of experiences to form relationships. The formation of relationships can then contribute to our cognitive development as other people can tell us things that add to our knowledge base. Here we have a lovely example of the complex interactions between developments in different areas: Language aids memory development and then language development helps memory development because it increases the motivation to form memories and be able to recall them.

Most experimental studies of children's ability to recall information suggest a substantial improvement with age (Kuhn, 2000). However, even very young children appear to remember information that they deem to be important. Rogoff (1998) suggests that young children have a problem with deliberate recall tasks because they can't see the point of remembering things because they are told to. Indeed, most of children's long-term memories are formed implicitly, as many adult memories are: Only occasionally do we actively try and remember things. When we do try and actively learn things it is usually because we are going to be formally tested on our knowledge of a particular area for some reason. Whether we acknowledge it or not, as adults we seem to work on the assumption that if something is worth remembering we'll remember it, if not then it's probably not worth remembering. Given that young children do not use generally use their memories purposefully, Rogoff suggests that we should focus our attention on how children use their memories in everyday life and not rely on evidence from deliberate recall tasks.

The memories of young children are obviously fairly fragile and become less so with age. Young children are also fairly suggestible. The extent to which children are open to suggestion is unclear, however, and this should be taken into account when using the testimonies of children in court, for example. The limitations of early memory also need to be taken into consideration when devising experimental procedures to investigate other cognitive developments. We also need to remain aware of the fact that constraints on long-term memory as well as working memory could affect development in other areas.

Understanding thinking

The evidence we have seen so far suggests that by the end of their first year infants have not only acquired a lot of knowledge about the world but that they have also developed the ability to represent information mentally. Although this allows for conscious access to knowledge it does not necessarily mean that infants know that they know anything. To do so, they would have to understand the nature of symbolism and what it *means* to think about something or remember something. This understanding is necessary if symbols are to be used to aid memory formation and retrieval. Children therefore need to develop *representational awareness*; an understanding of the relationship between a symbol and the thing that it symbolises (its *referent*); how thoughts relate to and describe the world.

As adults, we know what it is to *think*. To understand the nature of thinking one must understand that thoughts are *representations* of reality. This understanding is known as *representational insight*. To have representational insight we must recognise that thoughts are symbolic; that they are mental representations of external reality.

DeLoache (1987, 1989, 1991) looked at children's understanding of models as symbols. Children were shown a model of the room that they were in and the representational nature of the model explained to them. An object was then hidden in the model room and the child was asked to find a corresponding hidden object (it was something worth looking for, in case you were wondering !). Whereas two-and-a-half-year-old children didn't understand the correspondence between the model and real room, 3-year olds did. There seems, therefore, to be bit of a delay between the acquisition of symbolic thought and an explicit understanding of what it actually is, as is to be expected.

DeLoache's experiments suggest that the ability to understand the nature of symbols develops *after* the ability to symbolise itself. However, the nature of the symbolic system in question affects the specific age at which developments occur. For example, children understand the symbolic nature of pictures at an earlier age than those of models (DeLoache, 1987, 1991). DeLoache suggests that this could be because the understanding of pictures is a less sophisticated ability because pictures are not interesting as objects in their own right whereas models are; pictures are only bits of paper after all! It is therefore easier for children to see pictures as symbolic representations of objects, whereas models are not only symbolic representations; they are also objects in their own right. To recognise a model as a representation, the child therefore has to put aside his or her mental representation of the model as an object and concentrate on its symbolic function to pass the task. The competing mental representation of a picture as something in its own right is not as strong and would therefore be easier to resist.

Indeed, when DeLoache (1991) decreased the salience of the competing representation (the model itself) by asking children to view the model through a window so as to make it more like a picture, performance on the task improved. By contrast, increasing the salience of the model as an object of interest by allowing the child to play with the model prior to undertaking the task decreased performance. Seeing the model as an object in its own right therefore makes it more difficult for the child to treat it as a representation of something else. The mental representation of the model as a model is in direct competition with the representation of the model as a representation of the room.

Such an interpretation was confirmed by a version of the standard "model room" task (DeLoache, Miller, & Rosengren, 1997) in which symbolic abilities were not required. In this modified version of the task, children were led to believe that a strange "shrinking machine" had shrunk an *actual* room. Under these conditions, children found it much easier to treat the model as a representation, and thus they were able to find the hidden object (80 per cent versus 19 per cent). DeLoache attributed this increase in performance to the fact that no symbolic understanding is necessary in the modified task because the small room *was* the large room (as far as the child was concerned) and not a representation of it.

There seems to be a definite developmental pattern here. Children come to recognise symbols for what they are, that is, representations of something else. Understanding the symbolic nature of some things is easier than others. We have just seen that pictures are easier than models. The ability to understand the nature of symbols involves *dual representation*. To recognise a symbol as a symbol you need to both hold and acknowledge two simultaneous mental representations of the same thing, the representation itself and the representation as a representation. That is, you need to realise that you hold two representations that refer in different ways to the same object or event in the environment.

The capacity for dual representation underlies many subsequent developments. In the chapters that follow this one, we will look at how children's developing understanding of the nature of thought underlies the development of symbolic systems such as language, reading and writing, as well as the development of children's understanding of *mind*. The capacity for dual representation has been found to be fundamental in developing such abilities. Being able to reflect on the nature of thought is known as *metacognition*. Metacognition appears to be a very advanced cognitive ability that demonstrates the reflective nature of human thinking. It is also a very important ability to have. To progress with cognitive development we need to understand our thought processes, consider their effectiveness in different situations and adapt the way that we deal with information accordingly (Schneider & Pressley, 1999).

Metacognition and metamemory

When children come to appreciate that their thoughts are mental representations they can begin to understand the nature of memory. *Metamemory* is the conscious awareness of how much and what knowledge we have as well as an understanding of *how* our memories work (Flavell, 1971). It comprises of factual, declarative knowledge about the ways in which memory works and procedural knowledge that helps us to regulate our behaviour on an implicit level when we try to remember things. With increasing age and experience, we become both more aware of our own competencies and we engage in more self-monitoring.

Young children are not very good at assessing their own memory abilities, which seems to reflect a limited understanding of the processes involved in memory formation and retrieval. For example, Kreutzer, Leonard, and Fraser (1975) found that children often wrongly assume that learning pairs of unrelated words would be as easy as remembering pairs of related words, and also that delayed recall would be as easy as immediate recall. Indeed, young children often claim to have infallible memories similar to those of the proverbial elephant (Yussen & Levy, 1975) and negative experiences don't alter their perceptions significantly. Whereas DeLoache, Cassidy, and Brown (1985) found that 2-year-olds will point to or glance at an object they have been told that they would be asked to find later on, suggesting that they have at least an implicit understanding of the need to rehearse information, this understanding was procedural rather than declarative. It seems then that the development of procedural metamemory precedes the development of declarative metamemory. This is not surprising given that early cognition *is* implicit.

With age, the ability to recognise one's own competencies gradually increases. Three-year-olds realise that it is harder to remember larger numbers of items (Yussen & Bird, 1974) and 4-year-olds realise that they need to *actively try* to remember information; they no longer think that the brain works like a photocopier as they do when younger than 4 years old (Wellman, 1990) (this issue will be returned to later in Chapter 7).

With age, children become more proficient at estimating their own memory span (Yussen & Levy, 1975) and they come to realise that extracting the gist is an easier strategy than trying to remember things word-for-word (Kreutzer et al., 1975). This is something that even university students fail to realise, and if they do realise it they don't always act upon it! Children come to realise that if information is to be retained for a long period of time then more time should be spent encoding that information (Rogoff, Newcombe, & Kagan, 1984) and that categorisation increases memory abilities (O'Sullivan, 1996). Developments in metacognitive awareness result from experience and reflection upon strategy usage. However, knowing what strategies are effective in different situations does not necessarily mean that the strategy will be implemented. As we have seen, young children have problems planning and co-ordinating their behaviour and this is because of domain-general constraints on the development of executive function. It is therefore not surprising that, even when children have metacognitive awareness of a strategy and its usefulness, they do not always demonstrate this in their behaviour. Executive function develops during infancy, though, and therefore it does not constrain the development of metamemory for long.

Memory strategies

Strategies are deliberate, goal-directed, mental operations aimed at problem solving. Both an increase in memory capacity and an increase in conscious awareness of one's own thinking contributes to the implementation of strategies of many kinds, including memory strategies. The strategies that we employ when attempting to remember information demonstrate an awareness of the way in which our memories work. For example, if we acknowledge that organising information helps us to retrieve it when needed, we might impose organisation on what can seem to be unrelated pieces of information. Often, we make up rhymes or stories to help us remember things. For example, "naughty elephant squirts water" is a rhyme often used by children to help them remember the points on a compass. The use of such stories and rhymes also suggests that we understand, whether implicitly or explicitly, that our memories are organised in terms of scripts.

Evidence seems to suggest that children pass through a stage of implicit use of strategies prior to developing an explicit awareness of the strategies they employ. Schneider and Pressley (1999) reviewed over 60 studies that looked at the relationship between metamemory and memory behaviour and found that they consistently showed that the two were strongly related, with memory behaviour demonstrating that slightly more knowledge is stored at an implicit than at an explicit level. Obviously, the usefulness of strategies that are not available for conscious reflection is limited. If children are not aware of the fact that they are using a particular strategy they can't monitor the effectiveness of it. If the effectiveness of a strategy isn't monitored then informed decisions as to when and when not to use that particular strategy in different learning situations can't be made. Training children to use strategies and explicitly pointing out how they aid memory has proven effective, suggesting that the perception of strategy use is an important factor in the development of metamemory (Kail, 1990). Teaching children to use a strategy doesn't mean that they will use it, however. Flavell and Wellman (1977) found that the immediate improvements in memory behaviour that result from them having being taught a particular strategy soon disappear if the children are no longer encouraged to use the strategy. It seems that this is because they can't really understand the usefulness of such strategies, that is, they lack the necessary metacognitive awareness. Metacognitive awareness increases with age and becomes more consistent with memory behaviour. Whereas 4-year-olds rarely use strategies without being told to (Baker-Ward, Ornstein, & Holden, 1984), most 5-year-olds do (Flavell, 1985).

The fact that other people have a role to play in the development of metamemory and memory development shows how inter-related social and cognitive developments are. Other people can actively encourage children to reflect on their cognitions and this facilitates cognitive development. As social relationships are an environmental influence on development, this not only shows how environmental factors interact with innate predispositions to give rise to development it also shows how individual differences in competencies come about.

Bjorklund (2000) highlights the bi-directional relationship between metamemory and memory behaviour; we learn about how our memories work by *using* our memories and our knowledge of how our memories work affects the way in which we use our memories. However, the relationship is not as simple as this. Other factors, such as the amount of knowledge that a child has accumulated, also affect the efficiency of children's memories for specific types of information. We seem to remember things that make sense to us; something that might explain why it is so difficult for us to remember abstract concepts. Knowledge in our long-term memory is just one of the factors that affects the way in which we process information and store knowledge. Memory is not a passive store from which we retrieve information, it is actively involved in cognition.

Knowledge-based theories propose that an in-depth understanding of a particular domain is necessary before domain-general processes can operate effectively to develop further knowledge in this domain. Such theories emphasise the importance of the storage components of the memory system. By contrast, information-processing theories suggest that domain-general changes in information-processing *abilities*, such as the amount of working memory space available, enable the more effective use of information. Such domain-general processes are said to put an upper limit on cognitive performance. These limitations are biologically based, as physiological changes to brain structure affect the ability to store and recall information. The precise mechanisms that underlie such changes are as yet unspecified. Strategy use is said to come about as a result of domain-general changes to the cognitive system. It is likely that both are important, however, and that metacognitive awareness also contributes to development. Development of memory strategy use seems appears to be a result of changes in children's inclination to implement a particular strategy rather than their ability to use it.

Summary and conclusions

Brain growth during the first 2 years of life is greater than at any other time, as we saw in Chapter 1. It is these innate, architectural constraints on brain development that enable the rapid development and allow for the progression from perceptual to mental thought and from representations of perceptual features to representations that contain meaning. The complex inter-relationships between brain development and cognitive function can, however, be a problem when interpreting research findings, as developmental immaturities in some areas can mask competencies in others.

We have seen how an infant's knowledge and understanding of the world increases with age and development and how innate constraints on development predispose children to learn about some things earlier than others. Alongside these domain-specific abilities that allow for the interpretation and representation of specific things, there appear to be domain-general constraints on development. As domain-general changes occur these open up possibilities for development within different domains. One such domain-general mechanism is the ability to form mental representations, the development of which appears to be constrained by architectural constraints (brain development) to some extent. Although innate factors have a role to play, we cannot overlook the impact of environmental factors.

The development of the ability to form mental representations is of key importance. It allows for the representation of knowledge in a format that can be accessed on demand (knowledge is stored in an explicit form). It is at this point that cognition really begins, as it is here that infants develop the ability to remember things on a conscious level. Once children have conscious access to their thoughts they can begin to perceive similarities between experiences, evaluate their strategy use and develop more effective ways of processing information. This will inevitably lead to further knowledge acquisition.

The ability to categorise information forms the basis of the ability to form prototypical mental representations and thus forming concepts and categories is inextricably related to the development of memory abilities. The hierarchical organisation of concepts into conceptual hierarchies in which relations between concepts are specified allows for theory building. For a child's understanding of something to be theoretical in nature, concepts must be understood and the links between them understood to a level that allows the knowledge specified within them to be used to explain and predict events.

Once mental representations become explicit and grow in number they need to be organised so that they can be retrieved easily and in appropriate circumstances. They also need to be manipulated, so that thinking and reasoning can occur.

Chapter 4

Thinking and reasoning

Each day we are faced with problems and we spend much of our time and a lot of cognitive effort trying to solve them. Although some days might seem more fraught with problems than other days, we don't acknowledge *as* problems many of the problems that we are faced with. All of the decisions we make involve some sort of problem solving. Some problems have a fairly straightforward solution, for example we can get money out of a cash machine by following a series of learned steps (presuming that there is any money in our account!). Other problems are more complicated and require the careful analysis of many alternatives. For example, have you ever had to try and meet several social obligations without upsetting anyone while wanting to do only some of the things that you feel you should do? Indeed, many of the problems that we are faced with can be solved in more than one way and often we have to make compromises.

Problem solving involves several abilities. First, you need to identify both your aims and the nature of the problem, that is those things that need to be overcome if you are to solve the problem. You then need to devise and implement a plan. If you have the appropriate background knowledge and your reasoning is sound then the chances are that your plan will work.

As we have seen in previous chapters, the acquisition of knowledge is a gradual process. Infants are born with very little innate knowledge, just the ability to learn and a few simple principles to enable them to interpret their world at a perceptual level. Given that the rate at which we learn about things differs from domain to domain as a result of our experiences, it seems likely that our problem-solving abilities will be affected by whether we are familiar with the type of problem faced; the objects, people and situation involved. Innate constraints on information processing might preclude the effective use of such any domain-specific knowledge that has been acquired, however.

Piaget claimed that the way that children store, use, and manipulate their mental representations is different at each of the stages of development he described and that the different ways of thinking distinguish between the stages. Piaget's theory of development suggests that children pass through four distinct stages of development. In the sensorimotor and preoperational stages (birth to 6/7 years), children are said to be illogical in their thinking. Information is represented at a mental level during this second stage but it is poorly organised and not integrated into a coherent explanation of the world. The passing of a child from the preoperational to the next (concrete operational) stage is marked by the ability to represent information in a logical and ordered manner. During this stage children start to see the inconsistencies in their thinking and they re-evaluate their knowledge on the basis of this. Only on progression to the final stage (at around the age of 11 years) is children's thinking said to become "adult-like". It is only then that children begin to reason about the world in a scientific manner, carefully considering possibilities and testing hypotheses. Piaget claimed that cognitive development reflects domain-general changes that exist at a structural and therefore biological level, and that these are reflected in a child's thinking and problem-solving attempts.

In previous chapters we have seen how Piaget not only underestimated children's abilities but also how he placed too great an emphasis on innate constraints at the expense of knowledge acquisition. Although Piaget did acknowledge that children demonstrate thinking characteristic of different stages in different domains at any time, the strict stage-like description of development that he proposed has not withstood the test of time. Despite this, Piaget's theory and the research that he based it on have informed our understanding of the development of children's problem-solving and reasoning skills. More recent theories such as the information-processing accounts of Case (1985) and Fischer (1980), like Piaget, suggest that domain-general working-memory limitations put an upper limit on children's problem-solving attempts (see Chapter 1). Given that Piaget's theory has been so influential, his theory will feature quite heavily in this chapter.

Problem-solving and reasoning skills are applied across many different domains. When making sense of text and spoken language we devise rules and strategies to make our task easier. When faced with difficult social situations we similarly use our previous knowledge and devise strategies to enable us to deal with the problem. Thus long-term memory is also implicated in the development of problem-solving and reasoning skills. If we have insufficient knowledge we might not adopt the most effective strategy and therefore we might not cope with the problem very well. In the chapters that follow this one we will look at the development of language, reading, and writing skills and the development of a child's *understanding of mind*. Given that problem-solving skills are utilised in all of these domains (and that these will be discussed later) we will not discuss these in this chapter. Instead, we will consider the nature of problem solving in general and the processes and structures that are involved. We will then look at specific types of problem solving and reasoning and how these develop.

Early problem solving

When solving problems we have to bear in mind what we are trying to achieve while planning a course of action that will enable us to reach our desired outcome. Planning our response to a problem is known as *means–end analysis*. To plan a course of action to achieve an aim we have to chain together a series of subgoals, working backwards, starting from the outcome that we want to achieve.

Piaget (1976) claimed that problem solving is a characteristic of operational reasoning and thus that it does not develop until around the age of 6 or 7 years. Although he acknowledged that children in both the sensorimotor and the preoperational stage can solve simple problems by perceiving similarities between the situation they are currently facing and previous situations, and then acting upon the basis of these, Piaget claimed that *conscious* means–end reasoning is not involved and, as such, the problem solving involved isn't *real* problem solving.

We have already seen that children can solve simple problems in infancy. For example, infants can retrieve a hidden object from under a cloth at around the age of 8 months, and this requires means–end reasoning. Even younger infants can also perform actions in an attempt to control aspects of their environment or achieve a particular aim. The information that guides such behavioural reactions to problems in infancy is stored implicitly and therefore is not under conscious control. When considering early problem solving it is therefore easy for us to concur with Piaget's claim that such problem solving isn't *real* problem solving in the way that we as adults conceive of it. As with so many of the abilities studied by developmental psychologists, the answer to the question of whether infants are capable of a cognitive function depends on how you define it. Here, the way in which problem solving is defined determines any conclusions as to whether infants are capable of it.

The problem-solving attempts of infants are very easily disrupted (as we saw in Chapter 3). In Harris's (1973) study of object permanence, for example, infants soon appeared to forget what they were trying to achieve (reaching for the object under cloth B in the A not B task) when they were not allowed to retrieve the object immediately. It seems that Piaget's claim that domain-general constraints place an upper limit on the problem-solving abilities of infants is correct.

Working memory constraints

To solve a problem we first of all have to be able to hold the information that we need to solve the problem in our working memory. Although knowledge that we have stored in our long-term memory might provide us with valuable information as to how to go about solving the problem (a judgement that would be based on perceived similarities between the problem currently faced and those that we have faced in the past) often we hold only the information that we need to solve a problem for the amount of time needed to solve it; it is held in our working memory.

In the last chapter we saw how the amount of information that we can hold in our working memory increases as a result of our ability to organise or "chunk" information into meaningful units. We also saw how the amount of time for which we can hold information can be extended by the use of strategies such as rehearsal. As cognitive processes become automatic as a result of their repeated application, they no longer require attention and thus make no demands on working memory. Because processes only become automatic with experience, and young children have limited experience, things that require no conscious thought for us adults might be cognitively demanding for children. The application of automatic processes and the use of strategies are bound to have an effect on problem-solving abilities because they free-up working memory space. Given that this is where active cognition occurs, more space means more potential for the manipulation of information. One effect of this is that as our working memory capabilities increase we should be able to solve more complicated problems.

Means–end reasoning and alternative strategies

DeLoache, Miller, and Pierroutsakos (1998) suggest that problem solving doesn't necessarily have to involve means–end analysis. They suggested that a *hill-climbing* strategy, whereby each move towards a goal is considered independently, could be used instead. The use of such a strategy does not require any chaining of subgoals; instead a series of individual decisions is made. If a particular move takes the child closer to the solution, he or she will make that move. This strategy is not as effective as other strategies but it does work. When using a hill-climbing strategy, any one move could lead to a dead-end in terms of achieving the desired outcome. This would mean that the child would have to take a step backwards and try again. Eventually, however, such a strategy should prove successful, that is if the child doesn't give up!

Very few problems in real life can only be solved in one way, and whether we apply the most appropriate strategy depends on a number of factors. Some strategies are more effective than others, but they are all strategies and the fact that children can apply a strategy at all suggests that they are problem solving. They might not be very good at it, often selecting uneconomical strategies, but even young children demonstrate abilities in this area.

Siegler's (1996) overlapping waves approach (described in Chapter 1) proposes that children have a variety of strategies available to them at any time and that these compete for usage. With age, it is the frequency with which particular strategies are used that changes. Evidence seems to support this proposition, as it is the frequency with which children employ specific strategies that changes with age rather than the actual strategies that children *can* apply. With age and experience children learn to associate specific strategies with successful performance on specific tasks. This results in the more selective application of strategies, resulting in more efficient problem solving.

Generating rules

The ability to learn rules as well as the ability to apply these rules in appropriate circumstances is important for problem solving; it is one thing to remember a rule and keep this in mind when problem solving, it is another thing to work out a rule. Rules specify the relationship between two variables, and take the form "*if . . . then . . .*" To learn a rule you need to be able to perceive similarities between different situations. You also need to be able mentally to represent these similarities in an organised way. So, for an example, a rule might specify that to achieve a specific aim you have to perform a specific action.

As we have seen in previous chapters, the perception of similarities between different experiences results in the construction of prototypes. Prototypical representations of rules for problem solving specify the key characteristics of situations in which a particular rule has been applied successfully. To be able to implement a useful strategy we have to realise that the problem that needs to be solved at that point in time is similar to something that we've come across in the past. It is therefore useful if the problem we are confronted with is *obviously* similar to previous problems we have tackled. Contextual and environmental cues are important here because they trigger the recall of memories of similar problem-solving occurrences.

Lave (1988), for example, found that adults performed mental arithmetic better in a supermarket than a laboratory test. Given that adults rarely have to make mathematical computations in test situations but often have to tackle them in everyday situations, it appears that it was the context in which they had to solve the problems rather than the problems themselves that determined their success. Nunes (1993) similarly found that children made more errors solving problems if asked to write down a problem before they set about trying to solve it. It seems that asking children to do something that they wouldn't ordinarily do impeded their performance. The context-specific nature of cognition is something that Piaget failed to consider. Instead, he claimed that it was the underlying structures and the development of these that determines task performance. Whereas performance on tasks is partly determined by constraints that exist at a structural level, the context in which a task is presented determines whether cognitive processes are used to their full extent. Looking at the context in which cognition occurs and how this affects the extent to which available strategies and processes are applied can tell us a lot about the nature of cognition. By concentrating on this aspect of cognitive development we can ascertain what information children attend to when thinking. Because of this, many contemporary theories of development acknowledge this and focus more on processes than structures. After all, just because structures are available doesn't mean that they are used.

In the previous chapter we looked at how knowledge informs the strategies that we use when trying to remember and recall information. Using our memories (to actively try and remember things) is an instance of problem solving and so it goes without saying that the more knowledge you have acquired about a specific type of problem situation the more likely it is that the right rule or strategy will be called on. Domain-specific knowledge about the problem-solving situation and the type of problem to be solved therefore affects problem-solving abilities, in addition to the domain-general constraints that tend to exist at a structural level.

Following rules

Zelazo, Carter, Reznick, and Frye (1997) argue that a child's ability to follow arbitrary rules is dependent on executive function (the control and planning aspect of working memory). According to Zelazo et al., working memory abilities are equally, if not more, important than domain-specific knowledge when problem solving because they put an upper limit on performance. Such a suggestion was supported by a study in which Zelazo and Reznick (1991) asked children to sort a number of cards into categories; something that required following a rule. Although children understood the rule they could not follow it. This suggests that *knowing* what they should be doing doesn't mean that they actually *do* it. Knowledge alone is not sufficient for children to be able to plan and control their actions so that the rule is followed. It seems that actually *remembering* the rule required so much cognitive effort that there was none available for the child to use to actually plan and execute the behaviours that were needed to complete the task in hand. Although as adults we often know what we should do and yet we don't do it, this is not usually because we *can't* co-ordinate and plan our actions, it is usually because we don't really want to do whatever it is we know we should be doing.

In a further study, Frye, Zelazo, and Palfai (1995) asked children of between 3 and 5 years of age to sort a series of picture cards that differed along two dimensions, shape and colour, into categories on the basis of either their shape or their colour. Having done this, the children were asked to sort the cards along the other dimension (so, if they had sorted according to colour in the first trial they now sorted on the basis of shape). Frye et al. (1995) found that although young children have no difficulty sorting the cards in the first trial, they could not follow the rule in the second trial (whether this was colour or shape). This was interpreted as evidence of young children's inability to switch between different schemes of reasoning. They made what Zelazo and Reznick referred to as *perseverative errors*; they could not over-ride the first sorting rule and switch to another.

In a similar study, Gerstadt, Hong, and Diamond (1994) presented children with picture cards, one at a time. They were asked to respond "day" to a stimulus card depicting a night-time scene and "night" to a picture of a sun. To give a correct response, it was reasoned that the children must suppress a response based on their mental representation of what the picture card really depicts. If this response was not suppressed, the children would reply "day" to the picture card depicting the sun and "night" to that depicting a moon and stars. Gerstadt et al.'s (1994) results revealed developmental trends in the extent to which errors occurred (as measured by the amount of time it took for the children to respond to the whole series of pictures), with children under four having more difficulty than those over this age.

Response latency on the Stroop task could be construed as a measure of children's tendency to focus on reality at the expense of alternative representations (in this case, the representation of the rule that they must follow). To respond correctly to a given stimulus card, the child must resist the temptation to reply with reference to reality and give a reply based on a counterfactual mental representation. In other words, the child would have to resist giving a reply based on the prototypical mental model of what the card depicts. This model would have been constructed from previous experiences associating night-time scenes with the word "night" and daytime scenes with the word "day". Under this interpretation we would assume that the longer the child takes to give a response, the more difficulty he or she has overcoming such a tendency.

Gerstadt et al. (1994) offer a different interpretation of the results. They argue that the mechanism responsible for the difficulty that young children have with the Stroop task is that they are unable to switch their attention from one representation to another, the two representations in question being the correct response to the card (based on the prespecified rule) and what the card really depicts. Thus, their interpretation is in line with Frye et al.'s (1995) processing account.

Frye et al.'s findings suggest that it is limitations on children's ability to *process* information that constrains their early problem-solving attempts. Given that executive function is responsible for the planning and co-ordination of behaviour, and that this is dependent on the development of the prefrontal cortex (Diamond, 1985), it seems likely that brain maturation constrains the development of problem solving. Such a claim is consistent with Piaget's and information-processing accounts because domain-general processes, rather than knowledge, are said to limit problem-solving abilities.

Theory theory accounts (e.g. Gopnik & Meltzoff, 1997) see background knowledge as more important than innate domain-general constraints. They suggest that an in-depth understanding of a particular area is necessary before cognitive processes can operate effectively. That is, they claim that domain-specific knowledge constrains the use of domain-general mechanisms, rather than the other way. The effective operation of domain-general processes within a given domain then has the "knock-on" effect of allowing for more efficient knowledge acquisition. Theories such as this emphasise the *storage* components of memory (mental representations) rather than the processes that are applied to them.

It seems likely that both information-processing constraints and domain-specific knowledge have a role to play in problem solving. In situations where very little knowledge is required, such as in the sorting task described above (all the knowledge that you need to solve this problem is provided by the task itself) children appear to be constrained by working-memory limitations. In other situations, background knowledge is helpful and sometimes even necessary. It seems, then, that the way in which children's problem solving is constrained is dependent on the nature of the task to be solved and the context in which it is presented. That is, problem solving is context and situation specific.

In some areas at least, expertise has been found to compensate for low levels of general intelligence. For example, in a study by Ceci and Liker (1986) knowledge of "form" of the horses in a race is a better predictor of winning than IQ (which was taken to be an indication of the efficiency of cognitive processing). Many studies have been conducted, looking at the distinction between the problem-solving strategies of experts and novices (e.g. Chi, Feltovich, & Glaser, 1981; DeGroot, 1965) and they all suggest that experts and novices approach problem solving differently. This suggests that, with experience, we can learn rules and apply strategies that enable us to overcome information-processing constraints.

Planning and problem solving

Given that executive function has been implicated in the development of problem-solving abilities, we would expect that, as executive function develops, children would be able to plan their problem-solving attempts more efficiently. When young children face problems their attempts at solving them are often random and based on trial and error. They do not plan their actions or tackle the problem in a systematic way. Ellis and Siegler (1997) suggest several possible reasons for this. First, it could be that it is the young child's inability to inhibit a pre-potent response that is the problem. To solve a problem, they have to stop what they are doing and do something else; something that we have already seen is problematic for young children.

Alternatively, it could be that children are so obsessed with receiving praise that they rush to complete a task, seeing speedy completion as more important than accuracy. Let's face it, adults often help propagate this myth in the heads of young children, often congratulating them for "having a go" rather than getting it right. (Developmental psychologists must also put their hands up to this one! When testing children they rarely correct children if they get the answer to a test question wrong.)

It could also be that planning is seen as a bit too much like hard work. In adulthood we can appreciate the pay-off in terms of time spent on a task as a result of planning because we've learned from experience (hopefully!). Young children have very little experience to go on. Furthermore, any experiences that young children have are more likely to be negative ones. If they have formulated plans in the past, which because of cognitive limitations in other areas have failed to "pay-off" then they might see the trial and error approach as just as, if not more, effective than problem solving based on planning. It could also depend on how lucky they have been in the past. If trial and error pays off frequently then why would another strategy involving planning be seen as an important thing to develop? The same could be said for the hill-climbing strategy described earlier. A final possibility could be that trying out new possibilities is both a lot more fun and allows the child to learn new things and thus add to their domain-specific knowledge base.

Ellis and Siegler's account could be seen to suggest that children's attempts at problem solving are random. This is not the case. Although the strategies that young children employ might not be the best ones for use in a specific situation, they are by no means ineffective. Even very young children are capable of planning, although their abilities in this area are somewhat limited. The problem-solving attempts of young children are not characterised by the *means–end analysis* evident in the attempts of older children.

Fabricius (1988) used the Tower of Hanoi problem to investigate children's ability to "think ahead" (a problem also used by Piaget). In the Tower of Hanoi test, children are presented with three pegs. On one of the pegs are three discs. The child's task is to move the coloured discs from peg 1 to peg 3, so that they end up on the third peg in the same order as they were on the first peg at the start of the task. This might appear simple but there are rules to make it more difficult. The rules are that: (i) a larger disc cannot be placed on a smaller disc; and (ii) only one disc can be moved at a time. To successfully complete this task you need to be able to envisage the outcomes of individual steps in the process; you need foresight and the ability to imagine.

Fabricius found that, with age, children's need to backtrack becomes less frequent, suggesting that their ability to see beyond the next move, or next few moves, increases. Whereas younger children use the hill-climbing strategy described by DeLoache et al. (1998), older children rely on careful planning. This could be a result of the development of executive function or it could be that children have learned that planning does pay off in certain circumstances; this would be a result of experience.

Conclusions so far

In terms of the development of problem-solving abilities we can reach several conclusions. First, given that problem solving is a higher-level cognitive process it is dependent on many lower-level ones, such as the ability to perceive relationships, categorise experiences and manipulate this information. Familiarity with a problem or type of problems also contributes to abilities and thus domain-specific knowledge also plays an important role. Planning is a fairly late development and even as adults we tend to avoid doing it if at all possible! Remember all those times you've kidded yourself that "taking things as they come" is the best strategy; not because it actually is but because you can't be bothered to plan your course of action!

Given that so many factors contribute to the development of problem-solving abilities it seems that Piaget was wrong to suggest that development is stage like and limited by domain-general constraints on the way that information can be represented. Piaget was right to suggest that different types of reasoning involve different mental processes, however. This is because there isn't just one type of reasoning; it can take many different forms.

Reasoning

Reasoning is a particular type of problem solving and involves inference making. It goes beyond simple problem solving because it involves more than the perception of and application of rules. When making an inference we construct new knowledge using knowledge that we already have. Inference making is therefore *generative* rather than *reproductive*. The Tower of Hanoi puzzle described above requires this sort of reasoning; you have to generate a solution rather than simply act according to a specified rule (as in the card sort procedure). For Piaget it was this distinction that differentiates between preoperational and concrete-operational thought.

There are several different types of reasoning and these differ in terms of their complexity and usage. We will begin our discussion by considering analogical reasoning, as the development of this type of reasoning appears to precede other forms of reasoning. Given that we have already seen that even infants can perceive similarities between stimuli, first on a perceptual and then on a conceptual level, this is not surprising.

Analogical reasoning

Analogical reasoning enables us to use things that we already know to solve new problems. There are several different stages in reasoning of this sort. First of all we have to be able to understand how two things are related. This is obviously going to involve background knowledge. We then have to generate a rule that describes this relationship. Having generated a rule, the final step in the process is to apply this rule to something else. The process itself is known as *relational mapping*.

According to Piaget, such reasoning requires the capacity for logical thinking and therefore (in accordance with his stage model) does not become apparent until around the age of 7 years. By contrast, Goswami (1996) suggests that the ability to reason analogically is present at birth and forms the basis for the development of other problem-solving and reasoning abilities. Goswami argues that given that it is the ability to perceive relations that allows us to use knowledge that we have already acquired to cope with a new situation, it is a necessary skill to have, and therefore that evolution would have equipped us with this ability from birth.

Chen et al. (1997) presented 1-year-olds with a puzzle to solve. To obtain a desirable toy they had to pull a cloth so as to be able to reach and pull a string that was connected to the toy. All of the infants had to be shown how to solve the problem in the first instance but they soon transferred the knowledge they had acquired and applied the solution that they had been shown to similar problems. Twenty-nine per cent of the infants solved the first similar problem that they were presented with. This increased to 67 per cent on the third problem presented.

Chen et al.'s (1997) study shows that even infants are capable of problem solving and that they can perceive similarities between situations and base their behaviour on these, but many have questioned whether such abilities constitute *true* reasoning. Representations of the nature of the problem to be solved were based on both perceptual similarities between previous problem-solving situations and the one the child was currently faced with. They were also implicit. Similarly, the behavioural responses to the problem were implicit and procedural. As there is no conscious awareness either of the problem to be solved or the actions required to solve it, this is not true problem solving in a Piagetian sense. Again, whether it is true problem solving or not is dependent on the definition of problem solving that you adopt. It is, however, likely that such early abilities lay the foundations for subsequent development in the way that Goswami suggested.

In early infancy, analogical reasoning is limited to the perception of perceptual similarities and an implicit reaction to this when faced with a problem. *Relational similarity* problems are more difficult. Most researchers agree with Piaget on this issue; that only problems based on relational similarities demonstrate *true* reasoning because they involve the explicit identification and use of perceived relationships. To solve a relational similarity problem you have to consciously recognise the relationship between two things and then actively use this information to solve a problem.

In relational similarity problems, children need to identify a *conceptual* relationship between two items and then use this knowledge to solve a problem. For example, if presented with the pairing "cat: meow" we can work out that the second item is the sound made by the first. When presented with a third item, for example, "dog" we can then work out that "woof" goes with "dog" in the same way. Analogical reasoning of this type is a relatively complex cognitive process, involving the ability to perceive conceptual relationships and hold this knowledge in mind when solving the problem. This would make significant demands on working memory. Solving problems of this sort also requires domain-specific knowledge.

Goswami (1991, 1992) found that children are capable of making analogies between items at age four, as long as these are within familiar domains; that is, as long as the children have sufficient background knowledge to be able to work out the relation between the first two items in the problem. Such a finding suggests that domain-specific knowledge affects the ability to reason analogically. If causal relationships between items are involved, analogies are perceived and used to solve problems by 3 years of age (Goswami & Brown, 1989). Given that the perception of causal relationships appears earlier than the perception of non-causal ones, and therefore that children have knowledge of causal relationships before knowledge of non-causal ones (as we saw in Chapter 2), this is not surprising.

Analogical reasoning, like other types of problem solving, appears to be influenced by what the child already knows. Obviously in tasks such as those outlined above, children need to have sufficient knowledge to be able to perceive conceptual relationships between items. Familiarity with both the situation they are presented with and the nature of the items they have to reason with therefore increases children's performance on analogical reasoning tasks. Furthermore, it seems to be the case that it is a lack of domain-specific knowledge that prevents children from making analogies in certain situations rather than the lack of domain-general ability. The ability to make analogies seems to be in place by age three but is rarely used at this age. It seems that young children's representations of problems are deeply *contextually embedded* and that this makes it difficult for them to generalise from one situation to another. Young children do not recognise the similarities between situations because they lack knowledge, and it is this that constrains their analogical reasoning abilities. Although there might well be domain-general constraints on the ability to reason analogically, as Piaget suggested, it seems that these do not constrain children's problem-solving attempts.

We have to be very careful when interpreting studies of analogical reasoning. We need to ensure that children actually perceive the *relations* between items rather than just picking the item that "goes the best with" the other one. In many studies of analogical reasoning children are provided with several alternatives from which to select the item that goes with C in the same way that B went with A. Researchers therefore need to be very careful when selecting the items from which children have to choose!

As we have seen, knowledge stored in long-term memory affects the ease with which information can be dealt with in working memory. As a result, the development of problem solving appears to come about as a result of an interaction between innate constraints upon processing and experience. Metacognitive knowledge also has a role to play; the greater children's understanding of their own thinking, the more they can reflect on the strategies that they employ and how useful they are, and amend their strategy use accordingly. As a result, it seems inevitable that abilities increase with age and that abilities appear in different domains at different times.

According to Piaget, the ability to reason analogically develops during the preoperational stage of development, a stage he claimed is characterised by inconsistencies in children's thinking. Piaget claimed that at this stage children's thinking is not logical. For thought to be logical it has to be organised into a coherent system and follow a number of rules. We will now consider reasoning of this sort.

Logical reasoning

Piaget saw the development of logical reasoning as a key development, marking the transition from the preoperational to the concrete-operational stage of development. He concentrated his research on the age at which children apply logical rules, this ability being that which he claimed distinguished between the two stages. One of the logical rules that Piaget focused on was that of reversibility. There are two rules of reversibility. The first, *negation/inversion*, states that an operation can always be inverted. The second, *compensation*, states that for any operation there exists another operation that can compensate for the effects of the first. The ability to *conserve*, that is to realise that quantities cannot change unless something is added or subtracted, demonstrates an understanding of both of these principles and, as a result, Piaget spent a considerable amount of time investigating the development of this ability.

Conservation

According to Piaget, the ability to conserve not only demonstrates that the aforementioned rules of reversibility have been incorporated into a child's way of thinking, it also demonstrates the principles that underlie all rational thought.

Piaget (1965) devised a series of experiments to investigate children's ability to conserve quantity. The nature of the quantities under consideration varied; the ability to conserve volume, mass, and number were all tested. To test a child's understanding of volume, Piaget presented the child with two identical beakers of water. At this point the child was asked which beaker contained more water and most children rightly said that the beakers contained the same amount (those that didn't were excluded from the experiment). The content of one beaker was then poured into a taller, thinner beaker. Children were then asked which beaker contained more liquid, the tall thin one or the shorter fatter one. Up until the age of about six or seven children claimed that the tall thin beaker contained more water, despite the fact that they had just seen the same water being poured from one container to another.

Piaget claimed that young children reason in this way because they have not yet organised their knowledge into a coherent system. As a result, children fail to see any inconsistencies in their thinking. Children who fail conservation tasks obviously don't acknowledge that if the water has only been transferred from one beaker to another and that no liquid has been added then the second beaker must contain the same amount as the first.

Piaget claimed that children don't consider the whole picture when making judgements. Instead they fixate on one perceptual feature. Piaget suggested that in conservation tasks children fixate on the most obvious feature of the transformation and then make a judge-ment based on this. In the conservation of liquid task this would be the fact that the level of the liquid in the beaker was higher when the liquid was placed in the tall thin beaker.

This suggestion was later confirmed by Bruner (1966), who re-ran the conservation experiment but with the destination beaker hidden from view. He found that 4-year-olds could correctly conserve when there was no perceptual information available. It seems, then, that children were distracted from making correct judgements because they fixate on individual perceptual features rather than thinking about the problems itself. Indeed, when the second beaker was revealed in Bruner's experiment, children often changed their initial answer from a correct one to an incorrect one. This finding suggests that children did have the appropriate strategy available to them but that they opted to use an alternative one because other information distracted them and disrupted the decision-making process. It seems, therefore, to be a problem with focusing attention on the appropriate things when making a decision rather than not having access to a particular strategy.

Piaget's experimental procedures have been heavily criticised. Siegel (1997), for example, pointed out that the wording used in the conservation task, the questions asked, and the unfamiliar context in which the task was presented all put children at a disadvantage and thus they might not have reflected their true abilities. More realistic tasks that reflect the kind of judgements that children often have to make on a day-to-day basis might.

To investigate children's ability to reason on the basis of more than one perceptual characteristic, Kratochwill and Goldman (1973) presented children with photographs of people with their height manipulated. The children were asked to guess how old the people in the pictures were. Young children (under five) tended to base their judgements of age on the height of the person only: They did not take into account other factors (not even things like grey hair and wrinkles).

The tendency to focus on only one aspect of a situation is appar-ent in other errors that children make. For example, young children often tend to base their assumptions about whether things are alive or not on whether or not they move (Piaget, 1973). Thus, they have not constructed a complete concept of animate and inanimate objects;

they focus on one critical feature and make judgements accordingly. Often adults don't help. When asked questions about things such as why the sun is going down (this question asking often being a diversion tactic used by children at bedtime!), frustrated parents often respond with thing such as "because it's going to bed, as you should be". Such responses can only hinder a child's development, confusing rather than helping them to construct clear concepts specifying the key characteristics of inanimate and animate objects.

Syllogistic reasoning

The ability to solve *syllogisms* depends upon the ability to reason logically. A syllogism is a pair of statements that are said to be true. The task is to, on the basis of these two premises, make a judgement as to the accuracy of a third statement. For example;

Some monkeys are artists
All artists are female
So, some monkeys are female

This is an example of a *valid* deduction: The conclusion *necessarily* follows from the premises. The fact that monkeys don't tend to be artists is irrelevant; we can still solve the problem. To solve such problems, conclusions must be deduced from facts or *supposed* facts. The accuracy of the premises should not matter because the aim of the task is to calculate whether the final statement logically follows given the information contained in the premises. Piaget claimed that the ability to reason in an abstract way, that is about things that have no physical grounding in reality, does not develop until adolescence and is a characteristic of his formal-operational stage of development.

Hawkins, Pea, Glick, and Schribner (1984) found that 4- and 5-year-old children are capable of deductive reasoning but that realistic syllogisms (that contained premises that the children knew to be true) proved easier for them to solve than those that were unrealistic. Hawkins et al. also found that children's abilities increase with age, and at 4 and 5 years of age they can be easily disrupted. They presented real-world problems before presenting counterfactual syllogisms and found that this decreased children's tendency to accept the counterfactual premises. This led to incorrect responses. Dias and Harris (1988) also found that children of this age could solve counterfactual syllogisms if they were asked to *pretend* that the premises were true. These findings suggest that children do not have a problem with deductive reasoning *per se*. Rather, young children seem to have a problem accepting counterfactual premises and that it is this that prevents them from reasoning with them. If the context of the problem is changed so that it is easier for children to accept the premises, they can overcome this tendency and apply the appropriate deductive strategy. Piaget was wrong to suggest that the development of logical mental structures inevitably results in logical thinking. Helping children to over-ride their fascination with the accuracy of the statements enables them to reason logically.

This tendency to make *realist* errors has been well documented (and will be discussed further in Chapter 7). Young children seem to have a tendency to concentrate on reality at the expense of alternative representations of reality. Given that reality is something that we really need to get to grips with, whereas fantastical things aren't so important, it seems that such a bias might be adaptive during the early years. This finding also seems to concur with Piaget's suggestion that early logical reasoning needs support from reality. The distinction he made between concrete and formal operational reasoning reflects this.

It seems, then, that the ability to reason in a deductive way develops gradually. It is in place by about the age of four but becomes more robust thereafter. The development of deductive reasoning abilities seems to be dependent on the acquisition of domain-specific knowledge to some extent. If children *know* that the premises are true then they are more inclined to apply deductive processes to them.

Scientific reasoning

Solving syllogisms containing counterfactual premises requires the application of logic to make inferences. To respond appropriately you need to overlook the content of the premises and reach a logical conclusion. We don't often use logical reasoning of the type involved in syllogistic reasoning in our everyday lives because we usually reason with factual information (or information that we believe to be factual). As such, we could argue that studies looking at this type of reasoning are *disembedded*, that is, that they don't reflect the way in which reasoning is applied in the real world.

Piaget claimed that the capacity for scientific (or *formal*, as he called it) reasoning develops at around the age of 11 years (Piaget & Inhelder, 1958), marking the transition between the concrete-operational and formal-operational stages of development. However, subsequent research has shown that many adults cannot reason in a formal way and even those that can often don't do so spontaneously. Although Piaget was right to suggest that formal reasoning is a late development and therefore that it is more difficult than other forms of reasoning, formal reasoning appears to be a skill that only some people acquire and one that is only applied by individuals in some circumstances. This is probably because we don't really *need* to reason scientifically. One of the only areas in which the logical manipulation of abstract concepts is necessary is when we reason about scientific phenomena. Not surprisingly, then, in the real world we often use scientific reasoning only when reasoning about scientific phenomena.

Scientific reasoning involves hypothesis generation and the systematic testing of hypotheses. It involves a specific way of thinking that not only involves logic (a process) but also substantial background knowledge (representations to support the process). Although we can acquire scientific facts these are pretty useless unless they are organised into a theoretical framework and applied when solving problems.

Science: knowledge and processes

Often, young children have scientific knowledge but they have not yet integrated it into a *system*; that is, a *way* of thinking about things. For example, Nussbaum and Novack (1976) devised a study to investigate the difference between scientific knowledge and scientific reasoning. First of all they asked children to draw the world. If the children drew a circle, it was taken that they understood that the world was round. Given that the children seemed to know that the world is round, Nussbaum and Novack then looked at whether children can *use* their knowledge that the world is round and reason accordingly. Children were presented with pictures that showed, for example, a person stand-ing at the North Pole and at the South Pole. In one trial the person was holding a glass of juice (with a lid), in another he was holding a ball. Children were asked to draw the direction that the ball or juice would fall in it were let go/the lid was removed. Most of the children tested did not reason about the world as if it were round, despite understand-ing that it is. This was demonstrated by the fact that they tended to assume that the juice/ball would travel downwards, rather than towards the earth (and therefore apparently upwards when standing at the South Pole).

It seems that it takes time for children to organise their know-ledge into a coherent system. Although the children in the Nussbaum and Novack's experiment had scientific knowledge they did not con-sider its implications. On the surface it seems that they didn't think things through logically and therefore didn't recognise the contradic-tions in their own thinking; they knew the earth is round, they had some understanding of gravity, as was demonstrated by them drawing the juice/ball falling downwards, they just hadn't considered how the two related together. This could be a result of information-processing constraints. Although young children had accessed the correct infor-mation, and were therefore holding this in their working memory when solving the problem, they did not apply the correct processes (logic) to enable them to reach a logical conclusion. This suggests that recalling the scientific facts themselves put heavy demands on information pro-cessing, leaving no room for the manipulation of this knowledge. Simply explaining to students how scientists or mathematicians think is often not successful. Although they learn the terminology, formulae, and definitions they retain their previous ways of thinking and don't incorporate their newfound knowledge into their ways of thinking.

Scientific reasoning and concepts

As we have seen in previous chapters, the ability to understand the physical world in which we live is vital and, as such, it is an ability that develops rapidly. Innate constraints appear to equip infants with the ability to make sense of their environment to some extent. In Chapter 2 we saw how infants understand something of the nature of objects and in Chapter 3 we looked at how children come to form mental rather than procedural representations of them. We have also seen that young infants can perceive similarities and differences between experiences, and that they can use this to form prototypical representations of events. In early infancy, representations are implicit and therefore not available to consciousness. This precludes the development of any theories to explain how our world works. Once representations are available for conscious reflection, children can start to reflect upon their content and whether or not knowledge is consistent. This results in theory construction.

The theories that we develop to explain the way in which objects interact in the world are very different to those given by physicists. This is because physicists and non-physicists have *alternative* conceptions of the world. According to Gunstone and Watts (1985), these alternative conceptions affect the choice of events requiring explanation and the way in which they are explained. As was the case for the development of the ability to solve counterfactual syllogisms, we don't often need to reason like a physicist. All we need is a theoretical knowledge of physics that is sufficient for us to be able to explain and predict the behaviour of objects in our environment, at least to a level that enables us to interact with the world effectively. In some cases, having knowledge doesn't help us do this. For example, McClosky, Carmazza, and Green (1980) found that the ability to explain physical events does not necessarily mean that you can actually deal with the physical world more effectively. In their study, students were asked to judge where you would have to let go of a ball to get it to land in a bucket, if you were running past the bucket. They were given three alternatives; before you got to the bucket, as you passed the bucket or just after you had passed the bucket. Although 73 per cent of physics students correctly said that you would have to drop the ball just before you got to the bucket (only 13 per cent of non-physics students got this right), they were no better at actually getting the ball to land in a bucket when they tried it themselves.

Reasoning about scientific phenomena often requires reasoning about non-perceptible aspects of the physical world, for example, forces like gravity and friction. Piaget and Inhelder (1974) looked at children's understanding of the particulate nature of matter (that is, that things are made of atoms, etc.). In their study, children were asked to come up with theories to explain how sugar dissolves. Younger children claimed that the sugar had just disappeared, despite the fact that they could still taste it in the solution; children above 11 years of age acknowledged that the sugar must still be there in some form because it could be tasted. As we have seen, young children have difficulty reasoning about things that have no obvious basis in reality and even when scientific understanding does reflect reality it is often a reality that we cannot directly observe, such as the atomic structure of matter. It is this that makes reasoning about scientific phenomena a late development. When considering scientific knowledge we have to think about things that don't seem worth the cognitive effort. We are confronted with evidence that suggests the existence of things that we cannot see on a daily basis. For example, the force of gravity is working all around us and it affects the behaviour of objects in our environment. Very few of us would claim to care about knowing the precise way in which gravity works. This is because we don't need to, most of us just accept that things fall towards the earth.

For Piaget, the feature that distinguishes scientific reasoning from other types of reasoning is its internal consistency. According to Saxe (1982), when forming scientific concepts we learn general rules and apply these to specific cases, rather than extracting rules from particular cases as we do ordinarily. Although scientific reasoning hinges on *parsimony*, that is, the principle that simpler explanations are the best, we are often not parsimonious in our everyday explanations, often having different explanations for different phenomena, all of which are actually related and could be more economically explained with reference to one coherent theory. This is because we don't always reflect on our knowledge of things that do not interest us.

Hatano (1993) asked children a series of questions about heat. Although they could reason effectively on "real-world" problems, they gave answers to more abstract problems that were not only wrong but also contradicted the answers they had given to those questions that they had got right. For example, children understood that to reduce the temperature of bath water they should add cold water but they thought that adding equal amounts of water at 40 degrees and 20 degrees would result in water of 60 degrees.

Although Piaget argues that the capacity for scientific thinking is precluded until adolescence because of representational constraints that exist at a structural level and don't allow for the development of integrated theories, evidence suggests that background knowledge also affects problem solving in science (e.g. Smith & Good, 1984). Pilburn (1990), however, found a correlation between students' marks in science and their performance on other tests of reasoning. An item analysis revealed that only those items that required formal-operational reasoning were related to success in science. This seems to suggest that being able to reason in a scientific way helps students to learn science, and thus appears to support Piaget's suggestion.

Piaget claimed that when we reach the formal-operational stage of cognitive development we develop the capacity for abstract thought. The ability to reason logically no longer relies on concrete objects and the ability to think in this way generalises across contexts without the child having to learn anything new (specific to the new context). Things do not appear to be this simple, though. Experience and familiarity also have a role to play and, from what we have seen, domain-specific knowledge is more of a constraint on development than domain-general process availability. Domain-specific knowledge also makes it easier for us to solve scientific problems that are similar to those we have solved before (Cheng & Holyoak, 1985; Girotto, Light, & Colbourn, 1988). This is probably because it enables us to recognise that a specific mental process *should* be applied.

Summary and conclusions

In this chapter we have seen how both information-processing constraints and the acquisition of domain-specific knowledge affect the development of problem-solving abilities. The early problem-solving attempts of infants demonstrate some means–end analysis but require no conscious thought. Explicit problem solving develops gradually and its development is constrained by working-memory limitations. Background knowledge and experience are also important factors in determining whether a child will apply the appropriate strategy in a given situation. With development and experience, children become more proficient problem solvers and therefore employ appropriate strategies more frequently.

Both analogical and logical reasoning develop gradually over early and middle childhood, with the basic abilities required for such processes being available from about the age of 4 years. Other factors, such as the ability to overcome a bias to concentrate on individual perceptual characteristics and work with information that appears to contradict reality also affect reasoning abilities. The fact that analogical and logical reasoning appear to develop side by side contradicts Piaget's suggestion that they are characteristics of different stages of development. In fact, development doesn't appear stage like at all. Problem-solving and reasoning abilities do not appear to be constrained by domain-general mechanisms in the way that Piaget suggested. Rather, they appear to be constrained by a lack of knowledge and experience (as well as working-memory limitations). The more problems children have to solve, the more adept they get at applying the appropriate strategy in appropriate situations. Metacognition also has an important role to play. As children develop the ability to reflect on their problem-solving attempts they build up conceptual frameworks that specify when and where particular strategies should be applied.

Piaget was correct to suggest that scientific reasoning is a late development. Even many adults do not spontaneously reason in this way. This is because scientific reasoning is not needed on a day-to-day basis. One of the only areas in which we actually use scientific reasoning is when reasoning about scientific phenomena, and even then we don't always do so. Background knowledge seems especially important in the development of scientific reasoning skills.

Chapter 5

Language development

HUMANS ARE SOCIAL beings and, as such, need to communicate. To do this we have developed language, an infinitely flexible symbolic system whereby words are used to represent objects, actions, feelings, and the like. We don't just use language to communicate information to other people, though; often we use it to communicate with ourselves. We use our "inner voice" to regulate our actions and thought processes, often talking ourselves through situations. Although the specific language spoken by individuals varies from culture to culture, all humans acquire a language of some sort, with some people acquiring more than one.

Until recently, an interest in communicating information that is not directly related to the survival of the species, such as the warning signals used by monkeys to let others know that there is a predator in the vicinity, appeared to be a uniquely human development. New evidence (from the BBC TV programme *The life of mammals*) has, however, suggested that some species of ape chat to each other for no apparent reason. Although this claim is based only on observational data, evidence from studies of various species of primates suggest that the more similar to humans that they are genetically, the more complex the communicative abilities they have. The bonobo chimp, our closest relative from an evolutionary perspective, has demonstrated considerable ability (see Rumbaugh & Savage-Rumbaugh, 1994, for a review). This suggests that the capacity for language is biologically constrained.

Those studying language acquisition ask two basic questions. What do children have to *know* to be able to use language? And *how* do children acquire this knowledge? Given that human language is something that humans have actually invented, we would imagine that we would have made it as easy a thing to learn as possible, and therefore that it is easy for children to pick up. The fact that some of the great apes appear to have some capacity for language similarly suggests that the skills involved are not cognitively complex. But is this the case? Given that language is a symbolic system involving an understanding of relationships between abstract symbols (words) and either other abstract concepts or concrete objects, it is a higher-level cognitive function. The fact that there appears to be a relationship between language and consciousness also testifies to this. Species that show the ability to reflect upon their actions (and thus are consciously aware) seem to have linguistic abilities whereas those that can't reflect don't (Rumbaugh & Savage-Rumbaugh, 1994).

Knowledge

To be able to understand and use language effectively, four kinds of knowledge are essential. *Phonetic* understanding is the recognition of the basic sounds (phonemes) that make up the words of a particular language. Different languages differ in the amount of phonemes that are used. English is made up of 45 different sounds, whereas other languages use up to 60. *Semantic* awareness involves both an understanding of how these phonemes are combined to form words and an understanding of what these words mean. These meaningful units of language, words, are known as *morphemes*. To be able to combine words into sentences, an understanding of *syntax* is necessary. Syntactical knowledge is knowledge about the form and structure of language, e.g. grammatical rules. Finally, an understanding of *pragmatics* is needed. This is an understanding of how language is used in different settings and situations and for different purposes. For example, we talk to children in a different way to how we talk to adults. We also talk to different adults in different ways (I doubt you would talk to your tutor, your parents and your friends using the same sort of language and tone of voice!). We also often use different styles of communication when asking for a favour or admitting that we have done something wrong. All of this involves substantial *pragmatic awareness*; an understanding of what linguistic conventions we should follow in different circumstances.

Problems studying language development

The study of language development is problematic. Most of the research methods employed by psychologists tend to rely on language and we have a tendency to ask questions to try to understand what people are thinking. Such a tendency is not unique to psychologists, though. We all rely on language to communicate our thoughts and access those of other people because we cannot access thoughts directly. Measuring the linguistic competencies of children who cannot talk is therefore difficult. Just because a child cannot speak we cannot assume that he or she has no understanding of language, whether that is an understanding of phonetics, semantics, syntax, or pragmatics. We must always remain aware of the possibility that children might know something but cannot communicate their understanding; there might be difference between comprehension and production.

The technological advances made in recent years have allowed us to develop research procedures that enable us to measure children's *understanding* of language before they are able to use it (see Chapter 1). For example, the habituation techniques outlined in Chapter 1 have been used to investigate whether infants can distinguish between different words. These methods are open to interpretative biases, which can be problematic when interpreting research findings. We have to make assumptions about what infant behaviours tell us about the representations that underlie them. That is, we have to make informed guesses as to what knowledge guides the behaviour of the infants. Because of the limitations of experimental procedures, as well as the fact that experimental studies give us only "snap-shots" of a child's abilities, parents are often asked to keep diaries of their children's abilities. Although these are subject to many biases, the information that they provide does supplement the data obtained from experimental studies and this can't be a bad thing!

Prelinguistic competencies

The prelinguistic period is the time before an infant is able to speak. Cross-culturally, infants usually utter their first word at between the ages of 10 and 12 months. Although this is the age at which infants start to *use* words, even very young infants appear to understand something of the nature of language. Indeed, babies appear to come into the world equipped with several innate tendencies that predispose them to learn language. As we saw in Chapter 2, neonates come into the world ready to learn. They also have a working auditory system and innate guiding principles that enable them to identify individual sounds from a stream of noise. In addition, newborns prefer the sound of language to other sounds; they will suck harder on a dummy to hear spoken language (Butterfield & Siperstein, 1974).

This "preferential sucking technique" has been used to show that an infant's linguistic preferences become finely tuned very quickly. Within the first few days of life, infants develop a preference for their own language over others (Mehler et al., 1986). In Mehler et al.'s study, this preference was not apparent at birth, suggesting that limited exposure to a spoken language results in a preference for it and that the amount of exposure to language experienced in the womb is insufficient for the development of this preference.

The vocalisations that infants make suggest that they do have some language-specific knowledge, and changes in their vocalisations reflect a developing understanding of different aspects of language. Crying is an innate ability that has evolved to enable babies let their carers know they are in need; it is a reflex behaviour. Infants soon seem to realise that crying gets them attention; within the first few weeks of life they demonstrate *fake cries* (Wolf, 1969). In doing this, the infant is demonstrating an understanding of communicative intent. They know that vocalising gets them attention. This pragmatic knowledge is essential for the effective *use* of language.

The vocalisations of infants become progressively more complex with age. From the age of 1 or 2 months of age infants "coo". Cooing involves the repletion of vowel sounds. From the age of about 3 or 4 months, infants begin to add consonant sounds into their vocalisations, e.g. "Lalalalala". When they do this they are said to be babbling rather than cooing (Bates, O'Connell, & Shore, 1987). Interestingly, the babbling of infants contains phonemes not used in the language to which the child has been exposed, actually containing all of the phonemes used by humans. By 9 months of age this no longer occurs and children only produce vocalisations that contain the phonemes that apply to the language they are to speak. This phenomenon is known as *phonemic contraction* and many have argued that its existence suggests innate knowledge of language (Mehler & Dupoux, 1994); we will return to this issue later.

The vocalisations of infants are unlikely to reflect the full extent of their *knowledge* of language. In part this is because there are biological limitations upon the sounds that young infants can produce. During the first 3 months or so of the baby's life the size of the baby's tongue is proportionally large and nearly fills the mouth. Neonates are also fairly limited in their ability to manipulate their tongue. Given that it is the manipulation of our tongue that allow us to produce a wide range of phonemes, the large size and limited dexterity of the newborn baby's tongue limits the amount of sounds he or she can produce. Some sounds are more difficult than others. In many languages this seems to have been taken into account when deciding what word means what. Words for things that babies seem to want to talk about are often relatively easy to pronounce, for example *mama* and *dada*. Dada is easier to pronounce than mama (something that annoys many mothers because dada is usually said by babies before mama), and many different languages have very similar words for mother and father. Again, this suggests that attention has been paid to the abilities and wants of infants when making decisions about word meanings. A proportionally large tongue does have its advantages; it helps feeding and this enables babies to gain weight very quickly. This is obviously adaptive and more necessary than sound production during the early months. From about 3 months of age, the mouth-to-tongue ratio gradually increases and the vocal tract undergoes some structural changes. Together, these allow for the production of a greater range of sounds. Areas of the motor cortex associated with greater control over body parts also develops during this time and contributes to the ability to physically produce a wider range of sounds (Oates & Grayson, 2004).

Prelinguistic infants do appear to understand the meaning of some words and this suggests that they have a basic understanding of semantics, that is, the understanding that different words refer to different things. Harris, Yeels, Chasin, and Oakley (1995) found that infants comprehend their first word at around the age of 7 months and that this is usually their own name or that of another family member. Fenson et al. (1994) investigated the comprehension and production abilities of infants between the ages of 8 and 18 months and found the following: At 8 months of age, infants could comprehend approximately 40 words but produce only 3 or 4. By 18 months of age, the children's vocabulary had expanded to around 60 words and yet 200 were understood. Between the ages of 8 and 18 months a *comprehension spurt* seems to occur. Given that children's ability to understand words consistently exceeded their ability to produce them throughout the period of study, it seems likely that biological constraints on word production exist and prevent children from speaking words that they understand the meaning of.

The number of words both understood and produced by children of different ages described above are averages and, as such, we are not seeing the whole picture. Indeed, when Harris et al. (1995) examined their data they found that there were substantial differences in the ages at which children both produced and comprehended their first word. They also found that differences between production and comprehension varied considerably; some children could produce almost as many words as they could comprehend whereas other children could produce much fewer words than they could comprehend. The reasons for this were not clear. It could be that those children whose comprehension abilities were above average were not able to produce the words that they understood because of physical constraints on word production. Those whose comprehension abilities were below average would be less constrained; by the time they had learned the meaning of words they might well be physically able to pronounce them.

To learn the meanings of words, several abilities are required. The infant must be able to segment the constant stream of speech heard into individual words. Think about it; when you hear someone talk there are usually no apparent breaks between words. We have to determine where words end and begin, based on our knowledge of language and, more importantly, the words that make up language. Given that infants have very little knowledge of word meanings, their task is a difficult one. Johnson and Jusczyk (2001) found that 8-month-old infants were able to identify word boundaries, and that they do so on the basis of *syllable stress* and *transitional probabilities*. Ninety per cent of English words are stressed on the first syllable and this stress enables infants to identify the beginnings of words. Transitional probabilities are rules that specify the likelihood of syllables occurring next to each other in a speech stream. An understanding of transitional probabilities also helps infants to segment speech into words. Given that an understanding of transitional probabilities is dependent on experience and learning, it is not surprising that Johnson and Jusczyk found that, with age, more attention is paid to transitional probabilities and less to syllable stress when identifying individual words, with 8-month-olds relying primarily on syllable stress.

In addition to the ability to identify individual words, the ability to link words with their referents is essential if word meanings are to be learned. Infants from about the age of 9 months appear to understand (at least implicitly) that the object that a person is looking at or directing someone's attention to (by pointing at it, for example) is that to which the speaker is usually referring (Baldwin, 1991).

Hirsch-Pasek et al. (1985, 1987) found evidence to suggest that even prelinguistic infants have some understanding of the grammatical rules of the language that they are yet to actually speak. In one study

(1985) 17-month-olds who were not yet capable of producing more than single-word utterances could discriminate between linguistically relevant and irrelevant word orders, suggesting that they had some knowledge of the way in which sentences *should* be constructed. In a second study (1987) 7- to 10-month-olds reacted to inappropriately placed pauses in speech, suggesting that they had access to representations of linguistic rules that determine pause positions within sentences. Perhaps even more interestingly, Jusczyk et al. (1988) found that English-speaking 4-month-olds could recognise grammatical structures in Polish, but that by 6 months of age they had lost this ability. Taken together, these findings seem to suggest that we are born with some innately specified knowledge of grammar and that with exposure to spoken language we lose the knowledge that does not apply to the languages that we hear around us.

Young infants also appear to possess some understanding of pragmatics. During the early months babies tend to vocalise when another person is speaking. As adults we know that it is not appropriate to talk over other people but babies appear to react to the sound of speech by drowning it out with their own noise. From about 6 months of age they begin vocalising in a turn-taking manner (Bernieri, Reznick & Rosenthal, 1982). They thus seem to have acquired an understanding of the important linguistic rule outlined above. These turn-taking interactions are known as proto-conversations[1] because they have the appearance of a conversation but without the actual use of words on the infant's part. Other researchers and theorists (such as Schaffer, 1984) have suggested that infants are not nearly as competent as Bernieri et al's interpretation of his findings suggests. Instead, it is suggested that adult participants in such exchanges pre-empt the vocalisations of the infant and "frame" them accordingly; that is, the adults fit their vocalisations around those of the infant. This would serve to place the infant's vocalisations into a meaningful context. Whether infants understand the turn-taking nature of communication or not, during the early months it is clear that the social context in which language acquisition takes place is important for development.

When we want to direct people's attention to objects or events

---

[1] This term was coined by Bateson in 1976.

we often use gestures. Although the nature of the gesture used will vary from situation to situation, many of the gestures that we use are types of pointing. In early communications, pointing is often associated with object labelling. Often, adults point at the object that they are labelling and infants appear to pick up on this and use pointing to ask for a label to be applied to an object, usually at around the age of 10 months (Baldwin, 1993). The development of pointing and language appear to be related. Harris, Barlow-Brown, and Chasin (1995) found that infants who demonstrate pointing at an early age also demonstrate an understanding of object words. Norgate (1997) found that blind infants use fewer object words than sighted infants, suggesting that pointing contributes to an understanding of object names. Autistic infants often fail to understand that pointing is used to direct someone's attention to an object and their language abilities are also often impaired. This further confirms the suggestion of a relationship between the two. It could be that the same areas of the brain that is responsible for joint attention and language development is selectively impaired in those with autism, or it could be that autistic children's lack of understanding of joint attention prevents them from mastering language (we will return to the issue of the biological basis to autism in Chapter 7).

The development of language abilities

The way in which language develops appears to be consistent cross-culturally. Although children develop language at different rates, the ages at which developmental milestones are reached, as well as the order in which they are achieved, are remarkably consistent across individuals. This observation has led some theorists to suggest that language development is innately specified at birth and that only exposure to a language is necessary for its development (e.g. Chomsky, 1965, 1981).

As mentioned earlier, the first words tend to be spoken towards the end of the first year of a child's life. These tend to be nouns (e.g. teddy) with a few social words thrown in (e.g. bye-bye). Single words are uttered in isolation and are used to convey a whole sentence's worth of meaning; hence this period of language development is known as the "holophrastic"; holophrastic meaning "whole phrase". Often, gestures are combined with single-word utterances during this stage, presumably to clarify intended meaning. For example, a child might point and say "biscuit" meaning "give me that biscuit" (children of this age have no manners!).[2]

The fact that only the bare essentials are included in children's utterances suggests that their aim is to communicate meaning, and testifies to the social function of language. However, children often talk to themselves (Vygotsky, 1962). Sometimes it seems that children do this just for the fun of it. At other times, children use language to structure their own thoughts and direct their own behaviour. This suggests that whereas other people can encourage children's language learning and provide them with the information that they need (such as object labels), much of children's motivation to learn language is internal. Further evidence for this comes from Braine's (1971) finding that infants often repeat their utterances and improve on them, suggesting that they are trying to get their utterances correct. Again, these findings suggest that there might well be an innate predisposition for children to acquire language.

During this period, children often shorten difficult to pronounce words or add pauses between syllables; something that is known as *phonetic simplification*.

For example, my little brother used to call trumpets "bum-prints". This tendency to simplify words could suggest that the amount of cognitive effort required to produce even a single word is considerable and places huge demands on the infant's still-developing information-processing system. More probably, the physical constraints on word production, described earlier, preclude the production of some phonemes and therefore children work around these limitations and produce utterances that, although not completely accurate, are recognisable to those with whom they are trying to communicate. It is not until about the age of five or six that children can accurately produce

---

[2] Indeed, the mastery of politeness conventions is a late linguistic development and appears to take considerable parental effort. This is probably because young children can't see the point of words such as "please" and "thank you".

all of the sounds used in any particular language and this seems to be attributable to physical limitations in sound production (Oates & Grayson, 2004). The fact that children do simplify sounds that they have problems producing accurately, and that they do so in a way that allows for effective communication, testifies to the adaptive and reflective nature of human cognition.

At first, infants' vocabulary develops slowly, taking 3 to 4 months for them to learn their first 10 words. Things soon pick up though and infants add new words to their vocabulary at a much faster pace. By 18 months children have a vocabulary of about 60 words (Fenson et al., 1994). As with language comprehension, there are individual differences in language production, with girls consistently outperforming boys. During this stage, children go through a vocabulary spurt similar to the comprehension spurt described earlier. A word of caution is required here, however, Fenson's study was based on parental reports. Given that parents often want to give the impression that their child is rather special, they could overestimate their competencies. Indeed, my grandmother still insists that my father's first word was "stethoscope".

Young children often misuse words. Their errors are of two types. First, children often *underextend* words, applying them too specifically, for example they might use the word dog to refer only to the family pet. They also often *overextend* word meanings, that is they apply words too generally for example using "daddy" to apply to all men. Clark and Clark (1977) propose that children go through a series of stages in learning the meaning of a new word. Having just learned a new word, children underextend its meaning. Then they go through a stage of appropriate usage (albeit without awareness of the word's true meaning). A period of overextension follows until finally the child works out the true meaning of a word and applies it correctly.

The tendency of young children to make mistakes and either over- or underextend the meaning of words suggests that they are forming hypotheses about what words mean and then gradually modifying these early guesses until their understanding matches that of an adult. But how do children do this? What information do they attend to when forming their initial hypotheses about a word's meaning?

Both Markman (1992) and Pinker (1994) suggest that innate

tendencies help children to work out what words mean. Markman suggests that children work on the implicit assumption that words refer to objects rather than properties of objects or categories of objects. This would be a fairly successful strategy as the labels that adults apply to objects do appear to be object names; it is very rare for adults to point, for example, at a yellow car and say either yellow or vehicle. Perhaps adults do this because they are aware of young children's tendency to assume that labels refer to object names. More probably it is because we *all* have a tendency to describe objects at their intermediate level. Markman's suggestions are supported by research findings that suggest a relationship between the language abilities and the ability to categorise. The vocabulary spurt discussed earlier seems to coincide with an increase in infants' ability to categorise objects (Gopnik & Meltzoff, 1987).

Perhaps *overextension* occurs because children know very few words and are sort of asking to be corrected. For example, the word "dog" is often used as a label for all four-legged animals. However, many children that do this can pick out a picture of a dog from a selection of four-legged animals shown to them. Such a strategy would enable children to develop clearer conceptual categories for objects. In addition to the internal motivation to learn that young children seem to be born with, other people also contribute to the development of language and an understanding of word meanings by providing feedback, correcting children's attempts and encouraging language development. As we have seen, other people also label objects for children so that they learn word meanings more quickly.

Gleitman (1990) suggests that children use a process of *syntactic bootstrapping* to work out word meanings. This process involves making use of an implicit understanding of the grammatical structure of language. By making assumptions about the way in which sentences map onto events or objects that are being described, children are said to be able to learn word meanings. If this is the case then children have to understand the meaning of their experiences before they can identify word meanings. As we have seen (in Chapter 1), this ability does appear to be in place very early on in infancy.

During the holophrastic period, the child's priority appears to be to build up a substantial vocabulary. Having done this they can then begin combining words. Children at the end of the holophrastic period start to tie individual words together in a string, but each word still suggests more meaning than is actually included, e.g. "daddy . . . gone". Such two-word sentences are structurally correct in terms of the order in which verbs and nouns are positioned in relation to one another, thus suggesting substantial syntactic knowledge; that they understand the basic rules of grammar. Indeed, Hirsch-Pasek, Gleitman, Gleitman, Golinkoff and Naigles (1988) found that by around 27 months of age, children can make fine discriminations between similar sentences. Children were presented with either the sentence "Big bird is turning cookie monster" or "Big bird is turning with cookie monster". When presented with simultaneous video clips of both Big Bird turning Cookie Monster and Big Bird turning with Cookie Monster, the infants preferentially attended to the video that matched the sentence that was read to them.

Pinker (1984) suggests that the implicit awareness of the grammatical conventions of language teamed with a limited comprehension vocabulary enables children to learn the meanings of abstract words such as verbs. While acknowledging that syntactic bootstrapping enables children to work out the meanings of words that have an obvious referent, such as object names, he calls on the existence of another process to explain how children learn words for things that have no obvious basis in reality, such as abstract words like "think", "to", and "going". Children's innate grammatical knowledge is said to include an implicit understanding that different *types* of word are used in sentences, e.g. verbs, nouns, and that these tend to be organised consistently. Through a process that Pinker calls *semantic bootstrapping*, children apply their understanding of words to sentences. If children can work out the subject of the sentence using their understanding of a single word that appears in the sentence, then the relative position of the other words in the sentence can be used to work out the meanings of these words. This is dependent on their innate understanding of syntax. Through this process, children can also extend their understanding of grammar beyond that which is innately specified. Mapping an understanding of words onto grammatical knowledge allows for the identification of grammatical rules, such as the adding of an "s" at the end of a word to indicate that more than one object is being referred to or the "ed" rule that is applied to verbs to indicate that things have occurred in the past.

By the age of two the misuse of words (both under- and over-generalisations) is rare and children appear capable of matching words to the things that they refer to (even when these words refer to abstract, non-concrete things such as "gone"). Given little direct instruction children acquire language, they seem to have the ability to focus on the appropriate semantic and syntactic information at any given time with very little effort. Semantic and syntactic bootstrapping processes seem to allow for the development of syntactic and semantic knowledge, with developments in each area contributing to development in the other. This suggests that innate abilities and predispositions facilitate language development; the extent to which they do is much more controversial, however.

The telegraphic period

The combination of words into primitive sentences signals the transition of the child from the holophrastic to the telegraphic stage of language acquisition, usually at between 16 and 20 months of age (Brown, 1973). The name given to this stage highlights the fact that children tend to omit words that are not essential for the conveyance of the necessary information (such as in a telegraph); they use a sort of shorthand. Function words and verb endings are often omitted, whereas verbs are usually retained. Often quite creative, novel combinations are produced, e.g. "*all-gone . . . juice*". It was once thought that children speak like this because their memories are inadequate. Although evidence does suggest that the length of utterance that a child can string together does appear to be somewhat constrained by working-memory limitations, it is now thought that the bits of sentences that children omit are omitted because children don't yet understand their relevance.

Often, the same two-word utterance can convey different meanings. For example, the phrase "mummy sock" could mean either "mummy's sock" or "mummy I want the sock". To work out exactly what is meant by such a telegraphic sentence you therefore need to

135

look not only at the content of the utterance but also the context in which it occurs and any gestures that accompany it.

While continuing to expand their vocabulary, children at this stage appear to be concentrating on the acquisition of syntactic (grammatical) knowledge. Systematic regularities in word order and word use become apparent in their speech. The child's next accomplishment is to add extra words into these phrases so that they become more similar to the utterances of adults. This usually occurs at around the age of 2 years. This seems to indicate an increased reliance on the use of semantic bootstrapping. Once children start doing this they are said to have left the telegraphic period.

As children leave the telegraphic period they also begin to demonstrate the use of verb endings and plurals, thus demonstrating that their understanding of syntax is developing beyond an understanding of word order. The way in which children use verb endings progresses through the same stages as children's learning of words.

During this stage, children also learns how to tailor their language to a listener's level of understanding. By about 4 years of age children seem to have some understanding of pragmatics. For example, it is at this age that they begin to tailor their speech to their listener's needs, even mimicking the baby talk used by their parents when speaking to younger siblings.

Refinement of language skills

By about the age of 5 years children are pretty efficient users of language. Important strides in linguistic competence are, however, made during middle and late childhood. Children use progressively bigger words, form longer and more complex utterances and they also begin to think about and manipulate language in ways that were previously impossible.

During middle childhood children refine their *use* of language. They also begin to reflect on the nature of language and develop *metalinguistic awareness*, that is they come to consider the *nature* of language (Karmiloff-Smith, 1992) Although young children can use language in a way that suggests that they have an implicit understanding of words, sentences, grammar, pragmatics and the like, children do not have conscious access to this knowledge. Karmiloff-Smith suggests that the ability to reflect on language use develops at around age six and continues into adulthood. Children start to reformulate their utterances so as to make them more understandable at around the age of six and this coincides with an increase in their ability to explain why they have used certain words and even what a word actually *is*.

The development of metalinguistic awareness allows children to appreciate double-meanings, jokes, riddles and puns that are funny because of their play on sounds or words. Young children's understanding of jokes is very limited. They can recognise a joke as a joke but will laugh at a joke simply because they have recognised it as one; they don't seem to have cottoned on to the fact that you laugh at jokes because they are funny. A lovely example of this was shown in a BBC2 Open University programme. Here a young boy was told a classic "knock knock" joke. He then devised his own version which went as follows: "Knock knock", "Who's there?", "James", "James who?", "James Bond". Despite the fact that this isn't really funny because there is no play on words, which is the whole point of "knock knock" jokes, his friends all fell about laughing, presumably because they didn't understand that the content of a joke should be funny.[3] Language also becomes non-literal in middle and late childhood and statements such as "people in glass houses shouldn't throw stones" start to be used. Prior to the development of metalinguistic awareness, children cannot understand that statements like this are not just haphazard statements that people make.

Is language development predetermined?

The universality of language, common characteristics of spoken languages, and intertranslatability, as well as the consistency with which milestones are reached, all suggest that language acquisition is to some

---

[3] We should acknowledge here this joke *could* actually be funny to children and that we adults are missing something!

extent predetermined. All of the above evidence supports the idea of a biological preparedness to learn language as well as domain-specific biases in attention. However, it could be that language development is so uniform because it is learned in a logical way (and is therefore dependent more on nurture). Maybe, it is the *way* in which others teach children language that is the same across cultures. Alternatively, it could be that children have been genetically programmed to learn in a specific manner, and therefore that domain-general ability, rather than domain-specific ability, is responsible for the observed consistencies in language acquisition. If this were the case then substantial environmental input would be required. As we have seen, children do develop language at different rates and this suggests that experience has a role to play in language acquisition.

Many linguistic competencies are not present at birth and develop over the first few years of life. This seems to suggest that environmental input is necessary, but it could be that what we are observing is simply a result of the unfolding of a predetermined maturational pattern. This is unlikely, though, given that we have seen substantial evidence for differences in language development between individuals.

In sum, the evidence so-far discussed suggests that the environment does provide feedback to developing (biologically based) systems and that therefore both nature and nurture have a part to play in language acquisition. What we need to look at now is how much environmental input is required; we need to untangle the effects of environment and biology. To do this we have to look at how variations in environment affect language development.

Talking to babies

When talking to babies we often talk in a particular manner. We speak in a relatively high-pitched voice, exaggerate intonation patterns, repeat ourselves a lot and pose questions that we then answer on behalf of the child (Jacobsen, Boersma, Fields, & Olson, 1983). Such speech was originally referred to as *motherese*. However, mothers are by no means the only people to adopt this peculiar style when faced with an infant. This resulted in the terms *parentese* and *baby talk* being used to describe the same phenomenon in more recent years.

Newport, Gleitman, and Gleitman (1997) argue that the purpose of such speech is to simplify language so as to enable the baby to learn its basic structures and individual words. However, most mothers speak in *whole* sentences to their babies and tend to include a lot of questions and commands (25 per cent). The first utterances of infants, on the other hand, tend to be individual words and are declarative in nature. This suggests that babies do not imitate the "baby talk" they often hear. In addition, many studies looking into the relationship between the use of baby talk and the child's language development have failed to find a relationship between the two (e.g. Newport et al., 1997). Studies of this sort are hard to conduct and most are based upon observations of mother–child interactions. It is highly likely that interactions between mother and child vary considerably and that those actually studied are not representative of the interactions that occur between mother and child. Being observed or video-recorded is also likely to affect the nature of the interactions.

The use of baby talk is not universal. Many cultures and many individuals within cultures see the use of baby talk as ridiculous and argue that, if anything, the use of a style of language that does not reflect how language is usually used within a particular culture is going to be detrimental to a child's development. In England and America recently there has been a lot of media discussion about whether children's television programmes, such as "Teletubbies", where characters adopt an exaggerated form of "baby-talk", are harming children's language development.

Radical changes to the learning environment

There are ethical limits to what we can do to a child's learning environment. As a result, we often have to rely on case studies of children who have been deprived of environmental input for some reason, e.g. blind and deaf children.

Language development in deaf children

Sign languages have the same grammatical structure and same constituent parts as spoken languages (e.g. Klima & Bellugi, 1979). Deaf children who learn sign language from deaf parents follow the same developmental pattern and go through the same stages as hearing children (e.g. Newport & Meier, 1985).

A majority of deaf children are born to hearing parents, however, and this means that they are not exposed to sign language from an early age. Despite this, they tend to produce one-word gestures at around the age of 1 year and then go on to combine these gestures into sequences at around the age of 2 years (Goldin-Meadow & Mylander, 1984). Such sequencing of gestures is grammatically correct. The fact that deaf children appear to be internally motivated to use language and that they have some grammatical awareness without ever having been exposed to language suggests that there is a strong maturational component to language and that this develops in the absence of environmental input. However, it could be argued that the invention of a language is not the same as learning a specific language (such as English) and so such conclusions must be treated cautiously.

Language development in blind children

Learning a specific language depends on the understanding that specific words relate to specific objects and actions. Sighted children rely on visual cues to make associations between words and their referents (what the words refer to). From an early age, infants "tune in" to the fact that words tend to refer to things to which their attention is directed (by pointing or looking at it, for example). If this were true, then we would expect blind children to be substantially impaired in their language acquisition. However, blind children seem to reach developmental milestones at the same age as sighted children (Landau & Gleitman, 1985). Again, this seems to support the idea that there is a predetermined pattern to language acquisition and that only minimal environmental input is required.

Language development: the effects of environmental deprivation

Although deaf and blind children are denied access to environmental input associated with specific senses, it could be argued that other senses compensate and thus that they are not significantly impaired when it comes to the absorption of environmental input. But what about those children who are denied any exposure to language?

We cannot ethically impose environmental deprivation on young children for experimental purposes, so we have to look to case studies detailing the experiences of children who have suffered such deprivation. Such data suggest that the extent to which language acquisition is compromised depends on both the amount of time without stimulation and the age of the child when deprived. Davis (1947) describes the case of "Isabelle", who was found confined in a dark attic room, aged six but with a mental age of two. She showed no signs of being able to either produce or comprehend language. Despite the fact that she had been denied exposure to spoken language (apart from the occasional harsh word from her "carer") by the time she reached 7 years of age her linguistic and cognitive abilities were comparable to those of a child raised in normal social circumstances.

By contrast, "Genie" (described by Fromkin, Krashen, Curtiss, Rigler, & Rigler, 1974) was found at 13 years of age and her language development never approached normality. Although her language learning followed the same path as that of non-deprived children, her abilities never progressed beyond those of a "normal" 2-year-old.

Perhaps, a more depressing case is that of "Chelsea" (Curtiss, 1979). Chelsea was born deaf but was mistakenly diagnosed as "retarded" (something that is no longer a clinical diagnosis!). As a result, the people in her immediate social environment never attempted to communicate with her. At 31 years of age she was referred to a neurologist who identified her as "only deaf". Her language acquisition did not progress beyond that of a 2-year-old in terms of vocabulary and her speech lacked the basic grammatical structure apparent in the telegraphic speech of 2-year-olds.

It seems, then, that there is a sensitive period for language development. If exposure to language does not occur during the early years then the ability to acquire language is limited. Neurological evidence suggests that during the early years the brain seems to be especially receptive to linguistic input and preferentially processes information in the left temporal lobe (Bates, 1994). However, if no linguistic input is received, non-linguistic representations are formed in those areas of the brain that are more structurally equipped to deal with language processing. Although this means that language acquisition at an older age is a more arduous task, it does not mean that it is an impossible one. Evidence from studies looking at the learning of a second language further supports this suggestion.

Learning a second language

Many of us have attempted to learn a second language later in life (whether as a matter of choice or something we were subjected to while at school). Initially this seems fairly easy. Individual words are relatively simple to learn and in a short time we are often adept at producing primitive sentences (Snow & Hoefnagel-Hohle, 1978). Indeed, we speed through the early stages of language acquisition. But then something happens; we are faced with grammar. To be able to deal with learning the grammatical structure of a new language, it seems we have to work much harder than a child who, during early childhood, seems able to do this without any explicit awareness. This seems strange: Given that adults have had a lot of experience with language and young children haven't, we would expect that adults would find this an easier task, unless, of course, innately specified mechanisms are more important than experience.

Johnson and Newport (1989) studied native Chinese and Korean speakers who had moved to the USA 5 years previously. To test their understanding of the American language, participants were asked to distinguish between grammatically correct and incorrect sentences. Those who had moved to the USA before they were 7 years old performed as well as a native American control group. However, a negative correlation between performance and age at which the person arrived in the USA after age seven, was found. So, the older you are when you attempt to learn a second language, the harder it is to pick up. It seems that the age of about seven is again of critical importance here. When we were considering the case studies of severe deprivation, we came to the conclusion that if language wasn't acquired before the age of seven, it becomes progressively more difficult for children to acquire it after that age. The age of seven was also pinpointed in Johnson and Newport's study (just described). Together, these findings suggest that there may be innate constraints on language development that makes the brain less supportive of new linguistic representations after around the age of seven. However, learning a second language might be more difficult just because it *is* a second language. Our knowledge of the meaning of words and grammatical structure of our native language might interfere with incoming information. Anyone who has tried to learn two languages at the same time would testify to this.

Further evidence relating to the late acquisition of a first language comes from studies of deaf children. For example, Newport (1990) found that the ease with which deaf children picked up ASL (American Sign Language) varied in accordance with the age at which they were first exposed to it. Only those exposed before age six attained native-level proficiency. Again, this suggests innate constraints on the formation of linguistic representations.

Conclusions so far

So far, we have seen that the pattern of language development is remarkably consistent, both within and between cultures, despite the fact that children often have very different experiences. It could be argued that such findings are an artefact of the type of investigations that psychologists conduct. Often, studies take extensive samples of children and then calculate mean ages for specific development, such as the age at which the first word is produced. This could give a misleading impression of development and cloud individual differences and, in turn, environmental contributions to language development. However, the fact that there seems to be a sensitive period for language development, and that this appears to be constrained at a biological level, suggests that a domain-specific bias to learn language exists. Theories of language acquisition differ in terms of the importance they attach to innate predispositions to learn language and the extent to which our environmental experiences assist our language development.

Nativist theories

Nativist theories propose that the human capacity for language is innate. Proponents of this approach argue that language skills are incredibly complex and therefore could not be learned purely through observation and imitation, at least not as quickly as they are. They also point to the consistency with which language is acquired across cultures and populations. Given that the amount of and type of exposure to language differs from child to child, they claim that some domain-specific predispositions to language must be present. Nativist theorists also draw on evolutionary theory and argue that the social nature of our society has resulted from and given rise to advances in language skills. Given that language is so vital in today's society, they suggest that evolution is likely to have equipped neonates with the basic skills and abilities necessary for language to be acquired quickly.

Chomsky's theory

Chomsky (1965) was the first to suggest that humans (and only humans) are born equipped with an innate brain structure, the *language acquisition device (LAD)* that predetermines the development of language. The LAD consists of some innate knowledge about the structure of language, as well as a set of cognitive and perceptual abilities specialised for language learning. According to nativist theories such as this, these enable the child to *instinctively* work out the phonological patterns, word meanings and rules of syntax of the speech that they are exposed to. Given that such abilities are present purely to aid language acquisition, Chomsky's theory proposes that development is domain-specific.

Chomsky (1981) argued that the LAD contains information about the grammatical rules of all languages. He claimed that whereas some grammatical rules are common to all spoken languages, others differ between them. Those that are common to all languages, he called, *universal principles*.

Other grammatical features of language are not universal. These Chomsky called *parameters*. The child's task is to identify which of these principles are present in their native language. So, children don't have to learn grammatical rules from scratch, they match the rules present in the language they are to speak with the relevant ones specified by the LAD. Once a match has been detected, children can apply the rule: This process is known as *parameter setting*. Universal principles not relevant to the language being spoken in the child's cultural setting are lost. This suggestion seems to be supported by the findings that infants progressively lose the ability to be able to identify grammatical structures in languages that are not spoken around them. Given that such abilities are said to be based on innately specified knowledge, it is not suggested that children are aware of these processes; they are implicit.

According to Chomsky, then, the child's biology is in charge of language acquisition. The LAD equips the child with some basic knowledge of linguistic rules and a tendency to attend to language over and above other things (as well as to attend to specific features of language). As the brain matures, more cognitive resources (information-processing abilities) are available to the child and, as such, have the ability to process more and more linguistic input.

Although innate tendencies and biological maturation are thought to underlie language development, it is obvious that children actually need to be exposed to a specific language to learn it. However, unlike many other theories of language acquisition, nativist theories such as that of Chomsky, suggest that children are passive participants in the learning process and that they do not actively try and learn language. Likewise, it is thought that the role of other people in a child's language development is minimal and that other people must simply speak to the child or speak to someone else while the child is listening for the child to acquire language; no formal teaching or learning is required. Nativist theories such as Chomsky's stand in contrast to the next type of theory to be discussed.

Behaviourist theory

Behaviourist theories suggest that, rather than being born with any innate linguistic abilities or tendencies, children acquire language gradually as a result of learning. Other people are said to be the main contributors to this process. It is proposed that imitation and behaviour shaping are the main mechanisms underlying language acquisition. So the process is a two-way one; infants imitate others and other people shape the infant's attempts at language. Infants learn about the nature and function of language within the context of their early relationships. Their babblings become more "word-like" as a result of the selective reinforcement given by those with whom the infant interacts. For example, "dadadada" might be reinforced initially by the "other" but then reinforcement would be withheld until the child uttered something more "word-like", e.g. dada. Similarly, utterances that are not word-like would not be reinforced.

Behaviourist theory proposes that knowledge of language (words, grammar, pragmatics, and the like) is learned in much the same way as other things. No domain-specific processes or innate predispositions are said to be involved in language learning. All that is said to be necessary are domain-general learning mechanisms. In support of their argument, behaviourists point to the fact that adults do appear to talk in a manner that accentuates the rules of grammar (already discussed) and they do actively teach infants the meaning of words.

Syntax: the role of teaching and learning

Imitation and the selective reinforcement of utterances cannot be wholly responsible for language learning though, because children often produce grammatically incorrect phrases and sentences during the early stages of language development. Most adults talk in a grammatically correct way and so this means that infants aren't simply imitating the language of their older companions. Despite the fact that the utterances of young children are often grammatically incorrect, some understanding of the rules of grammar is apparent (for example, in the word ordering of holophrastic utterances). Overt corrections of children's grammatical errors are rare (Brown & Hanlon, 1970) and so it would be fairly difficult for children to learn grammatical rules in the rather simplistic manner proposed by behaviourist theories. However, adults do provide some feedback as to the grammatical appropriateness of the utterances of infants and young children (such feedback would not be necessary according to nativist theories). The way that adults respond to grammatically correct and incorrect grammar is different. When a child produces a grammatically incorrect utterance adults often expand on the utterance. This expansion includes a grammatically correct version (e.g. Bohannon, MacWhinney, & Snow, 1990).

This seems a rather uneconomical way of doing things, though, and evolution does not generally favour the development of complicated processes. Children would have to be able to instinctively work out (by listening to the expansion) which bits of their own utterance were correct and which were not. This is rather complicated and some people (e.g. Pinker, 1989) have claimed that it is *too* complicated for an infant mind.

It has been found that infants are more likely to repeat an adult expansion than any other type of utterance (Farrar, 1992) and that they are more likely to learn from expansions than example utterances (Saxton, 1997). So it seems that whereas children need to be exposed to language to learn it, they do not need to be actively taught grammatical rules. As no active teaching or learning is involved, it is likely that the children are oblivious to the fact that they are, in fact, learning grammar; it is implicit. Even in adulthood we cannot necessarily verbalise grammatical rules. Think about this one. You might well speak in a grammatically correct manner but could you explain the rules of grammar to somebody else?

It seems that "hypothesis testing" of some description is involved, and thus that the process of learning grammar is more active than the nativist account would have us suppose. Children do have to make informed guesses about the way in which words are strung together to form sentences. This is based on the feedback they receive.

Connectionism

Like traditional behaviourist theories, connectionist theories propose that language is something that is *learned* as a result of interaction with the social environment. Proponents of this approach claim that no innate knowledge is necessary for language acquisition and that no domain-specific learning processes are required. In fact, connectionist theories are best seen as a modern take on behaviourism, with a bit of biology thrown in. It is claimed that feedback, in the form of reinforcement, strengthens neuronal connections between words and their referents and allows for the learning of grammatical rules.

Evidence to support this approach comes from the computer modelling of neural networks. Computers are provided with examples of speech that contain a specific grammatical rule. The computer then generates sentences and is given feedback as to their grammatical correctness. The aim is to see whether, by giving such feedback, the computer can learn to apply grammatical rules. Rumelhart and McClelland (1986) equipped a computer with a basic learning network. The computer was then presented with a list of present-tense verbs (the input). The computer then had to work out the past-tense version of these verbs. Initially, the computer's outputs were random in nature. Feedback as to whether the computer had got the past-tense version right or wrong was given. Although direct associations between past and present tenses were not formed, a network of parallel associations was modified as a result of feedback. The researchers claimed that the learning demonstrated by the computer mimicked that of children. All that was needed for the computer to work out grammatical rules was simple feedback as to whether its "guess" was right or wrong, and it did not have to be corrected at all. The fact that no prespecified rules were needed for appropriate outputs to be generated, they claimed, severely undermines the claim that domain-specific, innate knowledge forms the basis of language acquisition.

More recent models (e.g. Elman, 1992; Plunkett & Marchman, 1993) have revealed that computer models, like children, go through several stages when learning about the past and present tenses of verbs. Initially, there is an error-free period. Here it is proposed that children and their computer counterparts connect past- and present-tense versions of verbs in a direct way (e.g. they learn that although they might be *going* swimming tomorrow, they *went* swimming yesterday). When several such relationships have been learned, the child or computer looks for similarities in the relationships between past- and present-tense versions of a verb. This results in the formation of a general rule, linking the two. Here, that would be that "–ed" is generally added to a verb to form the past tense. Although this is economical, in that individual connections between past and present forms of every verb in the child's/computer's vocabulary need not be stored individually, it also results in errors (in the example given above, the application of such a rule would result in the child/computer claiming that he "goed" swimming yesterday). The next stage, then, is for the exceptions to the rule to be learned and mentally represented (unfortunately these *do* have to be stored separately). When these are learned, speech will be again be error free.

Whereas evidence from computer modelling is helpful in that it shows that innate knowledge is not necessary for language learning, there are several reasons why we should be sceptical about such studies. First, the whole approach rests on the assumption that the human brain operates in much the same way as a computer. This is not so. Computer models are given very limited input to deal with. Human children do not deal with linguistic input in such a way. They are constantly being bombarded with sensory input of many different sorts. So, this begs the question, would a computer be able to work out the rules of language (or even *a* rule of language) if they had other information to process at the same time? In addition, the feedback given to the computers is much more consistent than that received by children. In studies such as that of Rumelhart and McClelland (1986), the computers were given feedback after every response they made. This doesn't happen with children.

Neurological evidence

Chomsky suggested that part of the brain is specifically wired-up for language acquisition: that there is a *separate module*. If there were, we would expect to be able to identify this area by monitoring brain activity when linguistic information is processed. Studies of brain activity suggest that the left hemisphere is more active in the processing of linguistic input than the right and that specific regions are more active than others (Neville et al., 1998). If it were the case that the left hemisphere is home to a specialised language module, we would expect that people who suffer brain damage to this area as a result of an accident or stroke would have specific problems with language. This does seem to be the case if damage occurs in adulthood, but studies of children who experience left-hemisphere damage paint a very different picture. Reilly, Bates, and Marchman (1998) studied a sample of children who had left-hemisphere damage that had occurred either before or during birth. Although these children showed significant delays in language acquisition at various points in their development, they soon caught up with children who had no such brain damage. Maratsos and Matheny (1994) suggest that these findings point to a genetic preference for language processing and representations to be located in the left hemisphere, but that other cortical areas can take over these roles if damage to the left hemisphere occurs during the course of development. The earlier-on in development that brain damage occurs, the more likely it is that language development will proceed normally because the plasticity of the brain allows for the localisation of language in areas of the brain not normally associated with language processing. Contrary to Chomsky's suggestion of an innate language module, it seems that a language module comes about as a result of development and experience. Although the left hemisphere seems better suited to the processing of linguistic data, which results in linguistic representations generally taking up residence here, other cortical areas can support language if necessary.

Conclusions so far

None of the theories that we have discussed so far offers a complete explanation for language acquisition. The evidence seems to support the behaviourist position with regards to the way in which children learn the meaning of words but it cannot account for the relative ease with which children work out the rules of syntax and pragmatics, given that children are not explicitly taught such things. If we were to assume that no such teaching is necessary, then we would have to acknowledge a role for innate predispositions and knowledge. If we did not, then how could we explain the speed with which young children work these things out?

Given that the meanings of words appear to be learned in the same way as many other things, that is, through the reinforcement of associations between words and referents, domain-general learning mechanisms seem to play an important role in language acquisition. However, the innate tendencies that predispose a child to concentrate on language over and above other auditory inputs, teamed with the apparent ability of infants to attend selectively to the most relevant features of language (syntactic and pragmatic rules), suggest that domain-specific mechanisms also have a part to play. Such conclusions undermine theories that propose that language development is attributable to *either* nature or nurture. They also challenge more general theories of development, such as that of Piaget, which present language development as a byproduct of more general cognitive developments. Piaget claimed that language development is restricted by, and so reflects, a child's cognitive abilities. This is evidently not the case; children with language problems are not necessary cognitively impaired (or vice versa). This suggests that development is to some extent domain-specific. Just because cognitive development does not *determine* language development, it does not necessarily follow that cognitive and language development occur independently. As both cognition and language involve the formation of mental representations, it is likely that a relationship between the two exists.

A compromise: representational redescription

Karmiloff-Smith's (1996) representational redescription model proposes that although the development of language is domain-specific, domain-general learning mechanisms contribute to it. Innate predispositions towards language acquisition provide the starting point. These determine what information is attended to and how it is computed.

Karmiloff-Smith proposes that within each domain (language being one), learning goes through three distinct phases. In each of these phases information is represented in a different format. Development comprises the reformatting of information (representations); that is, *representational redescription*.

During the first phase, learning is *data driven*; that is, it results from interaction with the external environment. Representations during this phase are stored separately. At this stage, environmental input triggers specific behaviours. This stage culminates in *behavioural mastery*; that is, children appear to react appropriately in response to specific stimuli. At this stage, though, information is implicit and unavailable to consciousness.

In the second phase, connections between representations are formed, giving rise to the generation of rules and principles. Internal representations over-rule information obtained from the environment. This can lead to behavioural errors because environmental information is ignored.

In phase three, equilibrium is reached between external and internal inputs. Children pay attention to both knowledge that they have acquired (internal) and environmental feedback.

In terms of language acquisition, Karmiloff-Smith proposes that syntactic and semantic information are processed separately and that these constitute different domains. Furthermore, she claims that each aspect of syntactic and semantic understanding is processed separately (in different *microdomains*). It is suggested that innate biases within each domain allow the child to process input. Domain-specific knowledge enables the child to make sense of grammar in the syntactic domain and the ability to identify word boundaries and associate words with the things that they refer to, in the semantic domain. We have already seen that infants can do these things at a very young age, which suggests that such biases exist. Children also seem to pass through a stage of apparent competence, followed by a phase of apparent regression, when learning both word meanings and grammatical rules. In terms of Karmiloff-Smith's theory this would be a result of children developing a rule and then overapplying it because of their reliance on internal information (knowledge) at the expense of environmental feedback, because their representations are stored in a phase two format. In phase three, children pay attention to both external information and internal knowledge allowing them to generate conceptual frameworks that specify the rules of language and also exceptions to those rules.

Summary and conclusions

Children acquire language at a rapid rate. Neurological evidence suggests that the left hemisphere is particularly receptive to the processing of linguistic input during the early months and to a lesser extent, years. Indeed, much of the evidence that we have considered seems to suggest that infants are predisposed to attend to language and that they are equipped with domain-specific abilities that enable them to make sense of language. While connectionist models of language learning suggest that language learning *could* occur without calling on any domain-specific knowledge or abilities, these models need a lot more input than children before they can learn rules and apply them appropriately. This suggests that whereas learning language does depend on domain-general processes to some extent, the speed with which children learn language is a reflection of the fact that it is preferentially and/or more effectively processed. This suggests that some domain-specific constraints on development exist.

Reading, writing and dyslexia

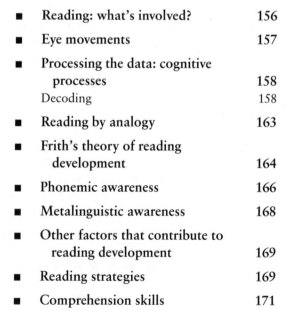

BEING ABLE TO read is a valued skill in most technologically advanced societies. The recent efforts by the UK government to increase levels of reading proficiency in school-leavers testify to the importance accorded to this particular ability. Decisions like this being made at such a high level suggest that reading is a skill that needs to be taught within a formal environment (unless the government has been misinformed!). This seems to be the case; whereas nearly all children develop the ability to speak a language, not all learn to read, and this seems to be attributable to a lack of experience and teaching. However, before you can learn to read, you do need to have a substantial understanding of language.

Reading: what's involved?

Reading involves the extraction of *meaning* from text and so substantial information processing is involved. When reading we do not aim to read and remember every word, rather we extract the gist and concentrate on content and meaning. To do this we not only have to process the visual data, we also have to understand it. While it is likely that the processing of visual data relies on domain-general processing mechanisms, comprehension relies on substantial background knowledge. Again, both structures and processes are important in the development of this ability.

When reading, we first have to input the data. We visually analyse the text, holding it in our working memory. We then need to recognise the words in front of us. Recognition involves matching the visual patterns apparent in what we have read with prototypical representations stored in our long-term semantic memory. As a result, the ability to form prototypes is a necessary precursor to reading development. We have already seen that this skill develops in infancy (see Chapter 2).

Having identified the words, we then can access information as to how to pronounce them and what they mean, providing that we have previously stored this information. If we have no information stored then we tend to make an informed guess.

We use information that we have acquired during the development of our reading abilities to make judgements as to pronunciation and, perhaps, meaning. Similarly, we often make informed guesses as to the meaning of a word based on the text that surrounds it (when we can't be bothered to go and look it up in a dictionary!).

Eye movements

When we read, our eyes jump from one point of fixation to the next, we don't focus on each individual letter. Usually, we fixate on points in the middle of words. Because our peripheral vision is quite good, fixating on points in the centre of words allows us to process letters either side of that which is focused on. Each jump is known as a *saccade*. Skilled readers do this automatically. This supports information-processing accounts of development that suggest that processes become automatic with experience (see Chapter 1). The number of saccades that we make when reading varies with both the complexity of the text and with practice. When reading complex text we often regress, that is, we go back to a previous point of fixation to double-check what we have read.

So how does this aspect of reading develop as we get more skilled at reading? There are several possibilities. First, it could be that as we get older we are able to take in more information per saccade. Rayner and Pollatsek (1989) suggest that this is not the case and that the amount of information that we take in per saccade is preprogrammed. Alternatively, we could develop the ability to make either bigger saccades or shorter fixations. McConkie and Rayner (1976) used a computer programme rigged up to an eye-movement monitor. By manipulating the amount of information available to the reader (on either side of the point of fixation) they found that the average reader processes fourteen characters to the right of fixation but only four to the left. The size of the font did not alter this and so they concluded that it is not just the amount of information that we can fit into our retinal image that determines saccade size. These results were consistent across both individuals and texts, suggesting that there must be an information-processing limitation. It is not the case that some individuals take-in more information with each saccadic jump they make, or that a case of saccade size is influenced by the complexity of the text, rather, saccade size seems to be innately specified. If this is the case then it must be that we become better readers because we spend less time on each fixation. If less time needs to be spent on each fixation then that would imply that our ability to process the information that we take in with each saccade increases. A limitation on the amount of information that we can read seems to be cognitive rather than perceptual. Given that we have seen that the perceptual skills of neonates are very sophisticated, this is not surprising.

Processing the data: cognitive processes

Two processes are involved in the processing of written information. *Decoding* a word involves matching the word to its underlying mental representation. We need to do this to identify it (and thus be able to read it). Having identified the word, we then have to put it into context to *comprehend* it. Decoding *must* therefore occur before comprehension.

Decoding

There are two ways in which we can decode text and identify the words that we are reading. Familiar words are stored in the reader's *lexicon* (word store). This lexicon is part of our semantic memory (see Chapter 4) and contains mental representations of words, which include information about their visual features, how they are pronounced and also their meanings. Given that we accumulate a lot of information about word meanings and pronunciation before we start to read, it is the matching of written words to their spoken form that is of paramount importance when learning to read.

When matching a word with its lexical representation, based on the visual features of the word, we can automatically access information relating both to how the word is spoken and to what it means (if this information is available). Such a route to decoding is known as *visually based retrieval*. The system that underlies this process is multidirectional and this allows us to use meaning to prevent or correct errors in reading. If we misread a word, often the fact that it doesn't make sense (given the context in which it appears) alerts us to this fact. However, words that are unfamiliar to us will not be stored in our lexicon. So how do we read words that we have never read before?

The second type of decoding is dependent on an understanding of what is known as the *alphabetic principle*. That means that the reader needs to understand that different words consist of different combinations of a limited number of basic units, i.e. the letters of the alphabet. The alphabetic principle is economical in that it allows us to construct a multitude of different words using only 26 letters (in English). To read words that we haven't come across before we have to translate the basic structural units that comprise a word into their phonetic equivalent; we convert letters into letter-sounds.[1]

Some languages are more transparent than others in terms of how letters map onto sounds. English is *partially* transparent. Some words are pronounced phonetically, others are not. Sometimes the context in which letters are presented affects the way in which individual letters sound in English. For example, the letter "a" is pronounced differently in "wag" and "late".

The process of breaking down language into individual letters and translating these into the sounds that match them is known as *grapheme–phoneme conversion* (or *phonological recoding*). To match

---

[1] We also use analogy and compare words with other words that we know, but we will return to this issue later because, for now, we need to concentrate on how we read words that *aren't* stored in our lexicon. As we shall see later, the use of analogy is dependent on making comparisons with lexical representations of words that we *do* know.

graphemes with phonemes, an understanding of the alphabetic principle is necessary; a child would need to understand that each letter represents a different sound. Such a skill requires the capacity for dual representation and an explicit awareness of the nature of symbols. Given that these abilities develop early on, that they are needed for the acquisition of language, and that the development of language necessarily precedes the development of the ability to read, the development of these abilities is unlikely to constrain reading development in any way. Children who are impaired in their understanding of symbolism and dual representation (such as those with autism) can and do learn to read eventually and, although they have problems with comprehension, their ability to map phonemes onto graphemes is unimpaired (Snowling & Frith, 1986).[2]

Several other skills are also required for grapheme–phoneme conversion. If you have an understanding of the alphabetic principle and an understanding of the way that particular sounds are associated with particular letters, you then have to identify the different letters that make up the word that you are reading. This is known as segmentation; you break the word down into its constituent parts. These are then held in working memory. Substantial information processing then has to occur so as to preserve the ordering of these units while converting the graphemes into phonemes. Having done this, the word then needs to be reconstructed, an ability known as *blending*. Given that substantial working memory ability is required to process text, we might imagine that the development of working memory could constrain reading development. We have seen that children's working memory abilities develop fairly quickly during the early years so it is not likely to have too great an impact on reading development because this tends to be a skill that children are taught *after* they have developed considerable language skills. If children have sufficient working memory abilities to process language, it is likely that they will also be able to process visually presented language.

There appear to be at least two possible ways in which we can read text. We can either use the lexical route, which we can only do if

---

[2] People with autism have been shown to have problems of this nature. We will discuss these later in Chapter 7.

we are familiar with the word, or we can use the sublexical route and use grapheme–phoneme conversion (e.g. Coltheart, Davelaar, Jonasson, & Besner, 1977). Faster word recognition (decoding) is obviously going to be the preferred option and, so where possible, the lexical route is used. If a word is not recognised on sight, the sublexical route is taken (Siegler, 1996).

Jorm and Share (1983) and Share and Stanovich (1995) suggest that children need to master the sublexical route first because it is this that enables them to *acquire* mental representations of individual words. Through the accurate sounding out of words using grapheme–phoneme conversion, associations between the printed and spoken form of the word are strengthened. Once associations between the printed and spoken word are formed, visual recognition of the spoken word results in the automatic retrieval of the spoken form using the lexical route.

The dual-route model, described above, is appealing because it is relatively simple and, as scientists, we adhere to the principle of parsimony (the idea that the simplest explanations are the best). However, it seems that it is too simple. Autistic individuals, for example, can read without understanding (Snowling & Frith, 1986). They must therefore be able to bypass the semantic part of the system. Funnell (1983) similarly found that some dyslexics[3] appear to be able to use the lexical route but not the sublexical but also fail to extract meaning from text, something that should be accessed automatically when using the lexical route according to the dual-route model. These findings led Ellis and Young (1988) to propose a third route to reading (Figure 6.1).

Hypothetical models like the dual- and triple-route models are very difficult to test in a direct way. There is very little neurological evidence to suggest that distinct areas of the brain are specialised for performing specific functions associated with reading. Given that the left hemisphere appears to be best suited for the processing of linguistic information, we might expect mental representations of visual forms of words to be located here as well. After all, they need to be connected to mental representations of semantic and spoken characteristics of

---

[3] Dyslexic individuals have specific problems with reading, writing and spelling. We will discuss dyslexia in more depth later in this chapter.

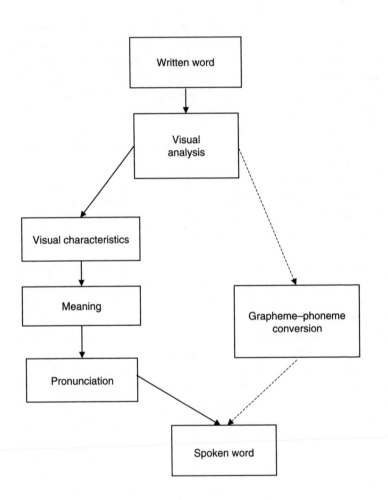

Figure 6.1 **Lexical and sublexical routes to reading**

words and these are typically located in the left hemisphere. Evidence does support this and much of the processing of text is concentrated in the left hemisphere (e.g. Galaburda, Sherman, Rosen, Aboitiz, & Geschwind, 1985; Flowers et al., 1991).[4]

Further evidence to suggest that the lexical and sublexical routes are not independent comes from studies that show that the way that we pronounce a non-word word depends on those that we have previously seen presented, (Kaye & Marcus, 1981). For example, whether we have been primed with the word *brown* or *known* before being presented with the non-word "*plown*", affects our pronunciation. This *priming effect* suggests that the sublexical route is affected by information stored in our lexicon and thus suggests that the two are far more integrated than is suggested by the aforementioned models. Furthermore, it seems uneconomical to build up a system for grapheme–phoneme conversion when all the information we need to pronounce new words is stored in our lexicon. Young children have no lexical store of words to draw on, however, and so grapheme–phoneme might prove invaluable to young children when starting to learn to read.

Reading by analogy

The priming effect described in the previous section suggests that we use analogy when reading. We compare the visual characteristics of new words that we see with those in our lexicon and transfer our knowledge of how words are pronounced. Such a strategy appears to be more economical than letter-by-letter reading but it is dependent on the ability to segment words into syllables or units. The use of such a strategy is therefore going to depend on substantial knowledge and therefore experience.

Both the use of analogy and the lexical route when reading require a well-stocked lexicon containing visual representations of many words. These methods are not available to children that are just

---

[4] Evidence of the neurological basis to reading will be discussed in more detail later in this chapter when we consider reading disorders.

starting to read. Perhaps the use of the alphabetic principle to convert graphemes into phonemes is the only option they have.

Frith's theory of reading development

Frith (1985) proposed that children pass through distinct stages when learning to read. In the first stage, which Frith called the *logographic* stage, children learn to read a few words as single units. A visual code is used to access the lexicon and words are stored separately (mental representations of the visual pattern). At this stage, children rely on the identification of one or two distinctive features that characterise a word. When beginning to read, then, children recognise a number of words because they focus on individual features such as the first or end letter, or on word length. Often, things like brand names appear to be being read but the child is only really recognising the distinctive font or pattern in which the word is presented. Sadly (in my opinion), an American survey recently reported that the most common word first "read" by American children was "Mcdonald's". This must be rather frustrating for parents! It might also be one factor that has contributed to both the recent rise in obesity in children and the constraints that have been imposed on child-directed advertising. The upshot of this is that children often get visually similar words confused. Obviously, such confusions are not particularly helpful and so a more effective and accurate way of reading is required. Furthermore, the creation of a separate mental representation for every word that we read is uneconomical in terms of memory. Having said that, the fact that children can begin to read at all before they have developed an understanding of the alphabetic principle has important implications for educators because it means that it is worthwhile teaching children individual words before they have acquired an understanding of sound–letter relationships. However, Connelly, Johnston, and Thompson (2001) found that if children are taught to sound out letters as soon as they begin to learn to read, they do not rely on a logographic strategy. Perhaps the key is making children aware of the relationship between graphemes and phonemes. This is something that we appear to do. At school, one of the first things that we are exposed to is the written alphabet and I'm sure we can all remember reciting it (or even singing it!).

There is plenty of evidence to support Frith's theory. Anyone who has spent time with young children will tell you that they often confuse similar words and that they don't appear to need phonemic or metalinguistic knowledge to be able to start reading. Yussen, Matthews, and Hiebert (1982) found that children can learn both the alphabet (sounds and symbols) and to read a few words logographically at the same time. The fact that children can read a few words logographically prior to developing an understanding of letter–sound relationships suggests that they are forming relationships between individual visual representations of words and their spoken equivalent.

Given that children are able to perceive similarities and differences (and therefore make analogies) between visual objects from a very young age (see Chapters 2 and 3) they eventually start to form concepts of what letters, sounds and words *are*. Karmiloff-Smith (1992) found that this ability tends to develop at around the age of 6 years. These concepts are then organised into a conceptual framework that specifies the way that the three are related. This allows for the development of an understanding of the alphabetic principle and progression into what Frith calls the *alphabetic* stage. That is of course assuming that children are exposed to written words. In many cultures they are not.

Earlier we discussed how an understanding of the alphabetic principle is essential for grapheme–phoneme conversion. Children come to realise that individual letters are associated with different sounds and that to read an unfamiliar word, the word must be segmented into a series of individual letters. These are then converted into sounds using grapheme–phoneme rules.

Using the grapheme–phoneme route when reading can be effective, but only when the word being read has a regular spelling. As we have already seen, English is only a partially transparent language and therefore it contains many words that are not pronounced phonetically (phonetic being one of them!). Often, the sounds of letters are affected by the context in which the letter appears, as we saw earlier. Relying on this route when reading is bound to lead to numerous pronunciation errors.

In the third and final stage of Frith's theory, children are said to break down words into orthographically standard "chunks" which are spoken via *letter-sequence* to *syllable-sound* rules. Such a strategy enables the use of analogy in reading, according to Frith. Children not only perceive relations between the word currently being read and those that they have previously encountered (and mentally represented in the lexicon), but they also transfer this knowledge. By about 7 or 8 years of age, children are capable of using grapheme–phoneme conversion rules and they do this consistently. This is demonstrated by the fact that they read typical words more easily than atypical ones, which tend to be misread in a typical way (Marsh et al., 1978). By 9 or 10 however, children can read regular and irregular words with equal efficiency, suggesting that they have progressed from the alphabetic to the orthographic stage at this age.

According to Frith's formulation, children's reading becomes more efficient with practice and repeated exposure to written and spoken language. Research evidence does support this claim and the general description of development that Frith described, although it seems that development is not as stage like as she suggests. We will return to this issue later.

Phonemic awareness

Children need to have an understanding of sound before they can develop an understanding of the alphabetic principle. Given that infants appear to be able to segment sounds (see Chapter 1) and that this is necessary for language development, it is highly likely that children will have substantial *phonemic awareness*, that is, they will have developed concepts of individual sounds and how these relate to spoken language *before* they begin to read.

Bradley and Bryant (1983) found that children who were insensitive to rhyme and other phonological characteristics of words had more difficulty learning to read. Phonological awareness training helped these children and, as a result, they concluded that phonological skills are important in the development of reading skills. Further support for this suggestion comes from Frith and Snowling (1983), who found that children of below-average reading ability tend to per-form poorly on other tasks that require the use of grapheme–phoneme rules. Maclean, Bryant, and Bradley (1987) also found that a child's knowledge of nursery rhymes at age three is a good predictor of later reading abilities, even when the IQ of both parents (who were the ones responsible for teaching their children the nursery rhymes) and the children were taken into consideration.

Although such findings seem to support the model proposed by Frith, we cannot necessarily claim that the relationship between phonological skills and reading ability is one way. It could be that learning to read increases sensitivity to sound. Indeed, Ellis and Large (1988) found evidence for this. It seems that there might be a reciprocal relationship between the two: Whereas phonemic awareness increases reading ability, reading development also contributes to phonemic awareness.

The phonics approach to teaching children to read is perhaps the one that has been the most successful (e.g. Chall, 1979; Johnson & Baumann, 1984). This method is based on the idea that children need phonemic awareness before they can read beyond the logographic level. When teaching children, the relationships between graphemes and phonemes are emphasised. Goldstein (1976) compared the reading abilities of 4-year-olds who were taught about letter sounds with those that were taught about letter names and letter orders (there was a 13-week training period). Those taught about letter sounds learned to read faster. Similarly, Lundberg, Frost, and Peterson (1988) found that children who were given training in breaking words into phonemes learned to read faster than those who were not.

Goswami and Bryant (1990) argue that there is no reason why phonological codes should operate at only the phoneme (single letter-sound) level. They suggest that we could capitalise on children's understanding of rhyme and relate sounds to spelling patterns (word segments) rather than individual phonemes when teaching children to read. This would enable children to understand similarities in spelling patterns. Once the children understand the relationship, they can use their knowledge to make inferences, providing, that is, their inference-making abilities are intact. Goswami and East (2000) used a teaching technique that involved emphasising rhymes and found that by the end of the training programme children had an average reading age that exceeded their chronological age by two months. However, although they claimed that this shows that such a technique has benefits, they did not report reading and chronological ages prior to the training period. This calls into question the conclusions they reached.

Metalinguistic awareness

In Chapter 3 we considered how both the knowledge that we acquire and the strategies that we employ often go through a stage during which they are applied implicitly, prior to us becoming explicitly aware that we are using them. Once explicit, we can reflect upon our knowledge and our strategy usage. This allows us to identify gaps in our knowledge and make judgements as to the appropriateness of different strategies.

The developments described above appear to apply to the development of reading. Oakhill (1995), for example, found that young readers are not "word conscious". Although they can read words they cannot tell you what a word *is*, or even point identify a word in a sentence. Bruce (1964) similarly found that neither 5- nor 6-year-olds could say what would remain if a phoneme is dropped from a word (e.g. s from spill), but that they could segment words into syllables.

It seems that whereas young readers might have substantial implicit knowledge about phonemes and how these relate to specific graphemes (enabling them to read phonetically), they are not explicitly aware of what phonemes *are*. Given that we have seen that there is often a substantial delay between implicit awareness and explicit awareness of a concept or strategy, this is not surprising. Phonemes are also rather abstract, they don't have obvious acoustic boundaries and often they are dependent on context. This makes the child's job of forming a clearly defined concept of what phonemes *are* all the more difficult.

Other factors that contribute to reading development

Although most children don't begin to learn to read or write until they go to school, they learn *about* these things beforehand. Whitehurst and Lonigan (1998) call this *emergent literacy* and they describe several things that children can learn, all of which facilitate reading development. First, a good command of spoken language is essential. Second, children must acknowledge the conventions of print. For example, English is written from left to right and from the top to the bottom of the page. Knowledge of individual letter names and sounds also helps, although Adams (1990) found that it is not an *essential* prerequisite for the alphabetic principle.

Children who show an interest in reading and writing, often demonstrated by them pretending to read or write, seem to develop their reading skills at a faster rate than children who show no real interest in reading. Bialystok (1996) found that parents have a large and very influential role in motivating children to learn to read and write. Those who take the time to teach their children the basics, and make this experience a fun one, give their children a head start when they start school. This suggests that being motivated to learn is a key factor in reading development. Educators should take note of this and make learning to read and write as fun as possible.

Reading strategies

Frith's theory seems to describe development to some extent. However, as Goswami and Bryant (1990) point out, it does little more than this. There is very little explanation of *how* development occurs and the processes and mechanisms that contribute to it. Goswami and Bryant also contest Frith's suggestion that reading development is stage like. Like Siegler's (1996) overlapping waves approach (see Chapter 1), Goswami and Bryant's account proposes that a number of different strategies are available to the child at any one time and that it is the frequency with which strategies are used, rather than their availability, that changes with age and experience. They propose that whereas children use logographic, alphabetic and orthographic strategies to different extents at different ages, they are not wholly dependent on any one strategy at any point in time.

Goswami and Bryant agree with Frith that phonological skills are important for reading development. However, unlike Frith (who suggests that these are essential for the development of the *alphabetic* strategy), Goswami and Bryant (1990) argue that phonological awareness allows for the categorisation of words by *orthographic* features (word segments). They also argue that the alphabetic strategy does not necessarily follow on from logographic reading. Instead, they suggest that children develop a strategy based on analogies. Initially, this relies on an understanding of rhyme and onset; rhyme being the part of a word that rhymes with another word and onset being the part of a word that distinguishes it from the word that it rhymes with. For example, magic rhymes with tragic; "qagic" is the rhyme and the onsets, "m" and "tr" are different. This strategy, they claim, enables children to overcome many of the problems associated with learning to read an irregular language, that is, one in which grapheme–phoneme conversion leads to pronunciation errors (like English). Goswami and East's (2000) study of the effectiveness of training children to recognise rhymes and onsets (discussed earlier) seems to support Goswami and Bryant's argument. Given the flaws in reporting that we also described, we cannot be sure that this is the case.

Like Frith, Goswami and Bryant identified learning the alphabet, alphabetic understanding and the use of an alphabetic strategy as essential for reading development. The important difference between theirs and Frith's theory is that Goswami and Bryant claim that the use of an alphabetic strategy does not initially confine children to the use of grapheme–phoneme conversion just because they have developed alphabetic awareness, as Frith does. They suggest that children could use this strategy only in situations where logographic and orthographic strategies aren't available, that is, in situations where the word isn't recognised immediately and where no orthographically similar words are stored in the lexicon. Such an account was supported by Goswami's (1986) finding that children as young as five are capable of reading by analogy. However, this doesn't necessarily mean that this strategy *is* employed spontaneously. As we saw in the previous chapter, children often have strategies available to them but don't use them.

Marsh et al., (1978) asked children to read nonsense words, e.g. "ephid". If they were using grapheme–phoneme conversion it was reasoned that they would pronounce the "p" and the "h" separately. However, if they were using analogy as a strategy they should pronounce p and h as f. Whereas 10-year-olds tended to use grapheme–phoneme conversion, adults were more likely to use analogy. So it seems that the availability of a strategy is not directly related to its use, in the way that Frith suggested.

Comprehension skills

As mentioned at the beginning of this chapter, the main aim of reading is to extract the meaning from what is being read. We do not remember text word for word, rather, we remember what it was about and the main points made. Indeed, Sachs (1967) found that adults cannot distinguish between sentences that had just been read and another with the same meaning 25 seconds after reading the original one.

This tendency to extract meaning from input is not restricted to reading, as we have already seen. It is an economical way of dealing with a lot of information. Children's episodic memory, for example, is based on the perception of and selection of central or key events. Likewise, semantic memory is based on the perception of similarities and differences between currently experienced and previously encountered stimuli (see Chapter 3).

Given that children have usually been using language for several years before they learn to read, it is usually the case that once children can decode written words enabling them to pronounce them, they recognise the word and understand what it means. However, some children have a specific problem with comprehension.

There are several possible explanations as to why comprehension might be particularly difficult. First, reading abilities are dependent on many more basic cognitive processes, such as working memory capacity. If this is limited then the task of decoding a word could use all of the available cognitive resources and therefore leave no mental effort available with which to put the word into context. As a result, as decoding becomes automatic comprehension would no longer be such a problem (Daneman & Blenerhassett, 1984; Daneman & Green, 1986). Second, it could be that information is rapidly lost from working memory, thus preventing children from keeping all the words in a sentence in there at once so that the gist (or meaning) can be extracted. Indeed, working-memory limitations have been associated with poor reading (Siegel & Ryan, 1989).

The fuzzy trace theory, put forward by Brainerd and Reyner (1993), proposes that young children have a tendency to try and remember things verbatim and that with development they begin to adhere to the *reduction to essence rule*, which specifies that the extraction of fuzzy traces (fuzzy traces being mental representations that are not clearly defined) is more efficient in terms of memory capacity. Working with fuzzy traces takes less cognitive effort and therefore leaves more working memory space free for the manipulation of information. This would explain why young children have a problem with comprehension; they expend far too much cognitive effort trying to retain photographic mental representations in their working memory, which takes up all their cognitive resources, leaving none left for them to use to put these representations in context.

To fully comprehend a piece of written text we need to be able to recognise which points are important and which aren't. As we have already seen, good comprehension depends on the extraction of gist rather than the ability to remember text word for word. Brown and Smiley (1977) asked 8- to 12-year-olds to classify ideas in text in order of importance (there were four levels). The 8-year-olds found this impossible whereas the 12-year-olds could only identify main point and irrelevant details but they could not distinguish between the intermediate levels. Despite this, recall was affected by importance, suggesting that although these children could not make explicit judgements as to importance, they had some implicit awareness. Overall, this seems to support theories, such as those of Karmiloff-Smith (1996), which suggest that the formats in which representations within domains are stored progress from being implicit to explicit.

Another factor that affects comprehension is the ability to monitor your own understanding and to adjust your reading strategy in response to this. As a result, metacognitive awareness is required (see Chapter 3). This is a late-developing ability and very few master it until adolescence, if at all. Evidence suggests that this skill is a learned one that improves with age, practice, and explicit instruction (e.g. Baker, 1994; Garner, 1990).

The ability to adapt our reading speed and the amount of care that we take when reading in response to the difficulty of the text is a late development. Although we can sometimes get away with skim reading, pulp fiction or magazines for example, there are times when such a strategy would not be advised, such as when reading legal documents with small print. Kobasigawa, Ransom, and Holland (1980) found that children are about 14 years of age before they begin to skim-read when only superficial information is required to answer a specific question.

Like other cognitive abilities, the accumulation of knowledge within a particular domain allows for the more efficient processing of information. Reading is a constructive process in which information previously represented at a mental level is used to interpret new input. As a result, *content knowledge* is related to comprehension. The more content knowledge we already have on the subject we are reading about, the more we can check the plausibility of what is being read. Such an ability also requires inference making and, as such, is pre-cluded prior to the development of these abilities. Given that these develop relatively early, as we have already seen, it is unlikely that inference-making abilities will constrain reading development.

Educators need to make use of the findings reported above when attempting to increase or maximise the comprehension skills of their students. For good comprehension, adequate background knowledge is necessary, as is metacognitive awareness. To improve metacognitive awareness it would be helpful for teachers to explicitly point out areas of possible difficulty and draw children's attention to the different strategies used when reading. This would not only serve to make students explicitly aware of the strategies they are using but also would encourage evaluation of strategy usage. Indeed, Rosenshine and Meister (1994) found that a technique based on these ideas and that they called "reciprocal instruction" results in an improvement in comprehension skills.

Overall conclusions: reading development

Reading involves the extraction of meaning from text and therefore it involves a lot of information processing. The information processing of text comprises of two abilities: decoding and comprehension. Given that we need to be able to decode words before we can comprehend them, teamed with the fact that working memory capacities are limited, children's early attempts at reading often focus on decoding at the expense of comprehension.

A child's ability to decode words seems to involve an understanding of the relationship between sounds and letters and/or orthographic units. These enable the child to break down written words and convert them into sounds (grapheme–phoneme conversion). This allows for the formation of mental representations of whole words and their storage in the lexicon. Decoding abilities increase as the lexicon comes to contain more representations, allowing for less reliance on grapheme–phoneme conversions (the use of an alphabetic or orthographic strategy) and more use of the lexical route. The use of the lexical route is the most efficient strategy and, with development, this becomes the preferred strategy.

As the process of decoding becomes less effortful and eventually automatic, more information-processing capacity is available for comprehension. Comprehension abilities increase as the child accumulates knowledge of: (i) language structure and written conventions; (ii) the subject matter; and (iii) the skills required for good comprehension.

Writing

The mechanical demands of physically writing something down are just a small part of the process of writing. We often have to bear in mind several things, such as what we are writing about, the specific points we wish to make, and who the likely reader of the composition is (so that we present the information in a clear and appropriate way). We have to call on information stored in our long-term memory and then organise this information (something that requires considerable working memory). The fact that long-term memory is implicated in writing means that knowledge and experience are important.

The actual act of writing demands considerable attention during the early years and takes up a good proportion of available cognitive resources. This often means that other aspects of writing suffer; young children often forget what they wanted to say before they have had time to write it down, or they forget the end of the sentence by the time they get to it. As the mechanical demands of writing become automatic, the cognitive resources needed to co-ordinate the physical act of writing decrease.

Given that writing makes considerable cognitive demands, it might well be that attempting to master this skill at the same time as learning how to compose a coherent piece of writing is not ideal. Bangert-Downs (1993) found that teaching children to use a word processor, which is physically an easier skill to master than writing, resulted in higher-quality pieces of writing. Furthermore, these abilities were generalised to written work. Obviously, teaching techniques like that suggested by Bangert-Downs concentrate on the development of one ability at the expense of another. In this case, children concentrate on the ability to compose a piece of writing at the expense of developing the physical skill of writing. As a result, some people don't think that such techniques should be used when teaching children. However, if children's ability to communicate their ideas is being constrained by the problems that they have writing, freeing children from these constraints can't be a bad thing as long as children also get the opportunity to develop their writing skills.

Scardamalia and Bereiter (1987) found that young children tend to use what they called a *knowledge-telling* strategy when composing a piece of writing. Instead of trying to achieve many goals simultaneously, children consider only one at a time. In response to a question they often answer the question first and then write down anything relevant that they can retrieve from memory (something that many university students also seem to do in examinations, presumably because the stress induced by the context interferes with the processing of task demands).

According to Bereiter and Scardamalia (1987), better quality writing (which comes about as a result of age and experience) is generally the result of the application of a *knowledge-transforming* strategy. Here the writer considers more than one aim simultaneously. The amount of time spent preparing before actually beginning writing is a reflection of the use of this strategy. Again, the lack of planning in university examinations suggests that many regress to a knowledge-telling strategy when under stress.

Dyslexia

Problems associated with reading, writing, and spelling are known as the dyslexias. Whereas acquired dyslexia is often the result of an accident or stroke that causes damage to the specific areas of the brain implicated in the reading process, developmental dyslexia becomes apparent as the child is learning to read. Miles and Miles (1999) estimate that between two and four per cent of the population is dyslexic (although they suggest that this would be higher if milder forms of the disorder are also included). Females appear to be less susceptible to dyslexia (about one female for every four males), possibly suggesting that this disorder has a genetic basis.

The World Federation of Neurology (1968) has defined developmental dyslexia as:

> A disorder in children who, despite conventional classroom experience, fail to attain the language skills of reading, writing and spelling commensurate with their intellectual ability

The important point to note here is that dyslexia is a disorder that affects only reading, writing, and spelling abilities and their development. The child is not generally cognitively impaired. It is therefore assumed that the problems experienced by dyslexics derive from impairment to a skill or cognitive component *specific* to the reading process. Given that it is assumed that to be dyslexic there must be a mismatch between general IQ and reading abilities, those children who have problems with reading but also have a relatively low IQ will not be given any specific help with their reading.

At this point in the discussion we need to distinguish between poor readers and developmental dyslexics. We have already seen that reading is a skill and, as such, it requires formal teaching and learning. A poor reader might just have not acquired adequate reading skills because of poor teaching. A dyslexic, on the other hand, fails to develop reading skills despite what is deemed to be appropriate teaching. It is therefore generally assumed that if a child fails to develop in the same way as his or her peers, despite having had the same experiences, then that child might well have dyslexia. One of the standard criteria for diagnosis in England is that a child is at least 18 months behind "normal" in their reading. This means that diagnosis often occurs late in childhood; something that could have negative implications for the child during the early school years because it would not be until late childhood that children *this* far behind would be identified.

To complicate things further, there doesn't appear to be only one form of developmental dyslexia. The most common distinction is drawn between those that are said to have *phonological* dyslexia and those that have *surface* dyslexia. Phonological dyslexics appear to have specific problems with grapheme–phoneme conversion, as is evidenced by the fact that they find non-words more difficult to read than real words (e.g. Grigorenko, 2001). Surface dyslexics, on the other hand, have problems with visual-based retrieval of word meanings and thus it appears to be the lexical route that is impaired. This finding seems to support the suggestion that the two routes are distinct (as was suggested by the dual-route model).

Dyslexics who have problems using one route to reading tend to have problems in using the other route. Thus any distinction drawn between the two types of dyslexia are more to do with the degree of impairment shown in each area. So, a surface dyslexic would be said to have more problems with the lexical than the sublexical route, whereas a phonological dyslexic would find the use of the sublexical route more problematic. Given that we have seen that the two routes are not as independent as is suggested by the dual-route model, it is not surprising that an impairment to one route will have a negative effect on the use of the other.

Given that the distinctions between a dyslexic and a poor reader, and between a surface and a phonological dyslexic are not clear-cut, checklists are often used for diagnosis. These list common errors made by dyslexics and, to be labelled a dyslexic, you have to demonstrate a certain number (but not all) of the specific impairments listed. Many dyslexics demonstrate a tendency to reverse and rotate letters, for example reading a "b" as a "d". This skill appears to be specific to the reading process, as we usually do not have to pay attention to the orientation of objects when identifying them. A spade is a spade whatever angle you look at it from. Other so-called symptoms include the omission of syllables and problems keeping place when reading. The use of checklists enables us to build profiles of the specific impairments of each individual dyslexic and thus enables us to develop intervention programmes that are specific to an individual's needs. They also demonstrate just how little is known about this particular disorder, if indeed it is just one disorder, which doesn't appear to be the case.

Theories of developmental dyslexia

Given that there appears to be more than one type of dyslexia, it is highly likely that there is more than one cause. Any theories of dyslexia should take this into account. It is very difficult to do this, though, because the distinctions between different types of dyslexia aren't clear and so many theories do not *attempt* to account for different forms of the disorder. This means that is highly likely that different theories are accurate explanations for different types of dyslexia.

The phonological deficit hypothesis (e.g. Bradley & Bryant, 1985; Snowling, 1996) proposes that dyslexics have a specific problem with phonology, the ability to represent or recall sounds. This would preclude grapheme–phoneme conversion and the use of an alphabetic of orthographic strategy when reading. Such a theory accounts for the fact that dyslexics often confuse perceptually similar units and have problems reading non-words, an ability that we have seen depends upon the use of this strategy (Grigorenko, 2001; Snowling, 2000).

Stanovich (1988) claims that phonological recoding is a relatively modular function and that it is this that is responsible for reading development and impaired in those with dyslexia. He points to the fact that few dyslexics have any other cognitive impairment to support his position. But is there any neurological evidence to support this suggestion?

Flowers et al. (1991) found that dyslexic individuals demonstrate abnormal patterns of blood flow around the left temporal lobe when asked to perform tasks that required phonological processing. The left temporal lobes, as we have seen, are the best suited to the processing of rapidly presented auditory information and therefore problems associated with the functioning in these areas would have an effect upon the processing of phonological information. Livingstone, Rosen, Drislane, & Galaburda (1991) also found evidence of abnormalities in the left hemisphere in an autopsy study in which the brains of dyslexic and non-dyslexic individuals were compared. Although such evidence does suggest that the left hemisphere has a role to play in phonological processing, we have already seen that the brain is developmentally plastic and, if there are problems with one area, representations usually associated with that area take up residence in different parts of the brain. In dyslexics it could therefore be that the processing of auditory information necessarily occurs in areas that are not ideally suited to such computations. This would result in poorer quality representations of individual sounds and therefore affected phonological processing; something that we have already seen is important for reading development. However, the phonological deficit hypothesis cannot account for the fact that many dyslexics also have auditory and visual problems. This has given rise to the magnocellular theory of dyslexia (e.g. Stein, 2001).

The magnocellular theory and the phonological deficit theory are not necessarily inconsistent with one another. Phonological problems could be caused by auditory problems and a visual deficit might independently contribute to reading difficulties further complicating the process of grapheme–phoneme conversion. However, not all dyslexics have auditory problems or visual deficits (e.g. Heath, Hogben, & Clark, 1999). In fact, the research seems to indicate that only about a third of dyslexics do.

Auditory deficits are likely to impact on phonological processing because they are part of the same system. The question is whether these are sufficient to cause a phonological impairment large enough to impact upon reading abilities. According to Ramus (2001), the evidence suggests that they are not, but he goes on to discuss a possible mediating factor. He suggests that auditory problems might be sufficient to cause reading problems if the child also has ADHD (attention deficit hyperactivity disorder), as many dyslexics do. However, many don't so it is not a complete explanation.

To sum up, there is a long-standing debate as to whether sub-types of the dyslexic disorder exist, or indeed whether dyslexia is just one disorder. We have very few clear answers as yet. Work looking at the causes of dyslexia is complicated by the fact that it exists in many different forms. The categorisation of reading errors is in itself problematic. Generally, phonological training has been the most successful intervention and there is some convincing neurological evidence to support the phonological deficit hypothesis. However, this does not necessarily mean that grapheme–phoneme conversion problems underlie all of the dyslexias.

Dyslexia is a very complex disorder and the fact that it exists in many different forms complicates things somewhat. As a result, it is going to be very difficult to reach firm conclusions as to its causes. However, as Snowling (2000) observes, dyslexia is characterised by significant levels of compensation. If certain strategies for reading are precluded by the dyslexic condition then alternative strategies can always be found. It seems, then, that we should focus on devising intervention programmes that can help dyslexics to overcome the specific problems that they are experiencing rather than looking for a single underlying cause for what appears to be more than one disorder.

Summary and conclusions

In this chapter we have seen how reading is a complex skill that involves several different processes. At different ages, children use different strategies to both decode and comprehend written material. With development we build up a lexicon that contains representations of the semantic, visual, and auditory characteristics of words. Visual recognition of a word stored in the lexicon provides immediate access to semantic and auditory representations of that word. If no recognition occurs, alternative strategies have to be used. If the unrecognised word is similar to one we have encountered previously we can use an orthographic strategy, if it is not we tend to use an alphabetic strategy. As the lexicon comes to contain more representations of words (as a result of experience) we rely on the use of alphabetic and orthographic strategies less. The use of the lexical route is automatic and thus not having to rely on it frees up working memory. We use our working memory to make inferences about what we are reading and to monitor our comprehension. As metacognitive awareness of the strategies that we employ and the things that we need to do to ensure comprehension increases, so too do comprehension abilities.

Developmental dyslexics have specific problems with learning to read and write. There appears to be more than one form of the disorder, with different dyslexic individuals displaying different patterns of impairment. The most common form of dyslexia seems to be phonological dyslexia, a disorder characterised by the inability to use phonological information (and therefore use both alphabetic and orthographic strategies) to read unfamiliar words. Other dyslexics have problems with visual retrieval and therefore the lexical route appears to be impaired (precluding the use of orthographic strategy). Some researchers have suggested that sensory impairments can account for this form of dyslexia. The debate continues, however. Dyslexia appears to exist in many forms and therefore trying to establish a single explanation is a rather pointless task. What we need to concentrate on is establishing the causes of individual impairments and intervening in a way that will minimise the impact of these on reading development.

Theory of mind

What is a "theory of mind"?

AS ADULT HUMANS we are continually striving to explain and predict the behaviour of other people. When doing this we often refer to what is, or what might be, going on in their mind; their mental state. For example, if you witnessed someone banging on a door, looking through the letterbox and repeatedly shouting someone's name, you would assume that they had reason to *believe* that someone was behind the door and that their *behaviour* would result in that person answering it. You might, however, know differently and that no one was at home.

Before we can make inferences of the sort described above, we obviously need to recognise that other people *have minds* that interpret incoming information in an active way. We need to recognise that people's beliefs are based on the information that they receive and that this can be inaccurate or incomplete. This understanding is known as *metarepresentational awareness*; that is the understanding that the mind is a representational entity and that the information represented therein is not necessarily an accurate reflection of reality.

Although we *passively* receive some information from the external environment, we *actively interpret* much of the information that our senses receive. Things such as our emotional state and past experiences affect the way that we interpret incoming information. Similarly, our minds often fill in details that are not directly available to us. Just think of all the conversations you have had with friends about television programmes, films, or books. It is highly doubtful that you all agreed on the intention of the writer, director, author, or any of the characters that they had created. This is because you would have all interpreted the material being discussed in different ways.

The fact that we often hold inaccurate beliefs testifies to the interpretative nature of representation. If we didn't interpret incoming information we could never hold an inaccurate belief and therefore people exposed to the same information could never disagree about its meaning. This is obviously not the case and it's not a bad thing. Imagine how boring life would be if everyone saw things in the same way!

If we understand that the mind interprets information actively and we can use this knowledge to predict and explain the behaviour of other people we are said to have a "theory of mind", that is, we have constructed a theory of how the mind works. We realise that different people interpret information that they receive in different ways, that such interpretations are not always right, and therefore that people's beliefs don't always accurately reflect reality. We also use our theory of mind to understand our own behaviour and how it relates to our own mental representations. Such metacognitive activity allows us to develop coherent explanations for our own behaviour and an understanding of how these relate to our thoughts, feelings, and desires. It also enables us to evaluate our thoughts and feelings because it allows us to reflect upon where they came from.

Premack and Woodruff (1978) coined the term "theory of mind" to describe the abilities of a chimpanzee called Sarah. They showed Sarah several video-clips of human actors trying to solve problems, for example, trying to obtain a banana that was out of reach. Sarah was then given a number of photographs showing possible solutions to the problem. On 21 out of 24 occasions Sarah selected the appropriate solution. Premack and Woodruff claimed that this showed that Sarah had interpreted the actors' behaviour and from this worked out what his or her intentions were. Given that intentions are mental states, Premack and Woodruff claimed that chimpanzees have a theory of mind (well, Sarah at least!). The publication of this paper triggered a debate as to whether chimpanzees possess a theory of mind. This is an important issue for those studying the development of such abilities in humans. If chimpanzees *do* possess such abilities it could suggest innately specified abilities in this area; something that we shall consider in more detail later. At this point, all that needs to be acknowledged is where the term originated.

Wellman's theory

Wellman (1990) proposed that to have a theory of mind we need to understand two important mental states; those of desire and belief. To explain and predict the behaviour of others we usually refer to these. Generally, we work on the assumption that what people *do* is directly related to what they *believe* and what they *want*.

So it seems that at the centre of our everyday psychological reasoning lies an understanding of three main concepts: beliefs, desires, and behaviour and an understanding of how these concepts affect each other; a "belief-desire reasoning framework" (Wellman, 1990; see Figure 7.1). We also need to understand where people's desires and beliefs come from if we are to be able to guess at what their beliefs and desires actually *are*. Wellman (1990) proposes that we generally assume that beliefs result from our perceptions and desires from our physiological and emotional disposition.

Although an understanding of desires and beliefs might form the basis of a theory of mind, Wellman suggests that for our understanding of the mind to be useable (to predict and explain behaviour), we also need to acknowledge that the mind is an active interpreter of information, that is, that our perceptions are not based solely on

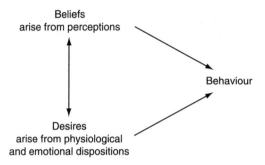

Figure 7.1 **The belief-desire reasoning framework** (adapted from Wellman, 1990)

environmental information. This understanding of the fact that humans are thinkers who process incoming information allows us to realise that beliefs can be formed in the absence of direct perceptual input. We also need to realise that intentions are not the same as desires; we might want something but not act on our desire because other factors stop us. Similarly, preferences affect how we act on our desires. It seems, then, that the links between beliefs, desires, and behaviours are not simple.

Recognition of false beliefs is the recognition of the fact that a person might mentally represent reality in a way that contradicts what actually *is* reality. To predict and explain the behaviour of others we need to understand this distinction. After all, other people often behave in ways that, although consistent with their own beliefs as to what is reality, are inappropriate in terms of what is actually the case.

It is clear that we need to construct a conceptual framework that specifies both the nature of beliefs, desires, behaviours, and the like and how they relate to and impact on each other. Such a framework constitutes a theory of mind. Wellman claimed that without a theory of mind, the prediction, explanation, and control of behaviour would be impossible, the social world in which we live would appear chaotic and an inevitable breakdown in communication would occur. Not everyone agrees with this claim. Some researchers (e.g. Dennett (1978), Harris (1991) claim that understanding of mental states is not necessary for the prediction and explanation of behaviour. Instead, it is proposed that all that is necessary for the prediction and explanation of behaviour is the ability to work out how we would feel or behave in a given situation. We could then project this explanation onto others. We will return to the issue later in this chapter. For now, we just need to acknowledge that Wellman's view is not the *only* view. It is a very popular view, though, for reasons that will become apparent in due course. We will therefore use it as a starting point for our discussion of the development of a theory of mind.

Measuring theory of mind abilities

So, at what age do children develop a theory of mind? Several experimental tasks have been designed in attempts to answer this question. These tasks are generally of a pass or fail nature. To pass them, children must demonstrate their understanding of the fact that reality can be misrepresented and therefore that the mind is a representational entity that actively constructs mental representations. All of the standard theory of mind tasks (described below) require the capacity for dual representation, that is, children need to be able to hold in mind two simultaneous representations of the same thing (see Chapter 3); one of reality and one of an alternative representation of reality (e.g. a false belief).

Standard "theory of mind" tasks

One classic test of false belief understanding is the "unexpected transfer task" devised by Wimmer and Perner (1983). The child is told a story in which a boy called Maxi places a bar of chocolate in a green drawer. Then, when Maxi is away, the bar of chocolate is moved from the green drawer to a blue one. Later Maxi wants some chocolate. The child is then asked where he will go to get it. Children under the age of about four consistently answer that Maxi will look in the blue drawer. Thus, they predict Maxi's behaviour on the basis of their own true beliefs rather than Maxi's false belief. Such an error is known as a "realist error"; responses are based upon reality rather than on an alternative (mis-)representation of reality. After about the age of four children predict that Maxi will act in accordance with his own false belief, demonstrating an understanding of the origins of beliefs and how beliefs affect behaviour.

Such a tendency towards reporting true beliefs when required to consider false ones has also been found to occur in children under the age of four when the beliefs concerned are those previously held by themselves, rather than those of another person. In the "deceptive box task" (Perner, Leekham, & Wimmer, 1987; see Figure 7.2) children are shown a familiar box (usually a "Smarties" tube[1]) and asked what they think is inside. The children reply with reference to the stereotypical box content, whereupon an unexpected content is revealed (typically pencils). This unexpected content is then put back in the box and the box is resealed. At this point the children are asked what they *thought* was in the box when it was first shown to them (before it was opened). Up until the age of about four years, children claim that they always

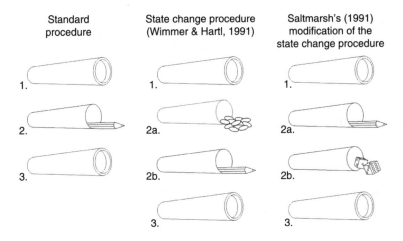

Figure 7.2 How the "Smarties" task (Perner et al., 1987) differs from Wimmer and Hartl's (1991) state change procedure and Saltmarsh et al.'s (1991) adaptation of the state change procedure.

[1] The version of the standard deceptive box task that utilises a Smarties tube with an unexpected content of pencils has become known as the "Smarties" task.

knew that the box contained an atypical content by referring to known reality when answering the test question; they made a realist error. This suggests that children have yet to realise that beliefs can be false.

Another task that has yielded results consistent with the view that young children are incapable of acknowledging a representation in conflict with reality is the "appearance/reality" task. Flavell, Flavell, and Green (1983) presented children between the ages of 3 and 5 years with ambiguous objects, such as a sponge painted to look like a rock. When asked the two test questions "What does this look like to your eyes right now?" and "What is this really, really?" children below the age of about 4 years tended to reply "sponge" to both questions, thus demonstrating a tendency to focus on reality at the expense of appearance.

The performance of young children on such tests of appearance/ reality has been found to correlate with their performance on tests of false belief, both those concerning the child's own beliefs (e.g. the deceptive box task) and those concerning those of another (e.g. the unexpected transfer task) (Astington & Gopnik, 1988). Children who tend to make realist errors on the rock/sponge task tend also to make realist errors when making judgements about beliefs.

Individual differences in theory of mind development

The studies outlined in the previous section all point to the age of about 4 years as the age at which standard theory of mind tasks are passed. Studies of performance on such tasks usually involve the testing of large samples of children and then the calculation of an average age at which the tasks are passed, and therefore any individual differences in performance would be glossed over. So are there any differences in performance and, if so, what factors are responsible for these?

The development of the ability to pass standard tests does seem to be fairly consistent both within and between cultures, with most children passing between the ages of three and six. For example, Avis and Harris (1991) gave an adapted version of the Maxi task to a tribe living in the Cameroon rainforests. Here, most children passed the task between the ages of five and six. Studies conducted on samples in

Western societies (such as those to be discussed in the next paragraph) have similarly found that whereas variations in the age at which tests are passed *do* exist, these are only slight variations. Such consistency suggests that innate mechanisms and predispositions have a role to play in the development of such abilities.

Several social factors have been shown to affect the age at which standard theory of mind tasks can be passed, suggesting that inter-action with other people is important for the development of theory of mind abilities. Ruffman, Perner, Naito, Parkin, and Clements (1998) found that the number of *older* siblings children have is positively correlated with theory of mind task performance and Lewis, Freeman, Kyriakidou, Maridaki-Kassotaki, and Breeidge (1996) found that social interaction with adults is important for the development of a theory of mind. Given that a theory of mind involves the recognition of the fact that other people might have different beliefs and desires to you, this is not surprising. Interacting with others is likely to make you more aware of this because you would be confronted with many situ-ations in which your views and wants are in conflict with those of other people.

If social interaction was important for the development of a theory of mind we would expect language to also be important, as much of social interaction is dependent on it. Indeed, we learn a lot about the minds of other people by talking to them, even as adults. There does seem to be a relationship between the two. Woolfe, Want, and Siegel (2002) found that deaf children who were not exposed to language from an early age (because their parents could hear and so did not communicate with them using sign language from birth) did not pass theory of mind tasks until substantially later than deaf chil-dren who were exposed to sign language from birth. Further evidence to support the relationship between theory of mind abilities and lan-guage comes from Charman, Ruffman, and Clements's (2002) finding that girls pass standard tasks at a slightly earlier age than boys and that this appears to be related to language development (as we saw in Chapter 5, girls outperform boys linguistically during the early years). Talking about the feelings of yourself and others also seems to be important. Dunn, Brown, and Beardsall (1991) found a relationship between the extent to which the mothers of children spoke to their child about their feelings at 33 months of age and the age at which the children passed standard theory of mind tasks.

Do standard tasks underestimate children's understanding of mind?

Wimmer and Hartl (1991) investigated the possibility that the extent of young children's understanding of mind was being underestimated by standard theory of mind tasks. They suggested that before we can be sure that children are failing these tasks because they have not yet developed a theory of mind, alternative explanations for young children's apparent incompetence must be ruled out.

Wimmer and Hartl proposed that children's inability to pass the deceptive box task could result from young children's tendency to claim that they always knew what was actually in the box so as not to appear stupid. This possibility was ruled out when children under the age of four were found to make realist errors for others as well as themselves. This is not surprising given that young children had already been shown to make realist errors for others as well as themselves in the Maxi task described earlier. Wimmer and Hartl also suggested that young children's poor performance could be attributable to them misinterpreting the time reference made in the test question ("*before* I opened it"). Owing to a superficial linguistic misunderstanding, young children might think that the experimenter is asking about the current state of affairs.

In an attempt to rule out this possibility, Wimmer and Hartl (1991) devised the "state change procedure"; a procedure based on the standard deceptive box task (see Figure 7.2). The only difference between the latter and the modified version is that, once the initial question "What do you think is inside the box?" has been asked, in the modified (state change) version the box is opened to reveal the *expected* content. Thus the child's initial expectation is confirmed. The expected content is then replaced with pencils (the unexpected content in the standard procedure) and the lid of the box is replaced. The child is then asked the test question "What did you think was in the box first of all, before we opened it?" All children were tested on both the state change procedure and the standard deceptive box task. These were presented in a counterbalanced order to prevent any order effects. It was reasoned that if young children's problems with the deceptive box task is due to a lack of a concept of beliefs as distinct from reality, they would ignore the reference to belief in the test question, thus interpreting "What did you *think* was in the box?" as "What *was* in the box?" This would result in the child getting the test question correct in the "state change" task (but, for the wrong reason) and wrong in the "deceptive box" task. If on the other hand, young children are misinterpreting the test question so as to refer to "What *is* in the box *now*?" rather than "What *was* in the box?" children should reply with the incorrect answer of "Pencils" to both test questions. This would suggest that the problem is a linguistic one rather than due to a lack of a concept of beliefs. Over 80 per cent of 3-year-olds passed the state change task, whereas only a third passed the deceptive box task. Wimmer and Hartl concluded that children's difficulty with the deceptive box task *is* therefore attributable to their lacking a concept of belief as distinct from reality rather than to any superficial linguistic misunderstanding. The findings of standard tasks were thus confirmed.

Why do young children have a problem with beliefs?

Wimmer, Hogrefe, and Perner (1988) suggested that young children have a problem with the concept of beliefs because they (wrongly) operate as if they think that information copies itself directly onto the mind. Thus, young children implicitly work on the assumption that information arriving via the sensory organs is converted in its original form into a mental representation of reality. They do not realise that individuals interpret raw perceptual data. If young children fail to acknowledge the existence of such a process intervening between sensation and cognition, they cannot acknowledge the possibility that people can fall victim to misleading information and consequently hold false beliefs. Failure to acknowledge false beliefs is, under this account, seen as symptomatic of a misunderstanding of the relationship between seeing and knowing.

Support for the aforementioned hypothesis comes from an

experiment in which Wimmer et al., (1988) found that 5-year-old children had no problem acknowledging the fact that a person with visual access to the contents of a box would know what is inside whereas those with no such perceptual access would not. In contrast, 3-year-olds revealed a tendency to attribute knowledge to everyone regardless of informational access.

Young children's tendency to overapply newly acquired concepts and rules has been well documented. One such example can be seen in young children's tendency to be overgeneral in their use of newly acquired linguistic rules, prior to their reaching an understanding of when and where adherence to such rules is appropriate (see Chapter 5). It seems plausible to suggest, then, that if Wimmer et al.'s (1988) explanation is correct, the sudden acquisition of a new rule linking seeing to knowing is responsible for children's false belief task competence, then they might well go through a phase where they overapply this rule before they work out when it should and when it should not be applied. This could result in the denial of the possibility that a person might obtain knowledge by any means *other* than seeing. Sodian and Wimmer (1987) revealed such a tendency. Children between the ages of four and six were first shown a bag that contained a number of sweets of the same type. The experimenter then transferred a sweet from the bag into a box, out of the sight of the child. When asked if they knew what the box contained, all children said that they did; they had made an inference. However, when asked if an assistant who was also present when the transfer was made and therefore saw the same as the child, knew what the box contained, they said that the assistant didn't. Children were effectively denying that one could know without seeing. Sodian and Wimmer (1987) labelled this phenomenon "inference neglect". It seems, then, that whereas children are capable of making inferences themselves, they deny that others can do the same. Children's understanding of the inferences made appears to be implicit and as such any metacognitive awareness of the processes involved in such problem solving is precluded.

"Theory theory" accounts

On the basis of the evidence reported above, Perner and Davies (1991) concluded that children, on reaching the age of about four years, acquire an understanding of the mind as an active interpreter of incoming information. At this age children realise that information received via the senses undergoes interpretation by the individual receiving it and is not simply copied. Hand in hand with this understanding comes the understanding that such a process can result in information being distorted or inaccurate. This allows for the acknowledgement of false beliefs. Such insight into the nature of human minds is said to occur suddenly.

Perner and Davies' view nicely exemplifies that of "theory" theorists in general and is supported by the research findings discussed in the preceding sections. Children under the age of four years fail standard theory of mind tasks whereas children over the age of four years pass them. This seems to suggest a sudden shift in children's understanding. This shift is said to occur because the child suddenly understands that beliefs do not necessarily reflect reality. To do this the child must be able to hold in their mind two different representations, one of reality and one of an alternative to reality (for example, in the Maxi task, one of where the chocolate *really* is and one of where Maxi *thinks* it is).

Theory theorists claim that, once the aforementioned shift in understanding has occurred, children can *use* their understanding of mind to predict and explain the behaviour of others and thus they now have a *theory* of mind similar to that of adults (Astington & Gopnik, 1988; Perner, 1991; Sodian & Wimmer, 1987). Prior to this shift in understanding, children are said to be constructing their theory, acquiring new concepts such as those of beliefs, desires, and the like, and making links between them. At this stage, children's knowledge of mind is not considered to be theoretical because it does not specify all of the links between concepts, which would enable the child to interpret and predict behaviour on the basis of a person's mental state (Slaughter & Gopnik, 1996). That is, young children's notions about the nature of mind are isolated as opposed to "conceptually coherent". Once isolated ideas about the mind become inter-related, a theoretical framework allowing for the explanation and prediction of behaviour, as well as the attribution of mental states, is in place. This is said to constitute a theory of mind.

Theory theorists state that the realist errors made by young children on standard theory of mind tasks are made because children do not yet understand that people can hold mental representations that conflict with reality. Thus it is claimed that realist errors are default responses that children give because they don't have the necessary understanding to give a correct answer.

The realism account

In contrast to "theory theory" accounts of theory of mind development, the "realism account" (Mitchell, 1996) proposes that young children *do* have an understanding of the interpretative nature of mind before the age of four, the age at which standard theory of mind tasks are passed. More importantly, the realism account argues that children do not *suddenly* acquire a theory of mind at all, rather they develop an understanding of other people's minds gradually. So, how can the realism account explain children's performance on standard theory of mind tasks?

Well, the realism account proposes that young children's early understanding of mind is masked by a realist tendency; a tendency to focus on reality at the expense of alternative representations of reality (such as false beliefs). With development, this bias towards reality decreases gradually, resulting in the ability to attend to an alternative representation of reality rather than to reality itself when this is appropriate. Such a bias is said to be responsible for the failure of children under the age of four to pass standard theory of mind tasks. The realism account claims that even children who fail such tasks have an understanding of the nature of beliefs (i.e. that they can be false) but that this is overwritten by the realist bias.

Under this account, realism is seen as a phenomenon in its own right rather than a default response given when the conceptual framework for explaining and predicting the behaviour of others is not available (because it has not developed yet), as is proposed by the theory theory account.

But why would children have such a realist bias? Leslie (1994) suggests that young children have a tendency to attend to reality over beliefs when the two are in conflict because beliefs are normally true. Thus children operate on this assumption when they make judgements about another person's beliefs. The strategy that children are applying has obviously proved effective in the past but is being overapplied. This would make sense given our discussion in Chapter 4 about the problems young children have working out when and where particular strategies are likely to prove successful.

The realism account claims that the realist errors demonstrated by children under the age of 4 years are the result of a domain-general bias towards reality rather than a specific problem with the concept of beliefs, as is proposed by the theory theory. Two processes are said to be working in tandem. On the one hand, children's understanding of the mind is increasing whereas on the other their realist bias is decreasing. Only when the former has reached a level sufficient for it to override the latter can a child use their understanding of mind to predict and explain behaviour.

Research evidence: facilitation studies

Evidence that appears to support the realism account comes from studies that show that children under the age of 4 years can acknowledge false beliefs when the contexts in which they are required to do so are more favourable than those provided by the standard false belief task. To create a context in which children could pass such tests, the realism account would suggest that the representation of reality must be made less "attention grabbing", allowing the child to acknowledge the existence of a representation that conflicts with reality.

Mitchell and Lacohee (1991), in what has now become known as the "posting procedure", enhanced the salience of children's initial false belief in the deceptive box task (Smarties version) by asking children to select and post a picture of the expected content of the Smarties tube before the unexpected content of pencils was revealed (thus giving the initial false belief held by the child a physical basis). This improved performance. Children of 3 years of age typically passed the test.

Robinson and Mitchell (1995) similarly found that explaining behaviour with reference to another person's false belief is easier than predicting it. They asked children to match the actions of each of two identical twins with their prior informational history. It was found that even those children who could not pass a standard false belief task could judge that a twin who was searching for a ball in a location where it had previously been was the one who had been absent when the ball was transferred to its new location. They argued that the behaviour demonstrated by the story character acted as a physical counterpart to their false belief, in the same way as the picture in Mitchell and Lacohee's posting procedure served as a physical counterpart to the child's false belief. They proposed that it was this factor that was responsible for the observed increase in task performance.

The aforementioned experiments have all resulted in children's performance on false-belief tasks being facilitated as a result of the salience of the false belief being enhanced allowing the realist bias to be over-ridden. Zaitchik (1991) instead *decreased* the salience of reality by indirectly communicating the nature of reality to the children by telling them about it rather than showing them. Under these conditions children found it easier to acknowledge false beliefs. It seems that changing the procedure used to test for a theory of mind affects children's ability to correctly answer test questions and, therefore, at least in early childhood, children's understanding of mind is *situation specific*; whether children can use the knowledge that they have depends on the situation in which they are required to do so. Whether this is attributable to a domain-general realist bias is less clear. It could be that children have more general working-memory constraints that affect their ability to pass standard theory of mind tests and those different variations of the standard procedure place different demands on working memory. In both the posting procedure and the twins study of Robinson and Mitchell (1995), demands on memory are substantially reduced because more perceptual reminders about the representations they need to refer to, to pass the test, are available.

Situation specificity

Steverson (unpublished) found that whereas children of below the age of four can be helped to acknowledge false beliefs if assisted, children of five and six can fail to acknowledge false beliefs if hindered. As in Wimmer and Hartl's (1991) experiment, Steverson's procedure involved children being asked to make a judgement as to the false belief of a notoriously stupid puppet in a standard deceptive box procedure. Children who could acknowledge the puppet's false belief under standard conditions were found to agree with the experimenter when it was suggested to them that the puppet had actually formed a true belief (despite them being given inadequate information), and thus they said that the puppet initially thought that there were pencils in the Smarties box. These children rejected a control suggestion as to what was in the box, implying that the children were not conforming to the experimenter's suggestions as a result of their eagerness to please, but rather because it meant that they would not have to acknowledge a false belief.

Mitchell (1994), in support of his realism account, suggested that the facilitation observed in circumstances such as those described above is attributable to the importance that young children attach to their representation of reality at the expense of anything that contradicts it. The realism account claims that young children *do not* lack a concept of belief.

Such a claim seems problematic in light of the rather convincing argument put forward by Wimmer and Hartl (1991) on the basis of their state change experiments. They argued that children fail the deceptive box task because they lack a concept of belief and thus they ignore the reference to belief in the test question. However, there is an alternative explanation. Perhaps, the children do acknowledge their initial belief as a belief and are assisted in this by the fact that their initial belief had a physical counterpart: The Smarties that were, as predicted, in the box. Under this account it matters not whether the belief that the child initially holds is true. Wimmer and Hartl's (1991) account, however, hinges on the fact that the children's initial belief is false. After all, if the children's initial belief were true then ignoring the reference to beliefs in the test question would have no effect upon the answer that the child gives.

199

Saltmarsh, Mitchell, and Robinson (1995) adapted the state change task (see Figure 7.2). In the amended procedure a deceptive box was first shown to the child and they were asked to predict its contents. The box was then opened and an unexpected content was revealed. This was then replaced with *another* atypical content and the box closed. The standard test question: "When you first saw the box, what did you think was inside it?" was then asked. Wimmer and Hartl's (1991) account predicts that children would ignore the word "think" and would thus report the first content of the box. However, the most common response given referred to the box's current contents; a realist bias was revealed. A vast majority of children correctly recalled the initial content of the box, suggesting that young children do not interpret questions concerning previous beliefs and previous reality in the same way.

The question as to whether children were giving correct responses on the state change task because their beliefs were being elevated to reality status as a result of their being supported by a physical counterpart remains an important one. An alternative explanation could be that success on the state change task is better than on the deceptive box task because in the state change procedure the children's belief is initially true. In an attempt to arbitrate between these two possibilities, Saltmarsh et al. (1995) again adapted the state change procedure, this time so that it referred to a *false* belief held by another person. To do this, children were first introduced to a puppet and asked both what they (the children) and the puppet thought was inside a deceptive box. The puppet was then hidden. In the puppet's absence the box was opened, the expected contents revealed, replaced, and the box resealed. The puppet then returned and the child was asked what the puppet thought was in the box "Right now". Wimmer and Hartl (1991) would predict that if the children ignored the word "think" in the test question they would make realist errors when judging the puppet's previously held true belief as they do in the standard deceptive box procedure. This was not the case. Saltmarsh et al. (1995) found that children were more likely to report the puppet's prior false belief if it was supported by a physical counterpart (state change) than when it was not (deceptive box), thus supporting the realist account.

Wimmer and Hartl (1991) would also expect that realist errors would be more common for judgements concerning another person's beliefs than for the child's own. After all, if children are giving right answers on the state change task due their failure to acknowledge beliefs as beliefs as they propose then correct answers would only be given (by default) in response to questions about prior true beliefs and not those about current false beliefs. However, Saltmarsh et al. (1995) reported no difference in the number of correct responses given when children were questioned about the puppet's previously held true belief and his currently held false one, thus undermining Wimmer and Hartl's explanation.

It seems, then, that children of 3 years of age can acknowledge false beliefs if the context in which the task is presented allows it; the ability is situation specific. The fact that context affects the answers that children give suggests that children's understanding of mind becomes stronger and more robust with age. As children mature, they can *use* their understanding of mind in more varied contexts.

Situation specificity and theory of mind in adulthood

There exists a wealth of research evidence to suggest that realist biases are not just a childhood phenomenon (e.g. Conway, 1990; Fischoff, 1975; Snyder & Uranowitz, 1978; Wilson & Brekke, 1994). Often, knowledge that we have already acquired affects our interpretation of incoming information (as we have seen on numerous occasions during the course of this book). Mitchell, Robinson, Isaacs, and Nye (1996) gave a test of false belief, adapted from Perner and Davies's (reported earlier in the chapter), to groups of 5- and 9-year-old children and a group of adults. Although none of the children made realist errors, the adults did. Realism is not purely a childhood phenomenon, then. However, it is likely that there are age-related changes in both the extent to which such tendencies are exhibited and the circumstances in which they arise.

Mitchell and Taylor (1999) presented an extensive sample of people ranging from 3 years of age through to adulthood a task designed to measure the *extent* of realist tendencies. In what they called the

"T-box task", participants were presented with a luminous circular disc that was inside a darkened chamber. The disc was presented at an angle so that when viewed it appeared elliptical. Participants were asked to replicate the *appearance* of the disc (using a computer programme). It was reasoned that as participants knew that the shape they were viewing was a circle, *if* a realist bias exists then this knowledge would contaminate their judgements of its apparent shape. Both children and adults demonstrated realist errors. However, the degree of overestimation of circularity was higher in early childhood than at any other age, thus supporting the realist accounts suggestion that realist biases decrease with age. Furthermore, the extent to which realist biases were demonstrated correlated with standard theory of mind task performance, supporting the claim that realist biases in early childhood prevent children from passing standard tests.

The fact that realist biases are also evident in the judgements of adults again testifies to the context and situation specificity of judgements about representations that conflict with reality. It seems that we all have a tendency to be biased by reality but that with age we become more adept at ignoring situational factors and focusing on the reasoning required to reach correct conclusions. Given that we saw in Chapter 4 that reasoning about things that have no basis in reality (or that don't *appear* to have a basis in reality) is a very late development and one that not all people develop, this is not surprising.

Factors that affect theory of mind task performance

Bloom and German (2000) point out that passing standard theory of mind tasks involves more than just a theory of mind. In addition to the capacity for dual representation and an understanding of beliefs, children also need sufficient working memory abilities so as to be able to both hold in mind the information that they are given and to process this information. For example, in the Maxi task children need to be able to follow a narrative, keep track of characters and the order in which events occur, focus on the correct information and then use this information to reach a conclusion as to the answer to the test question.

Given that standard theory of mind tasks are so complex, it is highly likely that information-processing limitations affect children's performance on such tasks (Case, 1985; Harris, 1991). The facilitation studies described in the previous section make fewer demands on working memory than do the standard versions of the tasks and this seems to affect performance. This could indicate that working-memory constraints mask children's understanding of mind during the early years. This suggestion is similar to that made by the realism account, which also proposes that domain-general constraints on processing prevent children from revealing their true understanding of mind. The difference between the two accounts is that the realism account suggests that it is a domain-general bias towards reality that masks children's abilities whereas information-processing accounts suggest that domain-general working memory abilities constrain children's judgements in some theory of mind tasks.

Given that executive function has been found to affect children's ability to reason, and that reasoning is involved in making the judgements that lead to correct answers on theory of mind tasks, it is likely that the development of executive function constrains young children's performance on standard tasks. As we saw in Chapter 4, reasoning is a complex ability that makes significant demands on working memory. We also concluded that reasoning about things that contradict what children know to be true is especially difficult for young children. It could be, therefore, that children's problems with standard tasks are attributable to more general problems with the reasoning required in theory of mind tasks. These problems are exacerbated in tasks that require reasoning with counterfactual information.

As their working-memory capabilities develop, children become more adept at resisting realist errors. Realist errors in standard theory of mind tasks are evidenced by a tendency to refer to one's own representation of reality at the current time, rather than either that held by another person or that previously held by oneself. Whether this is attributable to a domain-general realist bias, domain-general working-memory limitations, or a lack of domain-specific knowledge is not clear. It is likely that *all* of these factors have a part to play in determining whether children pass a specific theory of mind task. What is clear is that the complexity of the task being undertaken has an important role to play in determining whether errors are made. From the age of about 3 years, children seem capable of passing some tests of theory of mind understanding, suggesting that they do have a concept of beliefs as distinct from reality and therefore they recognise that the mind is a representational entity. In standard tasks, other factors prevent them from demonstrating this understanding.

Conclusions so far

It seems that there is ample evidence to support the suggestion that children's understanding of mind develops gradually. It is the *point* at which this understanding reaches a level where it could be called a theory (sufficient to explain and predict the behaviour of another on the basis of their mental representations) that is disputed. From what we have seen in this chapter so far, it is highly unlikely that there is *no* specific age at which theory of mind abilities are consistently applied. Children often demonstrate theory of mind abilities in one situation but not in others. We must therefore conclude that theory of mind is an area of reasoning that depends on substantial domain-specific know-ledge. Whereas domain-general constraints on working memory, and more specifically executive function, do preclude the passing of theory of mind tests by very young children, even when these are no longer there, domain-specific knowledge is required for theory of mind reasoning to be successfully undertaken.

When trying to evaluate the competing claims made by theory theorists and supporters of the realism account, it is important to remember that the emphasis of each is very different. Whereas theory theorists concentrate on the age at which a *theory* of mind develops, the realism account concentrates more on children's developing *under-standing* of mind. Indeed, proponents of the latter believe that concen-trating on a particular developmental point distracts from the remainder of the process.

The development of an understanding of mind

The prelinguistic years

Evidence of children's early understanding of mind comes from several sources. Infants of 9 months have been found to understand the significance of joint attention in communicative contexts as is evidenced by the emergence of pointing behaviour to direct attention to a specific object (Bruner, 1993). Children, thus, seem to possess a very basic understanding of the relationship between seeing and knowing. Such ability becomes more complex at around the age of 18 months, the same age at which language develops rapidly. Baldwin (1993) found that at this age children demonstrate sensitivity to their parent's line of sight in that they seem to realise that the object the parent is looking at when speaking is usually the one to which he or she is referring. Such an understanding suggests that very young children not only appreciate the relationship between seeing something and mentally representing it, but also that speech provides a vital key to another person's mental representations. Children's capacity for pretence also suggests that they have some conception of the distinction between reality and alternative representations of reality. After all, if children did not realise that the object that they were pretending was, for example, a hamburger, wasn't *really* a hamburger then they might end up choking or breaking their teeth! To pretend effectively, children must hold in mind a representation of both the object as it really is *and* a representation of what the object's pretend identity is. Children also need to recognise the difference between the two representations, that one is an inaccurate representation of reality—they need the capacity for dual representation. Pretend play occurs in children from about 18 months of age (Leslie, 1987). It seems, then, that even infants have *some* understanding of the minds of other people. It is a very basic understanding of the nature of mind and not sufficient to allow for the prediction and explanation of behaviour.

Early childhood

Before children could start to construct a belief-desire framework, it would be necessary for them to understand the difference between

205

reality and thoughts; that is, they need representational awareness (see Chapter 3). Thoughts differ from reality in many ways; they have no physical existence, can refer to things that do not (and even cannot) exist and they cannot be seen by other people. Very young children do not understand the distinction between mental states and reality and thus conceive of minds in the same way as they conceive of physical entities. An understanding of this distinction seems to appear at around 3 years of age. For example, at this age children realise that someone who *has* a dog can play with the dog whereas someone who is *thinking* about one cannot (Harris, Brown, Marriott, Whittall, & Harmer, 1991). Similarly, when asked to consider a thought about a raisin "in the head" versus a swallowed raisin in the stomach, children over three realise that only the latter is physically *in* the person (Watson, Gelman, and Wellman, 1988). Children also appear to understand the subjectivity of thoughts at around this age (Wellman, Hollander, & Schult, 1996).

But do these abilities constitute a theory of mind? The answer is no. Knowledge such as that outlined above does not allow children to predict and explain the actions of others. However, it *is* necessary for them to develop such an understanding before they can even start to develop *a causal-explanatory framework*. Children as young as 18 months of age have been shown to have a basic understanding of some of the concepts that later become conceptually linked (beliefs, desires, emotions, and the like) so as to *become* a theory of mind.

A basic understanding of emotions has been demonstrated in 18-month-olds (Denham, 1986). Children of this age also realise that people can have different desires for the same object. Repacholi and Gopnik (1997) presented 18-month-olds with two snacks to taste. It was assumed that one of these snacks would appeal to the children (an American snack known as "goldfish crackers") and one would not (broccoli). Just to make sure that their assumptions were correct, the children's reactions to each snack was observed. Unsurprisingly, very few children preferred the broccoli. An adult then tasted each of the snacks, saying "urghhh" to one and "ummm" to the other. In the first condition, the adult mimicked the reaction of the child to each of the snacks whereas in the second condition the opposite preference was demonstrated. The adult then placed her hands halfway between the two snacks and asked for more. In both conditions the children gave the adult more of what she wanted rather than what they would prefer. This suggests that even 18-month-olds understand that different people have different desires and that they can act on the basis of these perceived desires.

By the age of two, children spontaneously use different words to refer to people's internal states and their external behaviours, physical features, and facial expressions (Bartsch & Wellman, 1995). By about two-and-a-half years of age, children use the word "pretend" in their spontaneous utterances and show that they understand when other people are pretending (Harris & Kavanaugh, 1993). By the age of three, children's understanding of mind is becoming yet more complex. At this age, children begin to demonstrate an understanding of the relationships between some of the concepts that underpin a belief-desire reasoning framework, such as desires, perceptions, and so on. They can use information about what a person perceives to predict what they know or believe (e.g. Pillow, 1989; Pratt & Bryant, 1990) and predict a person's emotional reaction on the basis of their desires (e.g. Stein & Levine, 1989) or beliefs (e.g. Hadwin & Perner, 1991). To make such connections between concepts, children require substantial problem-solving abilities. Not only do they need to be able to hold the information needed to solve the problem in their working memory for the time needed to solve it, they also need sufficient executive function abilities to be able to manipulate this knowledge and make deductions such as those described above.

An understanding of the difference between thoughts and reality also continues to develop during early childhood. At age three, children understand that whereas physical forces are necessary to manipulate physical objects, thoughts are sufficient to manipulate mental objects and they can distinguish between the two (e.g. Wellman & Estes, 1989). They are also capable of referring to the false beliefs of both themselves and others *in some circumstances*, which suggests an understanding of the relationship between perception and beliefs.

Domain-specific knowledge and theory of mind tasks

Evidence suggests that social factors also have a role to play in the development of an understanding of mind. The age at which children pass tasks measuring an understanding or theory of mind varies as a function of various social factors, such as family size and amount of interaction with adults (e.g. Jenkins & Astington, 1996; Lewis et al., 1996; Ruffman et al., 1998). In Chapter 4 we discussed the effects of a lack of subject-specific knowledge on problem-solving attempts and came to the conclusion that, if children don't recognise the problem-solving situation as similar to one that they have previously encountered, they will not adopt the correct reasoning strategy. This is another factor that could be preventing children from revealing their true competencies. As is the case in many other areas of development that we have considered in this book, having a strategy available does not mean that it is used. These findings suggest that the acquisition of domain-specific knowledge is also important for the development of an understanding of mind. However, innate constraints on information processing prevent the effective use of this knowledge during the early years.

Despite individual differences in the ability to pass standard theory of mind tasks, the development of an understanding of mind does seem to follow a predetermined pattern. The ages at which children pass certain milestones in this understanding does appear to be very similar both within and between cultures (Wellman, Cross, & Watson, 2001).

A theory of mind module?

Some researchers (e.g. Fodor, 1992; Leslie, 1994; Leslie & German, 1995) have argued for the existence of a separate module that is responsible for the processing of social information. Leslie and German (1995), for example, propose that there are two independent modules, each preprogrammed to receive inputs of different types. One is said to receive and process information relating to inanimate objects and the other, the theory of mind module, is said to process information relating to animate objects. These develop according to an innately specified maturational pattern.

Given the evidence reviewed above, we must conclude that the ability to reason about the thoughts and beliefs of other people go beyond a simple understanding of mind. As we have seen in the preceding sections, general information-processing limitations constrain children's reasoning about mental states. This suggests that knowledge about the minds and behaviour of other people is not isolated from the rest of the cognitive system and therefore that a theory of mind module does *not* exist.

Brothers and Ring (1992) have suggested that the brain system responsible for the processing of information of a social nature incorporates the amygdala, the orbital frontal cortex (part of the frontal lobes), and parts of the frontal cortex. Studies of children with selective impairments to theory of mind abilities have often been used to substantiate this position. Autistic children are often the focus of such research.

Autism and other disorders

Autism is just one of a number of similar disorders, collectively known as autistic spectrum disorders (others include Asperger's syndrome, a milder form of the disorder). A recent study by the Medical Research Council (2001) estimated that six in every thousand children in the UK suffer from some form of the autistic spectrum disorder.

Kanner (1943: 242) was the first person to recognise autism as a distinct syndrome, he defined it as:

> The inability to relate in the ordinary way to people and situations . . . an extreme autistic aloneness that, whenever possible, disregards, ignores, shuts out anything that comes to the child from outside

Kanner's definition suggests that autistic children are cut off from the outside world. Even during infancy, autistic children do not engage with their environment or the people within it. They do not initiate or respond to physical contact with others and they do not show the desire for human contact that non-autistic children do from birth. Early symptoms of autism include not looking people in the eye (Nolen-Hoesksema, 2001) and a failure to develop imitation or engage in pretend play in the way that most young children do (Siegler, 1996). The primary impairment associated with autism therefore is the inability to respond to others appropriately. Secondary impairments include language and cognitive difficulties. An autistic child's language abilities are limited, although the extent varies. Severely autistic children might never learn to talk (about half of all autistic children) or understand language; mildly autistic children might use language minimally or inappropriately, whereas those at the lower end of the autistic spectrum, e.g. those with Asperger's, do develop considerable language abilities. In those autistic children who do learn to talk there is a distinct under-representation of mental state verbs in their vocabulary (e.g. want, believe, pretend, know) (Baron-Cohen, Leslie, & Frith, 1986) and they cannot discriminate between mentalistic words of this sort and non-mentalistic words (Baron-Cohen et al., 1994a). In fact, autistic children do not seem to be able to communicate effectively, if at all. For example, they do not use mimes or gestures (such as pointing) to make their needs known (Baron-Cohen, 1989b, 1996).

Some researchers have suggested that autistic children's limited language abilities are related to the fact that they fail to establish joint attention. Autistic children do not seem to be able to understand that the object to which someone is referring is the one that they are looking at, something that non-autistic children do from about the age of 18 months and, as we have already seen (in Chapter 5), appears to aid language acquisition. In fact, autistic children do not seem to pay *any* attention to the eyes of other people (Baron-Cohen & Hammer, 1997). Normally, eyes are treated as clues as to a person's mental state (their emotions, beliefs, etc.) and we pay considerable attention to them when interacting with others.

Impairments such as those listed above are bound to affect a child's ability to form relationships. Indeed, many autistic children fail to develop social relationships at all, although they don't actively avoid the company of others (Hermelin & O'Connor, 1970). Most autistic children show an improvement in social skills at around age five but relationships are still strained; personal friendships are not formed and co-operative group play is not engaged in.

The catalogue of impairments given above has led many psychologists to suggest that autistic children have a specific impairment to their theory of mind (e.g. Baron-Cohen, 1989b; Mitchell, 1996). There is ample evidence to support such a suggestion.

Baron-Cohen, Leslie, and Frith (1986) found that the mean age at which autistic children can acknowledge the false beliefs of others was 12 years (mental age five-and-a-half). This was not down to general cognitive impairments because children with learning difficulties (with a mental age of four or above) passed the task. Autistic children also have problems acknowledging their own, previously held, false beliefs in the "deceptive box" task (Baron-Cohen, 1989b) and distinguishing appearances from reality (rock-sponge task) (Baron-Cohen 1989a).

It seems, then, that autistic children's understanding of mind is at a similar level to that of non-autistic 3-year-olds, even though they have mental ages of well above 3 years. It is worth noting, though, that the linguistic demands made in these tasks might, at least in part, be responsible for autistic children's failure to pass them. This is unlikely, as findings concerning autistic children's problems with theory of mind tasks seem robust; many different procedures and variations on tasks have yielded consistent results (e.g. Leekham & Perner, 1991; Perner et al., 1989; Sweetenham, 1996).

Further evidence to support the suggestion that autistic children's deficits are specific to their understanding of mind comes from studies looking at their understanding of the mental–physical distinction. Whereas non-autistic children demonstrate such an understanding (e.g. by passing Harris et al.'s (1991) thinking-about-as-opposed-to-touching-a-dog task) at around the age of 4 years, autistic children do not demonstrate such an understanding until much later (Baron-Cohen, 1989b). Similarly, they do not understand the nature of "mind". When asked about the functions of the brain, autistic children describe it in physical terms only (Baron-Cohen, 1989b). Non-autistic 3- to 4-year-olds usually refer to at least some mentalistic functions, such as dreaming, thinking, wanting, when asked to do this (Wellman & Estes, 1986). Autistic children also come to understand the link between seeing and knowing at a later age than do non-autistic children (Baron-Cohen & Goodhart, 1994). Similarly, whereas non-autistic children can deceive efficiently by age four (Sodian, Taylor, Harris, & Perner, 1992), autistic children do not spontaneously attempt to deceive people, nor do they appear to understand when someone else is trying to deceive them (Baron-Cohen, 1992; Yirmiya, Solomonica-Levi, & Shuman, 1996). Again, this suggests a lack of understanding of the relationship between perception (informational input) and belief formation.

There is compelling evidence to suggest that autistic children's understanding of mind is limited. Mental age does not tally with theory of mind competencies and therefore it could be argued that the deficit is a specific one. However, it is only a partial description of the difficulties experienced by those with autism. For example, autistic children demonstrate insistency on sameness and intellectual impairments that are unrelated to their understanding of mind. This finding has given rise to the executive dysfunction deficit explanation. The executive function is responsible planning and regulation of behaviour in situations where normal routines will not suffice, for example, when we need to switch from one thing to another (as we do when attempting to do several things at once). Proponents of the executive function hypothesis suggest that it is an impairment to executive functioning that characterises autism (e.g. Hughes, Russell & Robbins (1994). Ozonoff, Pennington, and Rogers (1991) and Zaitchik (1990) found that some autistics who passed standard theory of mind tasks failed tests of executive function, therefore suggesting that the autistic participants' main problem was with executive function and not theory of mind abilities specifically.

Studies have found that autistic individuals often fail tasks thought to measure executive function, such as the Tower of Hanoi task and the card sort task (described in Chapter 4) (Ozonoff et al., 1991). This account can also explain autistic children's more specific problem with theory of mind. Theory of mind reasoning involves switching between two simultaneously held representations of the same object or situation and, as such, calls on the executive function.

Perhaps neurological evidence could help us to distinguish between the accounts. The prefrontal cortex is involved in the regulation and planning of behaviour and, as such, is associated with executive function. Whereas impairments to this area have consistently been found in the brains of *some* autistics (Rumsey & Hamburger, 1988), impairments to brain areas thought to play a role in understanding mind have been found less consistently (Johnson, 1997b). This seems to suggest that the problems of those with autism are more likely to be associated with deficits in executive function rather than specific theory of mind abilities, but things aren't this simple. Many children with damage to the frontal lobes are not autistic (Pennington & Ozonoff, 1996). Some of the abnormalities identified in autistic individuals have also been associated with other disorders, which suggests that although they might explain specific deficits associated with autism, they are an incomplete explanation of the disorder as a whole. For example, children suffering from ADHD have also been found to have problems with executive function and these are related to abnormal information processing in the prefrontal cortex (Rubia et al., 2001). Although there does appear to be a genetic basis to autism that affects the processing of information in specific brain areas, it is not clear exactly how this works and how different deficits contribute to different developmental disorders.

Williams syndrome is a disorder characterised by a high level of social intelligence but a poor level of general intelligence. In contrast to those with autism, children with Willliams syndrome do well on tests of false belief, with over 90 per cent passing (Karmiloff-Smith, et al., 1995). This has led many to suggest that Williams syndrome is a result of an impairment that affects the processing of non-social information but not the processing of social information. As such, it is thought to be the opposite of autism. Studies of brain function in those with Williams syndrome have produced mixed findings, however (Pober & Dykens, 1996). As is the case with autistic individuals, there does not appear to be a specific brain area associated with the impairments demonstrated by those with Williams syndrome.

The fact that the brains of autistic and non-autistic children appear to operate differently, teamed with the finding that the impairments of those with autism and Williams syndrome seem selectively impaired/unimpaired to their understanding of mind, lends *some* support to the idea that there is a specific module in the human brain responsible for understanding mind and that it is this that is damaged in autistic children (Baron-Cohen, 1995; Leslie, 1994) but remains unimpaired in those with Williams syndrome. However, the rather confusing neurological evidence suggests that this is not the case. Although it is possible that the knowledge needed to understand the nature of mind is *domain*-specific, the evidence we have reviewed in this chapter suggests that our knowledge of mind is not unconnected to other domains. As a result, it is unlikely that a specialist theory of mind module does not exist. More research is needed if we are to identify the genetic and biological factors responsible for autistic spectrum disorders.

Summary and conclusions

In this chapter we have seen how a theoretical understanding of mind is necessary for us to be able to explain and predict the behaviour of other people in an effective way. This appears to develop during the early years. With experience, children acquire knowledge about the behaviour of others, they form prototypical representations of central concepts (such as beliefs, desires, and behaviour) and they construct a conceptual framework that specifies how these concepts relate to one another.

Theory theory accounts of the development of a theory of mind emphasise the point at which children's understanding of mind becomes theoretical, whereas the realist account looks at the development of an understanding of mind and at how children's ability to demonstrate their understanding of the minds of other people is constrained by domain-general processing constraints that bias children to give responses to test questions that reflect reality rather than counterfactual representations of reality. Neither theory seems to provide a full account of the development of a theory of mind. As with other areas of development, the ability to reason about mental states is dependent on many different factors. Domain-general information-processing abilities constrain development and prevent young children from reasoning about beliefs in standard theory of mind tasks. Domain-specific knowledge also affects the extent to which and situations in which children can demonstrate their understanding of mind. The development of an understanding of mind is gradual and innate predispositions to focus on the social environment seem to facilitate development.

Autistic individuals have an impaired understanding of mind. However, this is not the only feature of autism. Autistic individuals demonstrate a range of impairments. Neurological evidence relating to autism is somewhat mixed but there is not evidence to suggest a selective theory of mind impairment. The frontal lobes appear to be implicated and this has led some theorists to suggest that domain-general impairments to executive function are responsible for the specific difficulties that autistic people have. Executive function impairments are also found in those with other disorders (such as ADHD), however. This suggests that neither a theory of mind or executive function deficits are sufficient explanations for autism.

Chapter 8

Conclusions

A T THE BEGINNING of this book we discussed why it is important for us to understand the way in which children's thinking changes with age. Not only can an understanding of the way that we develop enable us to understand some of the ways we might come to think as adults, it is also important for us to understand children's cognition so that we can do as much as we can to help them learn and develop.

It is also useful for us to understand the processes and structures that appear to be impaired in those with developmental disorders, so that we can ensure that their impairments affect their functioning as little as possible. In this book we have considered only a few developmental disorders. We have looked at autism, dyslexia, and briefly at Down and Williams syndromes, and at deafness and blindness. In doing this we have seen that each disorder has a characteristic pattern of development. Each of these developmental difficulties has a biological basis and, as such, we cannot "cure" those that experience them. By studying developmental disorders we have, however, learned a lot about the potential for development displayed by those with such disorders, and this seems to be considerable. We have also learned a lot about the process of normal development from the study of the impairments and biological bases to the aforementioned problems.

Studying cognitive development is by no means an easy task. It seems that asking questions about development often creates more questions as opposed to any answers. As is the case with many things, it appears to be a case of the more that we come to know, the more we realise that we don't know. Development appears to be the result of a complex interaction between a numbers of different factors. Given the complex nature of cognitive development, as well as the ever-changing nature of the environment in which we live, we might never be able to fully untangle the effects of our environment from those of our biology. Approaches such as the dynamic systems approach is attempting to unravel the complexities of development and construct a theoretical framework that explains how a multitude of factors interact and give rise to development in many cognitive areas. Although some researchers and theorists claim that such a task is an impossible one, it is an approach to be admired. All too often, developmental psychologists have oversimplified matters, concentrated on links between a limited number of factors and failed to see the whole picture. Human cognition is complicated, dynamic, and reflexive; the way that we study it must take this into consideration and study human cognition in real-life contexts as much as possible.

Studying cognition in the real world might have its benefits but it also has its limitations. Only by devising experimental procedures that isolate factors that influence specific abilities and developments can we reach firm conclusions as to whether they do influence development and the extent to which they do so.

Given that we will never be able to access thoughts directly, all we can ever hope to have is a "best guess" explanation for development based on our observations of behaviour and brain activity. Although this might seem a bit depressing, the future isn't as bleak as it might seem. The fact that we have realised that cognitive development is far from straightforward is a positive step in the right direction. So what can we conclude?

The nature of development

The overall pattern of development is very complex indeed. From what we have seen, children's behaviour often suggests that their thinking is remarkably inconsistent across both domains and situations. This is because there are always a number of factors influencing children's thinking at any one time. Some of these factors are external and others are internal. Those that are internal are determined by biology and innate constraints on development. The biological structures that underlie thought are themselves a product of experience to some extent, however. We have seen that learning results in structural changes to the brain and that experience is fundamental for brain development. Environmental factors also affect development. As we have seen, the experiences that children have determine the extent to which they acquire domain-specific knowledge. This, in turn, affects the extent to which domain-general processes can be applied in different situations. Given that children's internal motivation and capabilities, past experience, and the situation they are faced with at the time all affect their thinking, it seems that there are no simple relationships between individual factors and children's performance on a specific cognitive task.

Constraints on development

In Chapter 1 we considered how developmental psychologists have come to realise that innateness is best considered in terms of how it constrains development. The deterministic view that development is a result of brain maturation alone has now been discounted. Elman et al., (1996) described three types of innate constraint: architectural, representational, and chronotopic. We will consider each of these in turn. Before we do, though, we must remember that even these types of innate constraint seem to be related to each other in a complex way.

Development is constrained by brain development. The development of the brain is said to constitute an architectural constraint on development, according to Elman's description. Sensory and perceptual systems and the brain structures that support these appear to be nearing maturity at birth and require only minimal environmental input for them to become fully operational. By contrast, other cognitive systems are far from fully developed and need much more environmental input to develop. These cognitive processes tend to be those that rely on the development of cortical structures, the development of which occurs mainly after birth. Of particular importance seems to be the development of the prefrontal cortex, which is associated with the regulation and planning of actions; that is, it is associated with executive function. Executive function is a component of working memory. The development of working memory, a domain-general component of the cognitive system, constrains development. The manipulation of information depends on the development of executive function, and this is limited by the development of the brain systems that support such cognitive activity. The development of executive function also affects the capacity of working memory, because its development allows for information to be organised more effectively, which frees up more space in working memory for the manipulation of information. There is a two-way interaction between information stored in long-term memory and the activity that takes place in working memory. Given that working memory is where cognitive activity takes place, the more space available, the better. More space allows for more complex computations and therefore more complex thinking. The development of working memory and the acquisition of domain-specific knowledge limits reasoning and development in a number of areas, including reading, theory of mind, and language.

During the first year or so of a baby's life, the architecture of the brain does not allow for the formation of explicit memories (see Chapters 2 and 3). As a result, infants are constrained by a lack of conscious access to their representations. When such constraints are no longer there, children have the capacity to actively access their knowledge; both the representations that they have stored in the long-term memory and the processes that they apply to these when processing information. This allows for the construction of explicit concepts and theoretical frameworks specifying the relationships between these concepts. Representational constraints of development are not large, it seems. Once the structure of the brain has developed to the extent that it can support explicit representations, no further constraints on development appear to exist.

Architectural and representational constraints on development are related in that the development of the brain determines the types of representation that can be formed. Similarly, architectural constraints are related to chronotopic constraints that specify the order in which specific developments occur. Evolution appears to have done a particularly good job at ensuring that we are born with those abilities that are most likely to ensure our survival and kick-start development. Neonates are equipped with all they need to begin accumulating knowledge about their world. They have a full complement of neurons and the ability to learn. Their sensory systems are in pretty good working order and they appear to have the ability to impose order on the sensory information that they receive; that is, they have a well-developed perceptual system. Indeed, the perceptual abilities of infants are the only area in which we could claim that infants have some innate knowledge. Neonates appear to be able to apply a few basic guiding principles (implicitly, of course!) so that they can isolate individual objects and events in their environment.

Newborns are born with preferences for some stimuli over

others. This focuses their attention on these things, predisposing them to learn about some things before others. These biases are domain-specific. Infants focus on movement, on faces, and on human speech, suggesting that the formation of attachments with other humans is fundamentally important. Not only do these biases pave the way for the development of social cognitive abilities such as the development of an understanding of mind, they lay the foundations for language development, which in turn allows for the development of formal skills such as reading and writing. This is no surprise if we consider that humans have evolved to be social beings who communicate with each other both for fun and in the pursuit of knowledge. Other people figure highly in children's cognitive development because they both actually teach children things and they are often imitated. It is therefore in children's interest to form relationships with other people; the social experiences that a child has are invaluable.

The importance of experience

Innate constraints on information processing operate from the inside out, with the internal structure and functioning of the brain constraining the processing of incoming information. Obviously, the brain can only sort and process information that it receives. As a result, environmental input and experience is vital for development. From the outset, the information that we receive from the outside world affects the extent to which brain structures and knowledge can be operationalised. For example, biases in attention can operate only on incoming information; no cognitive development would occur if there were no experiences. The processes that we apply when thinking have to be applied to something and this is where representations come in. Although the format of these is somewhat constrained by brain structure, as we have seen, the content of representations depends on experience. From before birth children begin to accumulate knowledge, and this knowledge informs their behaviour and thought. Whereas innate constraints limit the extent to which we can represent and process information, the experiences that we have determine the pattern of cognitive development of each individual.

The domain-specific nature of development appears to be attributable to the amount of input received within different domains, to some extent at least. Children who have been exposed to many similar problem-solving situations, for example, are likely to be better at problem-solving that particular type of problem than their counterparts who have not experienced similar situations before. Whereas innate predispositions to attend to and learn about some things earlier than others appears to give us a kick-start in some domains, the knowledge base that children have seems to affect development within all domains. Background knowledge and experience have a big impact on children's competencies in all of the areas of development that we have considered in this book.

The brain and its function

Some areas of the brain are associated with specific functions. The areas responsible for motor control and sensory function are distinct from others, and these distinctions are present at birth. The cerebral cortex is the most underdeveloped part of the brain at birth. This is where representations are stored in the form of connections between neurons. Given that neonates have not had much of an opportunity to learn anything and therefore to form representations of anything (apart from a few sounds), it is not surprising that it is this part of the brain that develops the most after children are born.

Early neurological theories suggested that different parts of the brain are responsible for the processing of information within a specific domain and therefore that the brain and the development of cognition is modular. More recent evidence contradicts this suggestion on two counts. First, when performing specific cognitive tasks, brain activity appears to be spread across several brain areas at any one time; no one area seems to be implicated in the procession of say, theory of mind or language computations. Second, the specific areas of the cortex that come to support specific functions do not appear to be fixed. Rather, the brain appears to be developmentally plastic. Impairments in one area result in functions normally associated with it being localised in other parts of the brain. These brain areas are often associated with particular functions in adults. It seems that the brain is not modular at birth as Fodor (1983) suggests, rather it *becomes* that way; modularisation is progressive.

At birth there are differences in the neurological structure of different areas of the cortex. These differences seem to be specialised for specific computations. For example, the left temporal lobe seems suited to the processing of rapidly presented auditory information (as we saw in Chapter 5). The brain areas that are the best suited to the processing of different types of information do so preferentially. However, if a brain region is damaged, other areas take up those representations that are normally associated with the damaged area. This appears to be the case with language, for example. Although the left hemisphere tends to be associated with language (as evidenced by the finding that adults who suffer left-hemisphere damage tend to have problems with language), damage to the left hemisphere before or shortly after birth results in language being predominantly processed in the right hemisphere.

These conclusions paint a relatively optimistic picture for those who have problems as a result of genetic abnormalities to the brain, as plasticity will allow for the localisation of functions in parts of the brain not normally associated with them. Likewise, those who experience brain damage as a result of an accident can develop compensatory strategies that don't rely on the damaged areas; but only if it occurs early on in development.

Implications for theories of cognitive development

Piaget was the founder of developmental psychology and for that we should be grateful. He also made some very insightful observations that paved the way for other researchers and theorists. He was the first to acknowledge that the child is an active participant in development (at least academically), that both genes and environment interact in cognitive development, and to explain how a reflexive infant develops into a reflective adult. He thus pioneered the constructivist position. The evidence suggests that Piaget got a few things wrong, though. First, development is not stage like. The cognitive strategies that children use vary at any time across both domain and context because, as we have seen, other factors affect their implementation.

Second, innate constraints on development are not as tight as Piaget would have had us believe. Evidence from neurological studies has shown that although he was right to emphasise the transition from implicit to explicit thought, the later representational formats that he described to account for the development of things such as the capacity for logical thought and scientific reasoning, do not seem to be innately constrained.

More recent theories of development have taken these findings into consideration and differ in terms of the aspects of development that they concentrate on and the relative importance accorded to the influence of environmental and biological factors on development. Most theories that we have considered in this text are limited in their scope and focus. This isn't a bad thing though! Given the complexity of human cognition, we have to break things down and study processes in isolation. We can then fit the pieces together to get a clearer picture of development; it's a bit like a giant jigsaw!

Although computer simulations of cognitive processes inform our understanding of the way in which cognitive development *could* proceed in specific areas, they tend to be limited to the description of a few basic cognitive processes. For example, Siegler's overlapping waves approach seems to provide a good description of development in a few key areas but computer simulations have proved successful only at modelling processes that have clearly defined optimal strategies. Theory theory accounts (e.g. Gopnik & Meltzoff, 1997; Perner, 1991) provide a clear description of the processes involved in the organisation of information and the construction of theories, but pay little attention to innate constraints on development.

The dynamic systems approach seems one of the most promising because it seeks to describe the complex interactions involved in development. This involves incorporating all of the research findings that we have to date into one huge model. This is going to be a lengthy process given the amount of knowledge that we already have about cognitive development, let alone the amount of information that we don't have. Perhaps one day this dream will be realised; fingers crossed.

Educational applications

Given the complexity of development, educators have a lot to consider when devising education programmes to ensure the best for our children. Perhaps it is because of this that many of the systems that we have in place today are based on rather outdated ideas. For example, the UK government's recent numeracy strategy appears to have reverted back to a rather behaviourist approach whereby children are taught to recite times tables in a traditional way. This "Walton-esque" style of teaching was rejected in the 1970s in favour of a more progressive approach based on Piaget's theory of cognitive development (an approach known as discovery learning). The basic principle here was that children work things out for themselves and that the teacher's role is to provide suitable learning opportunities for children. This approach is still widely incorporated into educational policy today. However, the emphasis has shifted slightly in recent years with more actual knowledge-based teaching taking place. This has resulted from the recognition that domain-specific background knowledge also has a significant role to play in cognitive development. This is all rather speculative; the point being made is that research and theory *have* to inform educational policy if education is going to serve its purpose. After all, understanding the way that children's thinking develops is of little use unless we can cash-in on that understanding somehow. So what advice can we give to educators so that children's cognitive development is maximised?

From what we have seen in this book it seems that several things need to be taken into account when teaching children. First, we need to be aware of innate constraints on development and not push children beyond their capabilities. This would result in low self-esteem and a decrease in the motivation to learn, both of which have been shown to be important factors. Children also need to be provided with adequate background knowledge. The more knowledge that children have about a particular area or a particular type of problem solving, the more efficiently they can apply the appropriate strategy when dealing with a situation, whether that be reading, problem solving, or whatever. To maximise the amount of information that children represent and so incorporate into their conceptual frameworks (which is obviously an important part of cognitive development) we need to motivate children to learn. After all, one of the first steps in the chain of events that is cognition is attending to information in the first place. If children aren't attending to information, they are not going to learn. Motivating children to focus on the right information is the third thing that educators should aim to do.

Children's ability to reflect on their own thinking has repeatedly been shown to affect cognitive abilities. This metacognitive awareness allows for the conscious consideration of both what is already known and how new information is processed. By consciously considering the content of representations inconsistencies in thought can be identified. As a result of this, information is reorganised so that it is internally consistent. By consciously considering the way in which information is processed, strategy use is evaluated and this results in changes to the way in which these strategies are applied across different situations and domains. Teachers would therefore be advised to point out to children the strategy that they are using, suggest alternatives, point to inconsistencies in children's explanations and involve children in active consideration of the cognitive activities that they engage in.

Developmental disorders

One of the most important things that we have learned from the theory and research presented in this book is that the brain appears to be developmentally plastic. Impairments such as those suffered by dyslexics can often be compensated for providing that problems are identified early on and appropriate intervention programmes are devised. However, many developmental disorders appear to have a genetic basis. Those with autism or Williams syndrome suffer from specific impairments to abilities that cannot be taught or facilitated. Disorders of this sort seem to result from impairments to the ability to perform specific cognitive computations. As some computations are used in some domains more than others, this results in the distinctive pattern of impairment associated with each of these disorders.

Final comment

Cognitive development is not an easy thing to explain, but then again, interesting things are never easily explainable; maybe that's what makes them interesting! In recent years, technological advances have allowed us to access human thought in a way that was for a long time impossible. We can now simulate cognitive processes and measure brain activity directly. Although we can never assume that brain structure and cognitive function are directly related, studying brain function alongside cognitive activity and behaviour gives a more complete picture of cognition and its development. By combining our knowledge of the mind and brain we are working towards a more integrated and coherent explanation of the development of human thought. We are doing what children do, it seems; trying to develop a coherent conceptual framework to explain how various concepts are related to each other. Although we try and apply our advanced scientific reasoning to this problem, it is still proving to be a difficult one to solve!

References

Adams, M.J. (1990) *Beginning to read: Thinking about learning about print.* Cambridge, MA: MIT Press.

Astington, J.W., & Gopnik, A. (1988) Knowing you've changed your mind: Children's understanding of representational change. In J.W. Astington, P. L. Harris, & D. R. Olson (Eds.) *Developing theories of mind.* New York: Cambridge University Press.

Avis, M., & Harris, P. (1991) Belief-desire reasoning amongst Baka children: Evidence for a universal conception of mind. *Child Development, 62,* 460–467.

Baddeley, A. (1990) *Human memory: Theory and practice.* Hove, UK: Lawrence Erlbaum Associates.

Baddeley, A.D., & Hitch, G.J. (1974) Working memory. In G. Bower (Ed.) *The psychology of learning and motivation: Advances in research and theory* (Vol. 8). New York: Academic Press.

Baillargeon, R. (1986) Representing the existence and

location of hidden objects: Object permanence in 6- and 8-month-old infants. *Cognition, 23,* 21–41.

Baillargeon, R., Spelke, E.S., & Wasserman, S. (1985) Object permanence in 5-month-old infants. *Cognition, 20,* 191–208.

Baker, L. (1994) Fostering metacognitive development. In H.W. Reese (Ed.) *Advances in child development and behaviour* (Vol. 25). San Diego: Academic Press.

Baker-Ward, L., Ornstein, P., & Holden, D. (1984) *Influences on human development: A longitudinal perspective.* Boston, MA: Kluwer Nijhoff.

Baldwin, D.A. (1991) Infants' contribution to the achievement of joint reference. *Child Development, 62,* 875–890.

Baldwin, D.A. (1993) Infant's ability to consult the speaker for clues to word meaning. *Journal of Child Language, 20,* 395–418.

Bangert-Downs, R.L. (1993) The word processor as an instructional tool: A meta-analysis of word processing in writing instruction. *Review of Educational Research, 63,* 69–93.

Baron-Cohen, S. (1989a) Social and pragmatic deficits in autism: Cognitive or affective? *Journal of Autism and Developmental Disorders, 18,* 379–402.

Baron-Cohen, S. (1989b) The autistic child's theory of mind: A case of specific developmental delay. *Journal of Child Psychology and Psychiatry, 30,* 285–298.

Baron-Cohen, S. (1989c) Are autistic children behaviourists? An examination of their mental-physical and appearance-reality distinctions. *Journal of Autism and Developmental Disorders, 19,* 579–600.

Baron-Cohen, S. (1992) Out of sight or out of mind: Another look at deception in autism. *Journal of Clinical Psychology and Psychiatry, 33,* 1141–1155.

Baron-Cohen, S. (1995) *Mindblindness: An essay on autism and theory of mind.* Cambridge, MA: MIT Press.

Baron-Cohen, S. (1996) Autism: A specific cognitive disorder of "mindblindness". In P. Shattock & G. Linfoot (Eds.) *Autism on the agenda.* London: The National Autistic Society.

Baron-Cohen, S., & Goodhart, F. (1994) The "seeing leads to knowing" deficit in autism: The Pratt and Bryant probe. *British Journal of Developmental Psychology, 12,* 397–402.

Baron-Cohen, S., & Hammer, J. (1997) Parents of children with Asperger syndrome: What is the cognitive phenotype? *Journal of Cognitive Neuroscience, 9,* 548–554.

Baron-Cohen, S., Leslie, A.M., & Frith, U. (1985) Does the autistic child have a "theory of mind"? *Cognition, 21,* 37–46.

Baron-Cohen, S., Leslie, A.M., & Frith, U. (1986) Mechanical, behavioural and intentional understanding of picture stories in autistic children. *British Journal of Developmental Psychology, 4,* 113–125.

Baron-Cohen, S., Ring, H., Moriarty, J., Shmitz, P., Costa, D., & Ell, P. (1994a) Recognition of mental state terms: A clinical study of autism and a functional neuroimaging study of normal adults. *British Journal of Psychiatry, 165,* 640–649.

Baron-Cohen, S., Tager-Flusberg, H., & Cohen, D. (1994b) *Understanding other minds. Perspectives from autism.* Oxford: Oxford University Press.

Bartsch, K., & Wellman, H.M. (1995) Young children's attribution of action to beliefs and desires. *Child Development, 60,* 946–964.

Bates, E. (1994) *Language development in children after early focal injury.* Paper presented at the 9th International Conference of Infant Studies, Paris, France.

Bates, E., O'Connell, B., & Shore, C. (1987) Language and communication in infancy. In J. Osofsky (Ed.) *Handbook of infant development.* New York: Wiley.

Bateson, G. (1976) A theory of play and fantasy. In J.S. Bruner, A. Jolly, & K. Sylava (Eds.) *Play: its role in development and evolution.* New York: Basic Books.

Bauer, P.J., & Mandler, J.M. (1989) Putting the horse before the cart: The use of temporal order in recall of events by one-year-old children. *Developmental Psychology, 28,* 197–206.

Bauer, P.J., & Shore, C.M. (1987) Making a memorable event: Effects of familiarity and organisation on young children's recall of action sequences. *Cognitive Development, 2,* 227–238.

Bereiter, C., & Scardamalia, M. (1987) From conversation to composition: The role of instruction in a developmental process. In R. Glaser (Ed.) *Advances in instructional psychology* (Vol. 2). Hillsdale, NJ: Lawrence Erlbaum Associates, Inc.

Bernieri, F.J., Reznick, J.S., & Rosenthal, R. (1988) Synchrony, pseudo-synchrony and dissynchrony: Measuring the entrainment process in mother-infant dyads. *Journal of Personality and Social Development, 54,* 243–253.

Bialystok, E. (1996) Preparing to read: The foundations of literacy. In H.W. Reese (Ed.) Advances in child development and behaviour, Vol. 26. San Diego, CA: Academic Press.

Bjorklund, D.F. (2000) *Children's thinking: Developmental function and individual differences.* Belmont, CA: Wadsworth.

Bloom, P., & German, T. P. (2000) Two reasons to abandon the false belief task as a test of theory of mind. *Cognition, 77(1),* 283–286.

REFERENCES

Bohannon, J.N., MacWhinney, B., & Snow, C.E. (1990) No negative evidence revisited: Beyond learnability, or, who has to prove what to whom? *Developmental Psychology, 26,* 221–226.

Bower, T.G.R., Broughton, J.M., & Moore, M.K. (1971) Development of the object concept as manifested in the tracking behaviour of infants between 7 and 20 weeks of age. *Journal of Experimental Psychology, 11,* 182–193.

Bower, T.G.R., & Patterson, J.G. (1973) The separation of place movement and object in the world of the infant. *Journal of Experimental Child Psychology, 23,* 391–401.

Bradley, L., & Bryant, P.E. (1983) Categorising sounds and learning to read: A causal connection. *Nature, 301,* 419–521.

Bradley, L., & Bryant, P. (1985) *Rhyme and reason in reading and spelling.* Ann Arbor, MI: University of Michigan Press.

Bradley, L., & Bryant, P.E. (1985) *Children's reading problems: Psychology and education.* Oxford: Blackwell.

Braine, M. (1971) The acquisition of language in the infant and child. In C. Reed (Ed.) *The learning of language.* New York: Appleton-Century-Crofts.

Brainerd, C.J., & Reyner, V.F. (1993) Mere memory testing creates false memories in children. *Developmental Psychology, 32,* 467–478.

Brothers, L., & Ring, B. (1992) A neuroethological framework for the representation of minds. *Journal of Cognitive Neuroscience, 4,* 107–118.

Brown, R. (1973) *A first language: The early stages.* Cambridge, MA: Harvard.

Brown, R., & Hanlon, C. (1970) Derivational complexity and order of acquisition in child speech. In J.R. Hayes (Ed.) *Cognition and the development of language.* New York: Wiley.

Brown, A.L., & Scott, M.S. (1971) Recognition for pictures in preschool children. *Journal of Experimental Child Psychology, 11,* 401–412.

Brown, A.L., & Smiley, S.S. (1977) The development of strategies for studying texts. *Child Development, 49,* 1076–1088.

Bruce, D.J. (1964) The analysis of word sounds. *British Journal of Educational Psychology, 34,* 158–170.

Bruner, J.S. (1966) On cognitive growth. In J.S. Bruner, R.R. Oliver, & P.M. Greenfield (Eds.) *Studies in cognitive growth.* New York: Wiley.

Bruner, J.S. (1993) *Child's talk: Learning to use language.* New York: W.W. Norton.

Bushnell, E., Sai, F., & Mullin, J. (1989) Neonatal recognition of the mother's face. *British Journal of Experimental Psychology, 7,* 3–15.

Bushnell, I.W. (1982) Discrimination of faces by young infants. *Journal of Experimental Psychology, 33*, 298–308.

Butterfield, E., & Siperstein, G.N. (1974) Influence of contingent auditory stimulation upon nonnutritional sucking. In J. Bosma (Ed.) *Oral Sensation and Perception: The Mouth of the Infant.* Springfield, IL: Charles C. Thomas.

Butterworth, G. (1977) Object disappearance and error in Piaget's stage 4 task. *Journal of Experimental Child Psychology, 23*, 391–401.

Carroll, M., Byrne, B., & Kirsner, K. (1985) Autobiographical memory and perceptual learning. A developmental study using picture recognition, naming latency and perceptual identification. *Memory and Cognition, 13*, 273–279.

Case, R. (1985) *Intellectual development: A systematic reinterpretation.* New York: Academic Press.

Ceci, S.J., & Bruck, M. (1993) Suggestibility of the child witness: A historical review and synthesis. *Psychological Bulletin, 113*, 403–439.

Ceci, S., & Liker, J. (1986) A day at the races: A study of IQ, cognitive complexity and expertise. *Journal of Experimental Psychology: General 115*, 255–266.

Chall, J.S. (1979) The great debate: Ten years later, with a modest proposal for reading stages. In L.B. Resnick & P.A. Weaver (Eds.) *Theory and practice in early reading.* Hillsdale, NJ: Lawrence Erlbaum Associates Inc.

Changeux, J-P. (1985) *Neuronal man: The biology of mind.* New York: Pantheon.

Charman, T., Ruffman, T., & Clements, W. (2002) Is there a gender difference in false belief development? *Social Development, 11*, 1–10.

Chen, Z., Sanchez, R.P., & Campbell, T. (1997) From beyond to within their grasp: The rudiments of analogical reasoning in 10- and 13-month-olds. *Developmental Psychology, 33*, 790–801.

Cheng, P.W., & Holyoak, K.J. (1985) Pragmatic reasoning schemas. *Cognitive Psychology, 18*, 293–238.

Chi, M., Feltovich, P., & Glaser, R. (1981) Categorization and representation in physics problems by experts and novices. *Cognitive Science, 5*, 121–152.

Chomsky, N. (1965) *Aspects of the theory of syntax.* Cambridge, MA: MIT Press.

Chomsky, N. (1981) *Lectures on government and binding.* Dordrecht: Foris.

Clark, H.H. & Clark, E.V. (1977) *Psychology and Language.* New York: Harcourt, Brace, Jovanovitch.

REFERENCES

Clifton, R.K., Rochat, P., Litovsky, R., & Perris, E. (1991) Object representation guides infants' reaching in the dark. *Journal of Experimental Psychology: Human Perception and Performance, 17(2)*, 323–329.

Clubb, P.A., Nida, R.E., Merritt, K., & Ornstein, P.A. (1993) Visiting the doctor: Children's knowledge and memory. *Cognitive Development, 8*, 361–372.

Cohen, L.B., & Caputo, N.F. (1978) *Instructing infants to respond to perceptual stereotypes*. Paper presented at the Midwestern Psychological Association Convention, Chicago, IL.

Coltheart, M., Davelaar, E., Jonasson, J.T., & Besner, D. (1977) *Access to the internal lexicon. Attention and performance*. London: Academic Press.

Connelly, V., Johnston, R., & Thompson, G.B. (2001) The effects of phonics instruction on the reading comprehension of beginning readers. *Reading and Writing, 14*, 423–457.

Conway, M. (1990) On bias in autobiographical recall: Retrospective adjustment following disconfirmed expectations. *The Journal of Social Psychology, 130*, 183–189.

Curtiss, S. (1979) Genie: Language and cognition. *UCLA Working Papers in Cognitive Linguistics 1*, 15–62.

Daneman, M., & Blenerhassett, A. (1984) How to access the listening comprehension skills of prereaders. *Journal of Educational Psychology, 76*, 1372–1381.

Daneman, M., & Green, I. (1986) Individual differences in comprehending and producing words in context. *Journal of Memory and Language, 25*, 1–18.

Davis, K. (1947) Final note on a case of severe social isolation. *American Journal of Sociology, 52*, 432–437.

DeCaspar, A.J., & Fifer, W.P. (1980) Of human bonding: Newborns prefer their mother's voice. *Science, 208*, 1174–1176.

DeCasper, A.J., Lecanuet, J-P., Busnel, M-C., Granier-Deferre, C., & Maugeais, R. (1994) Fetal reactions to recurrent maternal speech. *Infant Behaviour and Development, 17*, 159–164.

DeCaspar, A.J., & Spence, M.J. (1986) Prenatal speech influences newborns' perception of speech sounds. *Infant Behaviour and Development, 9*, 113–150.

DeGroot, A D (1965) *Thought and choice in chess*. The Hague: Mouton.

DeLoache, J.S. (1987) Rapid change in the symbolic functioning of very young children. *Science, 238*, 1556–1557.

DeLoache, J.S. (1989) Young children's understanding of the correspondence between a scale model and a larger space. *Cognitive Development, 4*, 121–139.

DeLoache, J.S. (1991) Symbolic functioning in very young children: Understanding of pictures and models. *Child Development, 62*, 736–752.

DeLoache, J.S., Cassidy, D.J., & Brown, A.L. (1985) Precursors of mnemonic strategies in very young children's memory for the location of hidden objects. *Child Development, 56*, 125–137.

DeLoache, J., Miller, K., & Pierroutsakos, S. (1998) Reasoning and problem solving. In D. Kuhn and R. Siegler (Eds.) *The handbook of child psychology: Vol. 2. Cognition, perception and language*. New York: Riley.

DeLoache, J.S., Miller, K.F., & Rosengren, K.S. (1997) The credible shrinking room: Very young children's performance with symbolic and non-symbolic relations. *Psychological Science, 8*, 308–313.

Dempster, F.N. (1981) Resistance to interference: Developmental changes in a basic processing mechanism. In M.L. Howe & R. Pasnak (Eds.) *Emerging themes in cognitive development: Vol. 1. Foundations*. New York: Springer-Verlag.

Denham, S.A. (1986) Social cognition, prosocial behaviour and emotion in preschoolers. *Child Development, 57*, 194–201.

Dennett, D. (1978) Beliefs about beliefs. *Behavioural and Brain Sciences, 1*, 568–570.

Diamond, A. (1985) Development of the ability to use recall to guide action as indicated by infants' performance on AB. *Child Development, 56*, 868–883.

Dias, M., & Harris, P.L. (1988) The influence of the imagination on the reasoning of young children. *British Journal of Developmental Psychology, 8*, 305–318.

Dunn, J., Brown, J., & Beardsall, L. (1991) Family talk about feeling states and children's later understanding of others' emotions. *Developmental Psychology, 27*, 448–455.

Ellis, A.W., & Young, A.W. (1988) *Human cognitive neuropsychology*. Hove, UK: Psychology Press.

Ellis, N., & Large, B. (1988) The development of reading: As you seek so shall you find. *British Journal of Developmental Psychology, 78*, 1–28.

Ellis, S., & Siegler, R.S. (1997) Planning and strategy choice, or why don't children plan when they should? In S.L. Friedman & E.K. Sholnick (Eds.) *Why, how and when do we plan: The developmental psychology of planning*. Hillsdale, NJ: Lawrence Erlbaum Associates, Inc.

Elman, J. L. (1992) Grammatical structure and distributed representations. In S. Davis (Ed.) *Connectionism: Theory and practice*. New York: Oxford University Press.

235

REFERENCES

Elman, J.L., Bates, E.A., Johnson, M.H., Karmiloff-Smith, A., Parisis, D., & Plunkett, K. (1996) *Re-thinking innateness: A connectionist perspective on development*. Cambridge, MA: MIT Press.

Fabricius, W. (1988) The development of forward search in pre-schoolers. *Child Development, 59*, 1473–1488.

Fantz, R.L. (1961) The origin of form perception. *Scientific American, 204*, 66–72.

Farrar, M.J. (1992) Negative evidence and grammatical morpheme acquisition. *Developmental Psychology, 28*, 90–98.

Farrar, M.J., & Goodman, G.S. (1990) Developmental changes in event memory. *Child Development, 63*, 173–187.

Fenson, L., Dale, P., Resnick, S., Bates, E., Thal, D., & Pethick, S.J. (1994) Variability in early communicative development. *Monographs for the Society for Research in Child Development, 59*, 1–73.

Fernald, A., & Kuhl, P. (1987) Acoustic determinants of infant perception for motherese speech. *Infant Behaviour and Development, 10*, 279–293.

Fischer, K.W. (1980) A theory of cognitive development: The control and construction of hierarchies of skills. *Psychological Review, 87*, 477–531.

Fischhoff, B. (1975) Hindsight is not equal to foresight: The effect of outcome knowledge on judgement under uncertainty. *Journal of Experimental Psychology: Human Perception and Performance, 1*, 288–299.

Fivush, R., & Hammond, N.R. (1990) Autobiographical memory across the pre-school years: Toward reconceptualising infantile amnesia. In R. Fivush & J.A. Hudson (Eds.) *Knowing and remembering in young children*. Cambridge: Cambridge University Press.

Flavell, J. (1971) Stage-related properties of cognitive development. *Cognitive Psychology, 2*, 421–453.

Flavell, J. (1985) *Cognitive development*. Englewood-Cliffs, NJ: Prentice-Hall.

Flavell, J.H., Flavell, E.R., & Green, F.L. (1983) Development of the appearance-reality distinction. *Cognitive Psychology, 15*, 95–120.

Flavell, J., & Wellman, H. (1977) Metamemory. In R. Kail & J. Hagen (Eds.) *Perspectives on the development of memory and cognition*. Hillsdale, NJ: Lawrence Erlbaum Associates, Inc.

Flowers, D.L., Wood, F.B., & Naylor, C.E. (1991) Regional cerebral blood flow correlates of language processes in reading disabilities. *Archives of neurology, 48*, 637–643.

Fodor, J.A. (1983) *The modularity of mind*. Cambridge, MA: MIT Press.

Fodor, J. (1992) A theory of the child's theory of mind. *Cognition, 44*, 283–296.

Frith, U. (1985) Beneath the surface of developmental dyslexia. In K. Petterson, M. Coltheart, & J. Marshall (Eds.) *Surface dyslexia*. Hove, UK: Psychology Press.

Frith, U., & Snowling, M. (1983) Reading for meaning and reading for sound in autistic and dyslexic children. *Journal of Developmental Psychology, 1*, 329–342.

Fromkin, V., Krashen, S., Curtiss, S., Rigler, D., & Rigler, M. (1974) The development of language in Genie: A case of language acquisition beyond the "critical period". *Brain and Language 1*, 81–107.

Frye, D., Zelazo, P., & Palfai, T. (1995) Theory of mind and rule-based reasoning. *Cognitive Development, 10*, 438–528.

Funnell, E. (1983) Phonological processes in reading: New evidence from acquired dyslexia. *British Journal of Developmental Psychology, 74*, 159–180.

Galaburda, A.M., Sherman, G.F., Rosen, G.D., Aboitiz, F., & Geschwind, N. (1985) Developmental dyslexia: Four consecutive patients with cortical anomalies. *Annals of Neurology, 18*, 222–232.

Garner, R. (1990) When children and adults do not use learning strategies: Toward a theory of settings. *Review of Educational Research, 60*, 517–529.

Gerstadt, C.L., Hong, Y.J., & Diamond, A. (1994) The relationship between cognition and action: Performance of children 3½–7 on a Stroop-like day–night test. *Cognition, 53*, 129–153.

Gibson, J.J. (1979) *The ecological approach to visual perception*. Boston: Houghton Mifflin.

Girotto, V., Light, P.H., & Colbourn, C.J. (1988) Pragmatic schemas and conditional reasoning in children. *Quarterly Journal of Experimental Psychology, 40*, 469–482.

Gleitman, L. (1990) The structural sources of verb meanings. *Language Acquisition, 1*, 3–55.

Goldin-Meadow, S., & Mylander, C. (1984) Gestural communication in deaf children: The effects and noneffects of parental input on early language development. *Monographs for the Society for Research in Child Development, 49* (3–4, serial number 207).

Goldstein, K. (1976) The mental changes due to frontal lobe damage. *Journal of Psychology, 17*, 129–153.

Gopnik, A., & Meltzoff, A. (1997) The development of categorisation in the second year and its relation to other cognitive and linguistic developments. *Child Development, 63*, 1091–1103.

REFERENCES

Gopnik, A., & Meltzoff, A.N. (1997) *Words, thoughts, and theories.* Cambridge, MA: MIT Press.

Goswami, U. (1986) Children's use of analogy in learning to read: a developmental study. *Journal of Experimental Child Psychology, 42,* 73–83.

Goswami, U. (1991) *Analogical reasoning in children.* London: Lawrence Erlbaum Associates.

Goswami, U. (1992) *Analogical reasoning in children.* Hillsdale, NJ: Lawrence Erlbaum Associates, Inc.

Goswami, U. (1996) Analogial reasoning and cognitive development. In H.W. Reese (Ed.) *Advances in child development and behaviour.* San Diego: Academic Press.

Goswami, U., & Brown, A. (1989) Melting chocolate and melting snowmen: Analogical reasoning and causal relations. *Cognition, 35,* 69–95.

Goswami, U., & Bryant, P.E. (1990) *Phonological skills and learning to read.* Hove, UK: Lawrence Erlbaum Associates.

Goswami, U., & East, M. (2000) Rhyme and analogy in beginning reading: Conceptual and methodological issues. *Applied Psycholinguistics, 21,* 63–93.

Greenspan, S. (1997) *Growth of the mind.* New York: Addison Wesley.

Grigorenko, E.L. (2001) Developmental dyslexia: An update on genes, brains, and environments. *Journal of Child Psychology and Psychiatry, 42,* 91–125.

Gunstone, R., & Watts, M. (1985) Force and motion. In R. Driver, E. Guesne & A. Tiberghien (Eds.) *Children's ideas in science.* Philadelphia: Open University Press.

Hadwin, J., & Perner, J. (1991) Pleased and surprised: Children's cognitive theory of emotion. *British Journal of Developmental Psychology, 9,* 215–234.

Harris, M., Barlow-Brown, F., & Chasin, J. (1995) The emergence of referential understanding: Pointing and the comprehension of object names. *First Language, 15,* 19–34.

Harris, M., Yeeles, C., Chasin, J., & Oakley, Y. (1995) Symmetries and asymmetries in early lexical comprehension and production. *Journal of Child Language, 22(1),* 1–18.

Harris, P.L. (1973) Perseveration errors in search by young infants. *Child Development, 44,* 28–33.

Harris, P.L. (1991) The work of the imagination. In A. Whiten (Ed.) *Natural theories of mind.* Oxford: Blackwell.

Harris, P.L., Brown, E., Marriott, C., Whittall, S., & Harmer, S. (1991) Monsters, ghosts and witches: Testing the limits of fantasy-reality distinction in young children. *British Journal of Developmental Psychology, 9*, 105–123.

Harris, P.L., & Kavanagh, R.D. (1993) Young children's understanding of pretence. *Monographs of the Society for Research in Child Development, 58*, (Serial No. 231).

Hatano, G. (1993) *Children's concepts of heat and temperature.* Paper presented at SRCD biennial meeting, New Orleans, March 1993.

Hawkins, J., Pea, R., Glick, J., & Schribner, S. (1984) Merds that laugh don't like mushrooms: Evidence for deductive reasoning by pre-schoolers. *Developmental Psychology, 20*, 584–595.

Heath, S.M., Hogben, J.H., & Clark, C.D. (1999) Auditory temporal processing in disabled readers with and without oral language delay. *Journal of Child Psychology and Psychiatry, 40*, 637–647.

Hermelin, B., & O'Connor, N. (1970) *Psychological experiments with autistic children.* Oxford: Pergamon.

Hirsch-Pasek, K., Gleitman, H., Gleitman, L., Golinkoff, R., & Naigles, L. (1988) *Syntactic bootstrapping: Evidence from comprehension.* Boston, MA: Language Conference.

Hirsch-Pasek, K. Golinkoff, R., Fletcher, A., DeGasper Beaubien, F., & Cauley, K. (1985) *In the beginning: One-word speakers comprehend word order.* Paper presented at Boston Language Conference.

Hirsch-Pasek, K., Kemler-Nelson, D.G., Jusczyk, P.W., Wright-Cassidy, K., Druss, B., & Kennedy, L. (1987) Clauses are perceptial units for young infants. *Cognition, 26*, 269–286.

Hood, B., & Willatts, P. (1986) Reaching in the dark to an object's remembered position: Evidence of object permanence in 5 month old infants. *British Journal of Developmental Psychology, 4*, 57–65.

Howe, M.L., & Courage, M.L. (1993) On resolving the enigma of infantile amnesia. *Psychological Bulletin, 113*, 305–326.

Hughes, C., Russell, J. & Robbins, T.W. (1994) Evidence for executive dysfunction in autism. *Neuropsychologia, 32(4)*, 477–492.

Inhelder, B., & Piaget, J. (1958) *The growth of logical thinking.* New York: Basic Books.

Jacobsen, J.L., Boersma, D.C., Fields, R.B., & Olson, K.L. (1983) Paralinguistic features of adult speech to infants and small children. *Child Development, 54*, 436–442.

James, W. (1890) *The principles of psychology.* New York: Holt, Reinhart, and Winston.

Jenkins, J.M., & Astington, J.W. (1996) Cognitive factors and family structure associated with theory of mind development in young children. *Developmental Psychology, 32,* 70–78.

Johnson, C.N. (1997a) The neural basis of cognitive development. In W. Damon (Series Ed.) and D. Kuhn & R.S. Siegler (Vol. Eds.), *Handbook of child psychology: Vol. 2. Cognition, perception and language* (5th ed.). New York: Wiley.

Johnson, M.H. (1997b) *Developmental cognitive neuroscience.* Oxford: Blackwell.

Johnson, D., & Baumann, J. (1984) Word identification. In P. D. Pearson (Ed.) *Handbook of reading research.* New York: Longman.

Johnson, D.W., & Newport, E.L. (1989) Critical period effects in second language learning: The influence of instructional state on the acquisition of English as a second language. *Cognitive Psychology, 21,* 60–99.

Johnson, E.K., & Jusczyk, P.W. (2001) Word segmentation by 8-month-olds: When speech cues count for more than statistics. *Journal of Memory and Language, 44,* 548–567.

Jorm, A.F., & Share, D.L. (1983) Phonological recoding and reading acquisition. *Applied Psycholinguistics, 4,* 103–147.

Joseph, R. (2000) Fetal brain behaviour and cognitive development. *Developmental Psychology, 20,* 81–98.

Jusczyk, P., Hirsch-Pasek, K., Kemler-Nelson, D., Kennedy, L., Woodward, A., & Piowoz, J. (1988) Perception of acoustic correlates of major phrasal units by young infants. Unpublished. Quoted in A. Karmiloff-Smith (1992) *Modularity of mind.* Cambridge, MA: MIT Press.

Kail, R. (1990) *The development of memory in children* (3rd ed.). San Francisco, CA: Freeman.

Kanner, L. (1943) Autistic disturbances of affective contact. *Nervous Child, 2,* 217–250.

Karmiloff-Smith, A. (1992) *Modularity of mind.* Cambridge, MA: MIT Press.

Karmiloff-Smith, A. (1996) *Beyond Modularity: A Developmental Perspective on Cognitive Science.* Cambridge, MA: MIT Press.

Karmiloff-Smith, A., Klima, E., Bellugi, U., Grant, J. & Baron-Cohen, S. (1995) Is there a social module? Language, face processing and theory of mind in individuals with Williams syndrome. *Journal of Cognitive Neuroscience, 7,* 196–208.

Kaye, K., & Marcus, J. (1981) Infant imitation: The sensory–motor agenda. *Developmental Psychology, 17,* 258–265.

Kellman, P.J., & Spelke, E.S. (1983) Perception of partly occluded objects in infancy. *Cognitive Development, 15,* 483–524.

Klima, E.S. & Bellugi, U. (1979) *The Signs of Language*. Cambridge, MA: Harvard University Press.

Kobasigawa, A., Ransom, C.C., & Holland, C.J. (1980) Children's knowledge about skimming. *Alberta Journal of Educational Research, 26*, 169–182.

Kratochwill, T.R., & Goldman, J.A. (1973) Developmental changes in children's judgements of age. *Developmental Psychology, 9*, 358–362.

Kreutzer, M., Leonard, C., & Fraser, J. (1975) An interview study of children's knowledge about memory. *Monographs for the Society for Research in Child Development, 40*, 600–602.

Kuhn, D. (2000) Does memory development belong on an endangered species list? *Child Development, 71*, 21–25.

Landau, B., & Gleitman, L. (1985) *Language and Experience: Evidence from the Blind Child*. Cambridge, MA: Harvard University Press.

Lave, J. (1988) *Cognition in practice: Mind, mathematics and culture in everyday life*. Cambridge: Cambridge University Press.

Leekham, S., & Perner, J. (1991) Does the autistic child have a metarepresentational deficit? *Cognition, 40*, 203–218.

Leslie, A.M. (1987) Pretence and representation: The origins of "theory of mind". *Psychological Review, 94*, 412–426.

Leslie, A.M. (1994) Pretending and believing: Issues in the theory of ToMM. *Cognition, 50*, 211–238.

Leslie, A., & German, T. P. (1995) Knowledge and ability in "theory of mind": One-eyed overview of a debate. In T. Stone & M. Davies (Eds.) *Mental simulation: Evaluation and applications*. Oxford: Blackwell.

Lewis, C., Freeman, N.H., Kyriakidou, C., Maridaki-Kassotaki, K., & Breeidge, D.M. (1996) Social influence on children's false belief access: Specific sibling influences or general apprenticeship? *Child Development, 67*, 2930–2947.

Livingstone, M., Rosen, G., Drislane, F., & Galaburda, A. (1991) Physiological and anatomical evidence for a magnocellular defect in developmental dyslexia. *Proceeding of the National Academy of Sciences, 88*, 7943–7947.

Lundberg, I., Frost, J., & Peterson, O-P. (1988) Effects of an extensive programme for stimulating phonological awareness in pre-school children. *Reading Research Quarterly, 32*, 264–284.

Maclean, M., Bryant, P., & Bradley, L. (1987). Rhymes, nursery rhymes, & reading in early childhood. *Merrill-Palmer Quarterly, 33(3)*, 255–281.

Mandler, G. (1980) Recognizing: The judgment of previous occurrence. *Psychological Review, 87(3)*, 252–271.

Mandler, J.M. (1988) How to build a baby: On the development of an accessible representational system. *Cognitive Development, 3*, 113–136.

Mandler, J.M. (1990) Recall and its verbal expression. In R. Fivush & J. Hudson (Eds.), *Knowing and remembering in young children*. New York: Cambridge University Press.

Mandler, J.M. (1992) How to build a baby II. Conceptual primitives. *Psychological Review, 99*, 587–604.

Mandler, J.M., & McDonough, L. (1995) Long-term recall of event sequences in infancy. *Journal of Experimental Child Psychology, 59*, 457–474.

Maratsos, M., & Matheny, L. (1994) Language specificity and elasticity: Brain and clinical syndrome studies. In L.W. Porter & M. R. Rosenzweig (Eds.) *Annual review of psychology: Vol 45*. Palo Alto, CA: Annual Review, Inc.

Marean, G.C., Werner, L.A., & Kuhl, P.K. (1992) Vowel categorisation by very young infants. *Developmental Psychology, 28*, 396–405.

Markman, E.M. (1992) Constraints on word learning: Speculations about their nature, origins and domain-specificity. In M.R. Gunner & M.P. Maratsos (Eds.) *Modularity and constraints in language and cognition*: The Minnesota symposium on child psychology. Hillsdale, NJ: Lawrence Erlbaum Associates, Inc.

Marsh, G., Desberg, P., & Cooper, J. (1978) Developmental changes in reading. *Journal of Research in Reading, 1(2)*, 136–141.

McClosky, M., Carmazza, A., & Green, B. (1980) Curvilinear motion in the absence of external forces: Naïve beliefs about motion of objects. *Science, 210*, 1139–1141.

McConkie, G.W., & Rayner, K. (1976) Asymmetry in the perceptual span in reading. *Bulletin of Psychodynamic Society, 8*, 365–368.

McDonough, L., Mandler, J.M., McKee, R.D., & Squire, L.R. (1995) The deferred imitation task as a nonverbal measure of declarative memory. *Proceedings of the National Academy of Sciences, 92*, 7580–7584.

Medical Research Council (2001). In Chakrabarti, S. & Fomborne, E. (2001) Pervasive developmental disorders in pre-school children. *The Journal of the American Medical Association (JAMA), 285(24)*, 3093–3099.

Mehler, J., & Dupoux, E. (1994) *What infants know*. Oxford: Blackwell.

Mehler, J., Lambertz, G., Jusczyk, P., & Amiel-Tison, C. (1986) Discrimination de la language maternelle par le nouveau-ne. *Comptes Rendes Academie Des Sciences 303, serie II*, 637–640.

Meltzoff, A.N. (1985) Immediate and deferred imitation in fourteen- and twenty-four-month-old infants. *Child Development 56*, 62–72.

Meltzoff, A.N., & Borton, R.W. (1979) Intermodal matching by human neonates. *Nature, 282*, 403–404.

Meltzoff, A., & Moore, M. (1983) Newborn infants imitate adult facial gestures. *Child Development, 54*, 702–709.

Miles, T., & Miles, E. (1999) *Dyslexia: 100 years on* (2nd ed.). Buckingham, UK: Open University Press.

Miller, G. (1956) The magical number seven plus or minus two: Some limits on our capacity for processing information. *Psychological Review, 63*, 81–97.

Milner, B. (1963) Effects of brain lesions on card-sorting. *Archive of Neurology, 9*, 90–100.

Mitchell, P. (1994) Realism and early conception of mind: A synthesis of phylogenetic and ontogenetic issues. In C. Lewis & P. Mitchell (Eds.) *Children's early understanding of mind: Origins and development* (pp. 19–45). Hove, UK: Lawrence Erlbaum Associates, Inc.

Mitchell, P. (1996) *Acquiring a conception of mind: A review of psychological research and theory*. Hove, UK: Psychology Press.

Mitchell, P., & Lacohee, H. (1991) Children's early understanding of false belief. *Cognition, 39*, 107–127.

Mitchell, P., Robinson, E.J., Isaacs, J.E., & Nye, R.M. (1996) Contamination in reasoning about false belief: An instance of realist bias in adults but not children. *Cognition, 59*, 1–21.

Mitchell, P., & Taylor, L.M. (1999) Shape constancy and theory of mind: Is there a link? *Cognition, 70*, 167–190.

Nelson, K. (1988) Constraints on word learning? *Cognitive Development, 3*, 221–246.

Nelson, K. (1995) The dual category problem in the acquisition of action words. In M. Tomasello & B. Merriman (Eds.) *Beyond names for things: Young children's acquisition of verb meaning*. Hillsdale, NJ: Lawrence Erlbaum Associates, Inc.

Nelson, K. (1993) The psychological and social origins of autobiographical memory. *Psychological Science, 4*, 7–14.

Nelson, K. (1996) *Language in cognitive development: The emergence of the mediated mind*. New York: Cambridge University Press.

Neville, H.J., Bavelier, D., Corina, D., Rauschecker, J., Karni, A., Lalwani, A., Braun, A., Clark, V., Jezzard, P., & Turner, R. (1998) Cerebral organisation for language in deaf and hearing subjects: Biological constraints and effects of experience. *Proceedings of the National Academy of Science, USA, 95*, 922–929.

Newport, E.L. (1990) Maturational constraints on language learning. *Cognitive Science, 14*, 11–28.

Newport, E.L., Gleitman, H. & Gleitman, L.R. (1997) *Talking to Children:*

REFERENCES

Language input and acquisition. Cambridge, MA: Cambridge University Press.

Newport, N. L., & Meier, R. P. (1985) The acquisition of American sign language. D.I. Slobin (ed.). *The crosslinguistic study of language acquisition: Vol. 1. The data*. Hillsdale, NJ: Lawrence Erlbaum Associates, Inc.

Nolen-Hoesksema, S. (2001) *Abnormal psychology (2nd ed.)*. New York: McGraw-Hill.

Norgate, S.H. (1997) Research methods for studying the language of blind children. In N.H. Hornberger & D. Corson (Eds.) *The encyclopaedia of language and education: Vol. 8. Research methods in language and education*. The Netherlands: Kluwer Academic Publishers.

Nunes, T. (1993) Learning mathematics perspectives from everyday life. In R.B. Davis & C.A. Maher (Eds.) *Schools, mathematics and the world of reality*. Needham Heights, MA: Allyn and Bacon.

Nussbaum, J., & Novack, J.D. (1976) An assessment of children's concepts of the earth utilizing structured interview. *Science Education, 60*, 535–550.

Oates, J., & Grayson, A. (2004) *Cognitive and language development in children*. Oxford: Blackwell/The Open University.

Oakhill, J. (1995) Development in reading. In Lee, V.J., and Das Gupta, P. (Eds.) *Children's Cognitive and Language Development*. Oxford: Blackwell/The Open University.

O'Sullivan, J.T. (1996) Children's metamemory about the influence of conceptual relations on recall. *Journal of Experimental Child Psychology, 62*, 1–29.

Ozonoff, S., Pennington, B.F., & Rogers, S.J. (1991) Executive functioning deficits in high-functioning autistic individuals; relationship to theory of mind. *Journal of Child Psychology and Psychiatry, 32*, 1081–1085.

Paris, S.G. (1973) Comprehension of language connectives and propositional logic relationships. *Journal of Child Psychology, (16)*, 728–291.

Pennington, B.F., & Ozonoff, S. (1996) Executive funtion and developmental psychopathology. *Journal of Child Psychology and Psychiatry, 37*, 51–87.

Perlmutter, M. (1986) A life-span view of memory. In P. B. Baltes, D. L. Featherman, & R. M. Learner (Eds.) *Life-span development and behaviour* (Vol. 7). Hillsdale, NJ: Lawrence Erlbaum Associates, Inc.

Perner, J. (1991) *Understanding the representational mind*. London: MIT Press.

Perner, J., & Davies, G. (1991) Understanding the mind as an active information processor: Do young children have a "copy theory of mind?" *Cognition, 39*, 51–69.

Perner, J., Frith, U., Leslie, A.M., & Leekam, S.R. (1989) Exploration of the autistic child's theory of mind: knowledge, belief and communication. *Child Development* 60, 689–700.

Perner, J., Leekam, S. R., & Wimmer, H. (1987) Three-year olds' difficulty with false belief: The case for a conceptual deficit. *British Journal of Developmental Psychology*, 5, 125–137.

Piaget, J. (1951) *Play, dreams and imitation in childhood.* London: Routledge and Kegan Paul.

Piaget, J. (1954) *The origins of intelligence in the child.* London: Routledge and Kegan Paul.

Piaget, J. (1965) *Biologie et connaisance.* Paris: Gallimard.

Piaget, J. (1973) *The child's conception of the world.* (J. Tomlinson & A. Tomlinson, Trans.) London: Paladin.

Piaget, J. (1976) *The Child and Reality: Problems of Genetic Psychology.* Trans. Arnold Rosin. New York: Penguin Books.

Piaget, J., & Inhelder, B. (1958) *The psychology of the child.* New York: Basic Books.

Piaget, J., & Inhelder, B. (1974) *The child's construction of quantities.* London: Routledge and Kegan Paul.

Pilburn, M.D. (1990) Reasoning about logical propositions and success in science. *Journal of Research in Science Teaching,* 27, 887–900.

Pillow, B. (1989) Children's understanding of biased social cognition. *Developmental Psychology,* 27, 539–551.

Pinker, S. (1984) *Language learnability and language development.* Cambridge, MA: Harvard University Press.

Pinker, S. (1989) *Learnability and cognition: The acquisition of argument structure.* Cambridge, MA: MIT Press.

Pinker, S. (1994) *The Language Instinct: the new science of language and mind.* London: Penguin.

Plunkett, K. (1996) *Connectionism and development: Neural networks and the study of change.* New York: Oxford University Press.

Plunkett, K., & Marchman, V. (1993) From rote learning to system building: Aquiring verb morphology in children and connectionist nets. *Cognition,* 48, 21–69.

Pober, B.R., & Dykens, E.M. (1996) Williams syndrome: An overview of medical, cognitive, and behavioural features. *Child Adolescent Psychiatry,* 5, 929–943.

Poulin-Dubois, D. (1999) Infants' disctinction between animate and inanimate objects: The origins of naïve psychology. In P. Rochat (Ed.) *Early social cognition: Understanding others in the first months of life.* Mahwah, NJ: Lawrence Erlbaum Associates, Inc.

Pratt, C., & Bryant, P. (1990) Young children understand that looking leads to knowing (so long as they are looking into a single barrel). *Child Development, 61,* 973–983.

Premack, D., & Woodruff, G. (1978) Does the chimpanzee have a theory of mind? *Behavioural and Brain Sciences, 4,* 515–526.

Quinn, P.C. (1994) The categorisation of above and below spatial relations by young infant. *Child Development, 65,* 58–69.

Rakic, P. (1995) Corticogenesis in human and non-human primates. In M. Gazzaniga (Ed.) *The cognitive neurosciences.* Cambridge, MA: MIT Press.

Ramus, F. (2001) Outstanding questions about phonological processing in dyslexia. *Dyslexia, 7,* 197–212.

Rayner, K., & Pollatsek, A. (1989) *The psychology of reading.* London: Prentice Hall.

Reilly, J.S., Bates, E.A., & Marchman, V.A. (1998) Narrative discourse in children with early focal brain injury. *Brain and Language, 61,* 335–375.

Repacholi, B.M., & Gopnik, A. (1997) Early reasoning about desires: Evidence from fourteen- and eighteen-month-olds. *Developmental Psychology, 33(1),* 12–21.

Robinson, E.J., & Mitchell, P. (1995) Masking of children's early understanding of the representational mind: Backwards explanation versus prediction. *Child Development, 66,* 1022–1039.

Rogoff, B. (1998) Cognition as a collaborative process. In D. Kuhn & R. Siegler (Eds.) *Handbook of child psychology: Vol 2. Cognition, language and perception.* New York: Wiley.

Rogoff, B., Newcombe, N., & Kagan, J. (1984) Planfulness and recognition memory. *Child Development, 45,* 972–977.

Rosenshine, B., & Meister, C. (1994) Reciprocal teaching: A review of research. *Review of Educational Research, 64,* 479–530.

Rovee-Collier, C.K., Sullivan, M.W., Enright, M., Lucas, D., & Fagen, J.W. (1980) Reactivation of infant memory. *Science, 208,* 1159–1161.

Rubia, K., Taylor, E., Smith, A., Okasen, H., Overmeyer, S., & Newman, S. (2001) Neuropsychological analyses of impulsiveness in childhood hyperactivity. *British Journal of Psychiatry, 179,* 199–209.

Ruffman, T., Perner, J., Naito, M., Parkin, L., & Clements, W.A. (1998) Older (but not younger) siblings facilitate false belief understanding. *Developmental Psychology, 34,* 161–174.

Rumbaugh, D. M., & Savage-Rumbaugh, E. S. (1994) Language in comparative perspective. In N. J. Mackintosh (Ed.) *Animal learning and cognition* (pp. 307–333). New York: Academic Press.

Rumelhart, D.E., & McClelland, J.L. (1986) On learning the past tense of English verbs. In J.L. McClelland & D.E. Rumelhart (Eds.) *Parallel distributed processing: Explorations in the microstructure of cognition (Vol 2)*. Cambridge, MA: MIT Press.

Rumsey, J.M., & Hamburger, S.D. (1988) Neuropsychological findings in high functioning men with infantile autism, residual state. *Journal of Clinical and Experimental Neuropsychology, 10,* 201–221.

Russo, R., Nichelli, P., Gibertoni, M., & Cornia, C. (1995) Developmental trends in implicit and explicit memory: A picture completion study. *Journal of Experimental Child Psychology, 59,* 566–578.

Sachs, J.S. (1967) Recognition memory for syntactic and semantic aspects of connected discourse. *Perception and psychophysics, 2,* 437–442.

Saltmarsh, R., Mitchell, P., & Robinson, E.J. (1991) Realism and children's early grasp of mental representation: Belief-based judgements in the state change task. *Cognition, 57,* 297–325.

Saxe, G.B. (1982) Developing forms of arithmetic operations among the Oksapmin of Papua New Guinea. *Developmental Psychology, 18(4),* 583–594.

Saxton, M. (1997) The contrast theory of negative input. *Journal of Child Language, 24,* 139–161.

Scardamalia, M., & Bereiter, C. (1987) Higher levels of agency for children in knowledge building: A challenge for the design of new knowledge media. *The Journal of the Learning Sciences 1(1),* 37–68.

Schacter, D.L., & Moscovich, M. (1984) Infants, amnesics, and dissociable memory systems. In M. Moscovitch (Ed.) *Infant memory: Its relation to normal and pathological memory in humans and other animals*. New York: Plenum.

Schaffer, H. (1984) *The child's entry into a social world*. London: Academic Press.

Scher, A., Amer, T., & Tirosh, E. (2000) Object concept and sleep regulation. *Perceptual and Motor Skills, 91(2),* 402–404.

Schneider, W., & Pressley, M. (1999) *Memory development between 2 and 20*. Berlin: Springer-Verlag.

Shallice, T., & Burgess, P. (1991) Higher cognitive impairments and frontal lobe lesions in man. In H.S. Levin, H.M. Eisenberg, & A.L. Benton (Eds.) *Frontal lobe function and dysfunction*. Oxford: Oxford University Press.

Share, D.L., & Stanovich, K.E. (1995) Cognitive processes in early reading development: Accommodating individual differences into a model of acquisition. *Issues in Education: Contributions for Educational Psychology, 1*, 1–57.

Shinskey, J., & Munakata, Y. (2003) Are infants in the dark about hidden objects? *Developmental Science, 6*, 273–282.

Siegel, L.S., & Ryan, E.B. (1989) The development of working memory in normally achieving and sub-types of learning disabled children. *Child Development, 60*, 973–980.

Siegel, M. (1997) *Knowing children: Experiments in conversation and cognition* (2nd ed.). Hove, UK: Psychology Press.

Siegler, R. (1996) *Emerging minds: The process of change in children's thinking*. New York: Oxford University Press.

Skinner, B. (1957) *Verbal behaviour*. New York: Appleton-Century Crofts.

Slater, A. (1997) Visual organisation in early infancy. In G. Bremner, A. Slater, & G. Butterworth (Eds.) *Infant development: Recent advances*. Hillsdale, NJ: Psychology Press/Lawrence Erlbaum Associates, Inc.

Slater, A., Matlock, A., & Brown, E. (1990) Size constancy at birth: Newborn infants' responses to retinal and real size. *Journal of Experimental Psychology, 49*, 314–322.

Slater, A., & Morrison, V. (1985) Shape constancy and slant perception at birth. *Perception, 14*, 337–344.

Slaughter, V., & Gopnik, A. (1996) Conceptual coherence in the child's theory of mind. *Child Development, 67*, 2967–2989.

Smith, M.U., & Good, R. (1984) Problem solving and classical genetics: Successful versus unsuccessful performance. *Journal of Research in Science Teaching, 21*, 895–912.

Snow, C.E., & Hoefnagel-Hohle, M. (1978) The critical period for language acquisition. Evidence from second language learning. *Child Development, 49*, 1114–1128.

Snowling, M. (1996) Annotation: Contemporary approaches to the teaching of reading. *Journal of Child Psychology and Psychiatry, 37*, 139–148.

Snowling, M.J. (2000) *Dyslexia*. Oxford: Oxford University Press.

Snowling, M.J. (2000) From language to reading and dyslexia. *Dyslexia, 7(1)*, 37–46.

Snowling, M., & Frith, U. (1986) Comprehension in "hyperlexic" readers. *Journal of Experimental Child Psychology, 42*, 392–415.

Snyder, M., & Uranowitz, S.W. (1978) Reconstructing the past: Some cognitive consequences of personal perception. *Journal of Personality and Social Psychology, 36*, 941–950.

Sodian, B., Taylor, C., Harris, P., & Perner, J. (1992) Early deception and the child's theory of mind: False trails and genuine markers. *Child Development, 62,* 468–483.

Sodian, B., & Wimmer, H. (1987) Children's understanding of inference as a source of knowledge. *Child Development, 58,* 424–433.

Spelke, E.S. (1976) Infants' intermodal perception of events. *Cognitive Psychology, 8,* 553–560.

Spelke, E.S. (1988) Where perceiving ends and thinking begins: The apprehension of objects in infancy. In A. Yonas (Ed.) *Perceptual development in infancy.* Hillsdale, NJ: Lawrence Erlbaum Associates, Inc.

Spelke, E.S. (1998). Nature, nurture, and development. In J. Hochberg and J.E. Cutting (Eds.), *Handbook of perception and cognition, 2nd ed: Perception and cognition at century's end.* San Diego, CA: Academic Press.

Stanovich, K.E. (1988) Explaining the differences between the dyslexic and garden variety poor reader: The phonological-core variance-difference model. *Journal of Learning Disabilities, 21,* 590–604.

Stein, J. (2001) The magnocellular theory of developmental dyslexia. *Dyslexia, 7(1),* 12–36.

Stein, N.L., & Levine, L.J. (1989) The casual organisation of emotional knowledge: A developmental study. *Cognition and Emotion, 3,* 343–378.

Steverson, E. (unpublished). Cited in Mitchell, P. (1997) *Introducion to Theory of Mind: Children, Autism and Apes.* London: Edward Arnold.

Sweetenham, J. (1996) What's inside a person's head? Conceiving of the mind as a camera helps children with autism develop an alternative theory of mind. *Cognitive Neuropsychiatry, 1,* 73–88.

Thelen, E., & Smith, L.B. (1994) *A dynamic systems approach to the development of cognition and action.* Cambridge, MA: MIT Press.

Thornton, S. (2002) *Growing minds: An introduction to cognitive development.* New York: Palgrave/MacMillan.

Trehub, S.E., & Rabinovitch, M.S. (1972) Auditory-linguistic sensitivity in early infancy. *Developmental Psychology, 6,* 74–77.

Turkewitz, Z.G., Birch, H.G., & Cooper, K.K. (1966) Responsiveness to simple and complex auditory stimuli in the human newborn. *Developmental Psychobiology, 5,* 7–19.

Usher, J.A., & Neisser, U. (1993) Childhood amnesia and the beginnings of memory for four early life events. *Journal of Experimental Psychology, 122,* 155–165.

Uzgiris, I.C., & Hunt, J.McV. (1975) *Assessment in infancy: Ordinal scales of psychological development.* Urbana, IL: University of Illinois Press.

Vaughan, Jr. W., & Greene, S.L. (1984) Pigeon visual memory capacity. *Journal of Experimental Psychotherapy: Animal Behaviour Processes, 10,* 265–271.

Vygotsky, L. (1962) *Thought and language.* Cambridge, MA: Harvard University Press.

Watson, J.K., Gelman, S.A., & Wellman, H.M. (1988) Young children's understanding of the non-physical nature of thoughts and the physical nature of the brain. *British Journal of Developmental Psychology, 16,* 321–335.

Wellman, H.M. (1990) *The child's theory of mind.* Cambridge, MA: MIT Press.

Wellman, H.M., Cross, D., & Watson, J. (2001) A meta-analysis of theory of mind development: The truth about false belief. *Child Development, 62,* 655–684.

Wellman, H., & Estes, D. (1986) Early understanding of mental entities: A re-examination of childhood realism. *Child Development, 57,* 910–923.

Wellman, H.M., Hollander, M., & Schult, C.A. (1996) Young children's understanding of thought bubbles and thoughts. *Child Development, 67(3),* 768–788.

Whitehurst, G.J., & Lonigan, C.J. (1998) Child development and emergent literacy. *Child Development, 69,* 848–872.

Willatts, P. (1989) Adjustments of means-ends co-ordination and the representation of spatial relations in the production of search errors by infants. *British Journal of Developmental Psychology, 2,* 259–272.

Wilson, T.D., & Brekke, N. (1994) Mental contamination and mental correction: Unwanted influences on judgements and evaluations. *Psychological Bulletin, 116,* 117–142.

Wimmer, H., & Hartl, M. (1991). Against the Cartesian view on mind: Young children's difficulty with own false belief. *British Journal of Developmental Psychology, 9,* 125–138.

Wimmer, H., Hogrefe, J., & Perner, J. (1988) Children's understanding of informational access as a source of knowledge. *Child Development, 59,* 386–396.

Wimmer, H., Hogrefe, J., & Sodian, B. (1988) A second stage in the child's conception of mental life: Understanding informational access as a source of knowledge. In J. Astington, P. Harris, & D. Olson (Eds.) *Developing theories of mind.* New York: Cambridge University Press.

Wolff, P.H. (1969) The natural history of crying and other vocalisations in early infancy. In Foss, B.M. (Ed.) *Determinants of Infant Behaviour, Vol. IV.* London: Methuen.

Woolfe, T., Want, S.C., & Siegel, M. (2002) Signposts to development: Theory of mind in deaf children. *Child Development, 73,* 768–778.

The World Federation of Neurology (1968). In Critchley, M. (1970) Developmental dyslexia: a constitutional disorder of symbolic perception. *Research Publications Association for Research in Mental and Physical Disease*, 48, 266–271.

Yirmiya, N., Solomonica-Levi, D., & Shuman, C. (1996) The ability to manipulate behaviour and to understand manipulation of beliefs: A comparison of children with autism, mental retardation and normal development. *Developmental Psychology, 32,* 62–69.

Younger, B.A. (1985) The segregation of items into categories by 10-month-old infants. *Child Development, 56,* 1574–1583.

Younger, B.A., & Cohen, L.B. (1983) Infant perception of correlations among attributes. *Child Development, 54,* 858–867.

Yussen, S.R., & Bird, J.E. (1974) The development of metacognitive awareness in memory, communication, and attention. *Journal of Experimental Child Psychology, 28,* 300–313.

Yussen, S.R., & Levy, V.M. (1975) Developmental changes in predicting one's own span of short-term memory. *Journal of Experimental Child Psychology, 19,* 502–508.

Yussen, S.R., Mathews, S.R., & Hiebert, E. (1982) Metacognitive aspects of reading. In W.Otto and S. White (Eds.) *Reading expository material.* London: Academic Press.

Zaitchik, D. (1990). When representations conflict with reality: The preschooler's problem with false beliefs and "false" photographs. *Cognition, 35,* 41–68.

Zelazo, P.D., & Reznick, J.S. (1991) Age-related asynchrony of knowledge and action. *Child Development, 62,* 719–735.

Zelazo, P.D., Carter, A., Reznick, J.S., & Frye, D. (1997) Early development of executive function: A problem-solving framework. *Review of General Psychology, 1,* 198–226.

Author Index

Subject Index